# *The* Richardson-Stinstra *Correspondence*

AND

# Stinstra's *Prefaces* to CLARISSA

✵

*Edited by* William C. Slattery

*Carbondale and Edwardsville*
SOUTHERN ILLINOIS UNIVERSITY PRESS
FEFFER & SIMONS, INC.
*London and Amsterdam*

*For Marijke*

# Preface

FOR THEIR HELP before and after my locating the Richardson-Stinstra correspondence, I owe a debt of gratitude to a number of people and institutions. I am particularly indebted to Professor T. C. Duncan Eaves, who encouraged my study of Richardson in The Netherlands and who directed part of the present work as a doctoral dissertation. To Professor Ben D. Kimpel go my thanks for his advice and encouragement. To the libraries of Leiden University, to the Royal Library, The Hague, and to the State University of Amsterdam go my thanks for their help. Mr. H. W. Egter van Wissekerke, formerly with the Leiden University library provided invaluable assistance. I also wish to thank the British Museum for the use of its microfilm facilities.

The late Mr. S. de Clercq of The Hague gave his kind permission for the letters to be published; Mr. H. Brouwer, former Head of the Reading Room of the Algemeen Rijksarchief, The Hague, the former location of the correspondence, and Miss I. H. van Eeghen, Archivist at the Gemeentelijke Archiefdienst, Amsterdam, the present location of the letters, gave most helpful assistance.

The work of Professors Sale and McKillop has of course been of great help, particularly the latter's *Samuel Richardson: Printer and Novelist*. The recent work on Richardson by Professors Eaves and Kimpel has also been a valuable aid.

To Professor Roy E. Cain, who read and made valuable comments on the Introduction and on my efforts to reflect Stinstra's style in my translation of his Prefaces, go my deepest thanks. Professor John I. Ades, who read an early draft of the Introduction, made helpful suggestions for which I am grateful. To Professor W. A. Wage of Leiden University go my thanks for his gracious aid. I must add, of course, that I alone am responsible for any factual errors in the entire work or for any infelicities of language in my translation of Stinstra's Prefaces. The editors of *Papers on Language and Literature* have given me their kind permission to reprint parts of an article which appeared in that journal. Biographical information in the Notes is from the *Dictionary of National Biography, La Grande Encyclopédie,* the *Biographie universelle,* and *Der Grosse Brockhaus,* unless indicated otherwise. I am grateful to Southern Illinois University for a research grant for the later stages of the manuscript preparation, and for assistance in preparing the manuscript my thanks go to Martha Harris, Kathryn Kennedy, Virginia Kesl, Joan Powell, Shirley Raymer, Carole Rezabek, and Don Christy. The portrait of Richardson is reproduced by permission of the National Portrait Gallery, London; that of Stinstra by the kind permission of the Mennonite Congregation, Harlingen, from a photograph of the original in possession of the congregation.

My wife has given not only her moral support in patience and understanding, but also has given very practical critical advice and assistance concerning my translations of Stinstra's Prefaces.

*Katwijk aan Zee*                                           W. C. S.
*May 1968*

# Contents

## PART 2 *Johannes Stinstra's Prefaces to* Clarissa

# List of Illustrations

between pages 32–33

# Introduction

SAMUEL RICHARDSON's extensive correspondence has long been a valuable source of information for scholars working on his life and novels. After the general acclaim of *Clarissa*, while Richardson was writing *Sir Charles Grandison*, he received a letter in praise of *Clarissa* which was to be the beginning of a three-and-one-half years' correspondence [1] with one of his most ardent champions on the Continent, Johannes Stinstra, Mennonite clergyman of Harlingen, The Netherlands. This important group of letters has been for the most part unavailable for more than a hundred years. Even though five of the letters have previously been printed, in whole or in part (Letters Nos. 1, 3, 5, 11, and 13), the location of the correspondence in this work has remained unknown. Christiaan Sepp used the letters when he was writing his biography of Stinstra, *Johannes Stinstra en zijn Tijd* (Amsterdam, 1865–66) He printed the rough draft of Stinstra's first Latin letter in full and stated that he had the body of the correspondence before him (II, 248–49) but failed to give its location; further, Stinstra's original letters have disappeared. The correspondence had passed, on Johannes Stinstra's death (January 8, 1790), to Isabella Stinstra, daughter of Johannes Stinstra's elder nephew, Simon Stinstra. Isabella Stinstra had married Pieter de Clercq on August 4, 1782,[2] and it was through this branch of the de Clercq family that the correspondence found its way into the de Clercq Family Archives.[3]

Richardson's attitudes towards his own work are clearly revealed in the correspondence, both as regards *Clarissa* and the forthcoming *Sir Charles Grandison*. While Stinstra shows himself to be a staunch advocate of Richardson's method, he does, at times, show an independence of opinion concerning the details of plot and intent. It is not surprising that Richardson again reveals his vanity, but the exchange of letters concerning Stinstra's quoting the "five bishops" passage from Richardson's letter of December 6, 1752 has a comic overtone to it that points up Stinstra's level-headedness just as much as it does Richardson's inordinate fear of being thought vain by his friends. The reasons for Richardson's writing his autobiographical letter become clear when one reads Stinstra's letter of April 2, 1753 (Letter No. 3), in which he responds to Richardson's interest in him by writing his own autobiographical letter and by posing questions to Richardson concerning his life and method of writing. Further, the letters are of particular interest because, even though Richardson's novels were translated widely, there is no other known extended correspondence between Richardson and a translator.

Stinstra's letters reveal his efforts in translating *Clarissa*, his critical interest in the novel as a moral force, and his successful search for competent translators of *Sir Charles Grandison*. Also, his independence of mind is shown, particularly as regards his relationship with the Mennonite Church.

Stinstra's role in furthering Richardson's European reputation and influence began when he set himself to the task of translating *Clarissa* into Dutch as *Clarissa, of de Historie van eene Jonge Juffer* (8 vols.; Harlingen, 1752–55). Along with his first letter to Richardson, he sent the first two volumes of his translation, including the first of four Prefaces he wrote for it. By the time his eight-volume translation was completed, he was one of Richardson's most trusted correspondents, in possession of Richardson's autobiographical letter of June 2, 1753 (Letter No. 5), which gives details of his early life unavailable anywhere else. Although they never met, the development of their sympathetic relationship is revealed in the twenty-one letters which passed between them.

It is impossible to say precisely why Stinstra broke off the correspondence; perhaps he was disappointed because Richardson was unable to aid either of Stinstra's friends (see Letters Nos. 21, 22, and 23).

Richardson's first letter shows that he took the precaution of making enquiries into Stinstra's background. Part of that background is much to the point. Johannes Stinstra was born on August 11,[4] 1708, in Harlingen. He was the younger son of Simon Johannes Stinstra, a well-to-do businessman engaged in the lumber trade and an active member of the Harlingen Mennonite Congregation.[5] Stinstra enrolled at the University of Franeker about 1725, where he remained for several years studying theology, philosophy, and languages, including Hebrew and related dialects.[6] Upon his return to Harlingen in 1733 he offered to preach four sermons a year there. In August, 1734, he received a part-time appointment at an annual salary of four hundred guilders. Originally he was to have received six hundred guilders for offering three-eights of the services for a year, but he found this offer unsatisfactory because he wanted both a free hand in deciding the number of services for three years and the right to resign the position whenever he so chose.[7] This independence of mind, later revealed in a different way, was to involve him in difficulties with the church authorities. The church board agreed with his request but proposed a two hundred-guilder reduction in salary, to which he agreed. He offered to serve as full-time pastor if after three years he remained satisfied with the position;[8] this was the case, and he remained as pastor of the Harlingen Congregation until 1785, when he resigned because of ill health,[9] even though there was a long period during which he was not allowed to preach.

In April, 1735, the bij 't Lam en den Toren Congregation in Amsterdam offered Stinstra a pastorate without the necessity of his preaching a trial sermon; after long deliberation, he turned down the offer because he felt he had more freedom in the Harlingen Congregation than was possible

in Amsterdam. The offer was repeated in 1738 and this time
he refused immediately because he could not in conscience
agree with all the rules of the Amsterdam Congregation, in
particular a stipulation against the taking of oaths, which
Stinstra felt to be the right of a Christian.[10]

In October, 1739, the Mennonite Conference of Friesland, which Stinstra served as moderator, called a special
meeting in Leeuwarden to defend two Mennonite clergy-
men, Wytse Jeens and Pieke Tjommes, who had refused to
sign four articles of faith because they insisted on freedom
of religious belief. Their refusal had led to charges against
them of Socinianism.[11] Stinstra wrote a defense, pleading
for liberty of conscience, belief, and religion [12] and submit-
ted it, with the approval of the Conference, to the Frisian
government in January, 1740. The reaction of the government was equivocal, no firm decision being made.[13] In May
of the following year Stinstra published five sermons [14]
which led to an attack on him as an advocator of Socinian
views. At the request of the Frisian government the theological faculties of several Dutch universities gave opinions
on Stinstra's supposed heretical position. The findings being
almost unanimous against him, on January 13, 1742, the
government ordered him to cease preaching.[15] For a number
of years frequent requests for lifting the suspension were
made by the Harlingen Congregation, the Conference of
Friesland, and Stinstra himself; but it was not until 1757
that he was reinstated with the full duties of his pastorate.[16]
Stinstra discusses the situation at some length in his letter of
April 2, 1753 (Letter No. 3).

It was during this period of restricted duties that Stinstra
turned to translating *Clarissa*. An active man who could not
remain intellectually idle, he was greatly impressed by
Richardson's moral approach and his emphasis on reason and
virtue in *Clarissa*. Though Stinstra was widely read in several languages, there is little fiction to be found in the
*Catalogue* of his library. Printed after his death for the
auction sale of his library, the 304-page *Catalogus Biblio-*

*thecae...Joannes Stinstra* (Harlingen and Franeker, Oct., 1790) lists more than forty-six hundred items, many of which are multivolume works. The sale lasted for eleven days, with two sessions per day. The books cover a wide variety of Stinstra's interests: theology, history, anatomy, biology, mathematics, and languages are all well represented. All of Richardson's works of fiction as well as the *Familiar Letters* are listed but no works by Fielding,[17] Smollett, Sterne, or other English novelists, with the odd exception of Thomas Amory's *Memoirs Containing the Lives of Several Ladies of Great Britain* (1755) and his *The Life of John Buncle, Esq.* (1756–66). The following representative works give an indication of Stinstra's interest in literature: works by Corneille, Molière, Racine, Malherbe, La Fontaine, Boileau, Shakespeare, Thomson, Butler's *Hudibras*, Marmontel's *Belisaire, Don Quixote* (English trans.), *Telemachus* (Dutch trans.), Erasmus' *Moriae Encomium*, Addison's works, bound volumes of the *Tatler, Spectator, Guardian,* twenty-five years of the *Monthly Review* (1760–84), thirty-five years of the *Gentleman's Magazine* (1750–84), *De Hollandsche Spectator, De Nederlandsche Spectator* (the latter two Dutch publications were widely-read imitations of the *Spectator*), Milton's *Works,* Young's *Night Thoughts,* MacPherson's *Ossian,* Gellert's *Fables,* and editions of Homer, Aeschylus, Euripides, Sophocles, and Aristophanes. Besides the portrait of Richardson, portraits of Samuel Clarke, James Foster, and George Washington are listed. Finally, under "Rariteiten" are listed mathematical instruments, a telescope, a prism, two air pumps, and two microscopes.

Stinstra's role as regards Richardson's reputation in The Netherlands was twofold: first, as translator of *Clarissa,* he made available to the Dutch public a novel of strong moral force; second, because of his Prefaces, some anonymous Dutch critics were brought to accept *Clarissa* as a serious moral work of fiction. Stinstra well understood the difficulty of being a clergyman and a translator and promoter of

*Clarissa* at the same time. He also felt the necessity of suggesting to the reader how the novel should be read and used; further, he found it necessary to justify the novel as an art form which would not be in conflict with the middle-class mores of its readers. In order to achieve these aims, he wrote lengthy prefaces to the first, third, fifth, and seventh volumes of his translation.[18]

Each of the Prefaces takes up a specific series of topics. The first Preface deals with Stinstra's defense of himself as translator-clergyman, the moral value of novels, the distinction between good and bad novels, praise of *Clarissa*, its influence on youth, and the difficulties in the translation. Three major topics are discussed in the second Preface: reading for pleasure, relaxation, and refreshment of spirit; the proper reading of moral novels, *Clarissa* in particular; and using such novels beneficially. The third Preface consists entirely of Stinstra's discussion of Imagination and Reason and the proper balance between the two. The last Preface justifies the death of Clarissa and the pathos which accompanies it.

Professor Alan D. McKillop, commenting on Stinstra's Prefaces, writes: "No contemporary critic gives a clearer description of the transition from didacticism to psychology in Richardson's work. Stinstra takes from current English criticism the comment that Fielding dwells on the general and the external, while Richardson works with the specific and the internal. He anticipates Diderot when he ranks Richardson with Milton, Newton, and Addison. But his commentary is essentially first-hand; he is sensitive to the detail and the vividness of Richardson's work, and reports what he has felt. If this discussion had been written in a more accessible language, it would, in spite of its verbosity, have become a *locus classicus* of Richardson criticism." [19]

While Stinstra in his Prefaces sees *Clarissa* basically as a moral novel, to be used for moral purposes, he nevertheless indicates a certain concept of literary criticism which indicates a broader view on his part than the term "moral critic" might imply. His recognition of Richardson's realistic approach in fiction and the importance of such an approach is seen in his first Preface, where he comments on Richardson's dealing with the ordinary actions of human lives. His understanding of the necessity of realism in conjunction with moral aims is seen in his comment on the lewd remarks of Lovelace in Preface I. At the same time, his distinction between Richardson and Fielding is reminiscent of Dr. Johnson's distinction between the two in which he saw Fielding as a man who knew how to read the dial of a clock and Richardson as one who knew the inner workings of it. His liberal view of knowing the attributes of virtues and vices, seen in his analogy of the steersman and the use of maps is also reminiscent of Milton's concept of individual freedom of knowledge as expressed in the *Areopagitica.* Finally, in the first Preface, Stinstra clearly perceives the aim of Richardson in delineating his major characters in *Clarissa* by a distinct style for each of them in their letters.

In his second Preface, Stinstra writes at great length to express to his readers the necessity of their understanding the relationship between usefulness and relaxation and the fact that they combine in everyone's life to make reading more purposeful. It is perhaps easy to forget that while the concept of instruction and entertainment was a standard dictum of literary approach in the eighteenth century, it was not standard for a theologian whose knowledge, not of literature, but of prose fiction, was somewhat limited. Further, by combining a sense of humor, as indicated by the passage in the second Preface concerning card players, with the highly perceptive comment (for his time) that when a libertine speaks as a libertine, we should not attribute his attitudes to the author, Stinstra continues his emphasis on the importance of the moral value of literature in general and *Clarissa* in particular. His insistence on the reader's paying attention to the details of *Clarissa* in order for him to distinguish between the comical and the serious in dialogue is then related at the end of the second Preface to his equally strong insistence that the reader must apply Richardson's view of life to himself if he is really to gain the moral value that the novel offers.

While much of the third Preface deals with the necessary balance between Reason and Imagination in a general way, the implication of this Preface is that in order for the reader to fully appreciate *Clarissa*, he must transfer this knowledge of the function of Reason and Imagination to the novel itself. Stinstra's own ability to see clearly this balance is perhaps indicated by his reference to the preacher in his pulpit who, instead of serving his congregation, becomes so enamored of himself, so infused with the feeling of his power over others' lives, that he in fact loses touch and further displays a complete lack of understanding of what the Imagination is capable of doing to a human being —in this case, to himself.

The fourth Preface is perhaps weakened by Stinstra's dealing too much with the moral implications of death rather than with a literary defense of Richardson's ending of the novel. But here again, Stinstra writes of what *he* feels is most important to consider in the novel: and in the view that he takes, he is not far removed from that of Richardson, who clearly saw the ending as a powerful moral force. Stinstra does make two significant points in this Preface: first, the reader learns from adversity, both real and vicarious, and second, Clarissa logically should not be elevated above the common lot of mortals in her earthly happiness —the contrary should apply, as indeed it does in Richardson's ending.

Contemporaneous comments on Stinstra's Prefaces were consistently laudatory. They reflect the fact that Stinstra, more than any other person, was responsible for the favorable reception of Richardson's works in The Netherlands, even though *Pamela* had been translated earlier. A reviewer of the first two volumes of the Dutch translation of *Clarissa* wrote: "One sees from the title page of this work that Mr. Stinstra is the translator. Because it will undoubtedly seem

strange that a minister of the Gospel would put his hand to
the translation of a fictitious history dealing with the love of
a young couple, one of whom plays the role of a libertine, in
which it is necessary to show many adventures of a bad sort;
and because novels in general are considered to be writings
which bewilder the young, Stinstra shows in a Preface of 37
pages . . . what a beautiful picture of an oppressed and
tormented virtue is given." [20]

In a letter to *De Nederlandsche Spectator*, a correspondent named Lugthart complained about the reading of novels
by young people. Lugthart was living as a boarder in the
home of a widow who had a young daughter for whom he
had developed a fatherly affection; in a discussion of novel
reading, Kootje, the young girl, had suggested that Lugthart would be as well off buying wine as novels for all the
moral good *he* was capable of receiving from reading. Lugthart then described a particular novel, "a History of a
Miss Catrina Bardowe, the English lady . . . [which] was
translated by a man whom she named, but whose name I
have forgotten. I almost believe that he was a minister. . . .
The more I think about it, the stranger it appears that one
can get moral lessons from novels, which, after all, are
written in order to make dull-spirited conversations happy
ones and to make young people gallant. You can now see
how wrong my Kootje's reasoning is and how little inclined
she is toward the right direction; and I do not need to tell
you how you must instruct her—moral lessons from novels,
indeed!" [21]

In his "answer" to the objections of Lugthart, the editor
took the opportunity of giving Stinstra a strong recommendation as a moral critic: "I would have willingly answered
the question of Mr. Lugthart, whether moral lessons can be
drawn from novels, and would have shown what use one
must make of such writings; but because this answer has
already been furnished us by the translator of the history of
*Clarissa Harlowe* (whom my droll correspondent calls Catrina Bardowe) in the Prefaces which are to be found in the

first and third parts of the novel [the last four volumes not
yet having been published], I shall ask him to see them for
himself. And if he also reads *Clarissa* itself, he will find
described in it the career of an adventurer, or libertine—
yes, of a general of debauchery, as well as the life of a
virtuous young woman. Whether he will have the patience
for it, because he demands that a novel be not too tedious,
will depend on the interest that he takes in the adventures
of the chief characters of the history." [22] The possibility
that the editor wrote the letter from Lugthart as well as his
own answer indicates either a strong liking for Richardson
or a necessary manipulation to fill up space—perhaps both.
In any case, the play on Clarissa's name indicates that it had
become a household word in The Netherlands.

Another instance of the influence of Stinstra's Prefaces is
seen in the attitude of a writer who said that in preparing an
article about the reading of "adorned histories and novels,"
he reread Stinstra's Prefaces with such enjoyment that he
then lost courage to continue with his own critical remarks.
After regaining his courage, he stated that he would risk
Stinstra's reading his comments because, while Stinstra
might feel the writer to be forward in commenting on his
Prefaces, the writer himself felt that there were many people who did not own a copy of *Clarissa* and who would
profit a great deal from his instructions. He added that the
number of novels in the same class with *Clarissa* was small
in comparison with the great quantity of novels published. [23]

When Mrs. Barbauld's edition of Richardson's correspondence appeared in 1804, [24] those letters between Richardson and Stinstra which had been included were immediately translated into Dutch and commented on thus:
"From the several prefaces placed by the honorable Mr.
Stinstra before his translation of *Clarissa*, it is known only
to those who have read these beautiful volumes that this
worthy man, who died on the 8th of January, 1790, at the
age of 88 [81], was in correspondence with the English
writer whose work it is not necessary to praise here. Some

inclinations of such praise are put before us—inclinations which serve to arouse our curiosity rather than give us complete satisfaction. Our interest was stirred by the six volumes which were published this year in London. . . . With the translation of these letters between Stinstra and Richardson, we judge that we are able to do our readers a service. It will allow us to be able to know Stinstra and Richardson in the best way. As friends, they pour their whole hearts out to each other; and it appears remarkable to us that in the very detailed *Life* of Richardson, preceding his correspondence, his letter to Stinstra tells us of his early life, from which we learn more about the highly-praised English writer." [25] The anonymous reviewer then asserted —and one can only agree with him—that "we do not judge necessary more than these few lines to justify printing the letters in our *Miscellany*." And he added: "It is apparent that there are more letters which were exchanged between the gentlemen. . . ."

Several other translations of Richardson's works as well as imitations and parodies appeared in The Netherlands during the eighteenth century and the first half of the nineteenth century. These works reflect the favorable reputation which Richardson enjoyed in The Netherlands, even though some of the critical comments on the value of the novels as moral guides for youth were overdone.

*Pamela, of de Beloonde Deugd* was first published in The Netherlands in four volumes (Amsterdam, 1742–44); in a Foreword to Volume I, the Dutch editor commented on the importance of the work in England and advised the Dutch reader that he no doubt could better follow Richardson's style were he able to read the work in the original. The editor added that two or three inoffensive plates from the original were included in the Dutch edition.[26] A second edition followed during the same years, 1742–44, and a third appeared between 1751 and 1759. A cut version of Pamela entitled *Pamela Bespiegeld* ("Pamela Observed") was brought out in 1741 by Dirk Swart, an Amsterdam publisher; following it is a Dutch translation of *Pamela Censured* (*Pamela, Zedelyk Beoordeeld*). In the copy I have seen, a translation of Eliza Haywood's *Anti-Pamela* is bound in the same volume.

New editions of both *Clarissa* and *Sir Charles Grandison* were announced in the *Algemeene Konst en Letterbode* in 1796: "Two moral novels, both of which must be viewed as the first and only ones of their kind, are continually held in all of Europe to be the greatest of masterworks by people of judgment and taste. The reading public seeks them with great eagerness. This acclaim is apparent not only by the many editions of the original works in England but also by so many translations of them in almost every European language. The Dutch translation of *Clarissa* was given to us, as people know, by the reverend and learned Johannes Stinstra and is enriched by him with suitable laudatory Prefaces concerning the use and proper employment of moral novels in general and of this history in particular. . . . Its appearance also had a perceptible influence on the improvement of taste for works of this kind here in Holland; and in spite of the following rash of novels of various worth which overflowed Holland as well as all of Europe, those of Richardson were not discarded with the others but held firmly the respect accorded them. For many years it has been difficult to buy a new copy of the Dutch translations of *Clarissa* and *Grandison*, a fact which made the present owner and publisher of them decide on *new editions*, an undertaking which should be praised and promoted because of the intended improvement of them. . . ." [27]

Both editions were completed, *Sir Charles Grandison* from 1797 to 1802 in seven volumes, and *Clarissa* from 1797 to 1805 in eight volumes. In a comment on the first volume of *Grandison* in *De Algemeene Vaderlandsche Letteroefeningen*, the reviewer wrote that it was to the honor of The Netherlands that a new translation had been made of such an exemplary work. He felt that the novel had been improved by the new translation and indicated confidence that it would find a ready sale, since the first, more expensive translation had proved to be so profitable. He went on to say that it would be rather pointless to praise a novel or an author so well known, not only because of the earlier translation but also because of Stinstra's Prefaces to *Clarissa* and a two-part biographical sketch of Richardson which had appeared in a predecessor of *De Algemeene Vaderlandsche Letteroefeningen.*[28]

*Sir Charles Grandison* was translated into French in seven volumes at Leiden and Göttingen simultaneously (1755–56).[29] The Prévost translation was published in Amsterdam at the same time.[30] Richardson mentions the requests for sheets of *Grandison* for these translations in Letter No. 5. A second printing of Prévost's translation appeared in 1770. A French translation of *Clarissa* appeared in The Hague much later in 1846.[31]

An abridged version of *Sir Charles Grandison* was published at Leiden in 1793.[32] This shortened version, written especially for young people, is narrative rather than epistolary and is but 219 pages long.

Inevitably, an abridged version of all three of Richardson's novels appeared in one volume; this work, *Pamela, Clarissa en Grandison Verkort,* which was published at Amsterdam in 1805, also is not epistolary but does use extracts from the letters. A Dutch reviewer gave it brief, favorable mention and added that it would be useful for anyone to read and that it was a better translation, even considering the fact that it was an abridgment, than the Dutch translation of *The Paths of Virtue Delineated.*[33] A second edition of this abridgment was published in 1808 at Amsterdam with the addition of three plates depicting a scene each from *Pamela, Clarissa,* and *Grandison,* that from *Clarissa* being the death-bed scene.

*The Paths of Virtue Delineated* was loosely translated into Dutch in 1766.[34] In general, no direct quotations were used except for occasional quotations in *Clarissa.* This single-volume work is 450 pages long, with 106 pages of *Pamela,* 180 of *Clarissa,* and 164 of *Grandison.*

The various editions and abridgments of Richardson's works which followed the original translations serve as an indication that Richardson's popularity in The Netherlands continued for a considerable time after his novels were first published and also continued well after his death.

Direct imitations of Richardson's works followed the translations of the originals. The critical reception of these imitations sheds further light on Richardson's eighteenth-century reputation in The Netherlands. The first direct imitation was published, it is true, more than ten years after the publication of the translation of *Pamela* into Dutch; but by this time *Clarissa* had been partially translated, and it is my opinion that the appearance of *Clarissa* influenced the writing of *De Hollandsche Pamela,* published at Amsterdam in two volumes in 1754. Professor McKillop quite properly refers to it as "an inferior version"; [35] it is a long, tedious tale of a young servant girl who, after many tribulations, finally ends her trials by marrying a count.

Two years after its publication, *Joseph Andrews* was translated into Dutch and appeared in two volumes, with plates, in 1744.

Sophie von La Roche's *Fraulein von Sternheim* was translated into Dutch in two volumes in 1772 as *De Hoog-duitsche Clarissa, of Geschiedenis van de Freule van Stern-heim.* It received a very favorable review as a moral novel in *De Hedendaagsche Vaderlandsche Letteroefeningen:* "If one ever saw, in any novel, virtue described in its greatest splendor and vice exhibited in its most odious form, it is in this history of the *Freule van Sternheim.* A lady of virtuous upbringing, with a religious heart, is brought to court with the intention to engage her cunningly in a romance with the prince; she is scandalously deceived by a refined dissembler . . . to deprive her of her honor and by the same man cruelly abused. . . . The story of all this, mixed with a

multitude of striking occurrences, which often give rise to
various moral thoughts, captures the reader continually so
that he could not refrain from esteeming highly the *Freule
van Sternheim*, even though it might appear to him somewhat gushingly sentimental. He detests the man who harms
her with an inward abhorrence. One might therefore fear-
lessly place this work in the rank of readable novels; and a
person would have to be immovably prejudiced if he in
reading this adventure of life yet kept insisting that it is
inconsistent with a healthy moral philosophy to be at leisure
with this sort of writing."[36]

A French imitation of *Clarissa*, *La nouvelle Clarice*, by
Madame Le Prince de Beaumont, which appeared in 1767,
was translated into Dutch in two volumes in 1768. In an
overall favorable review of the first volume one critic felt
that Madame de Beaumont was even more prolix than Richardson but had succeeded in eliminating entirely the somewhat imprudent scenes of the latter. He maintained that
there were some rather tedious digressions in the French
novel which should have been improved; for the remainder,
he felt that it was a very good novel which could be counted
among those which were able to incite its readers to good
morals.[37] In his comments on the second volume he again
complained that the work was too drawn out, though it was
well worth reading because of the heavenly virtue which
enlightened it, and objected to the authoress' carrying the
reader into a sort of Utopia, because he felt that the moral
lessons in the novel were thereby somewhat weakened.[38]

A parody of *Grandison* entitled *De Nieuwe Grandison*
appeared in 1770–71 in two volumes. The main character is
a sort of Don Quixote who has with him his Sancho: a
German nobleman gets it into his head to follow in the
footsteps of the famous Grandison, and a teacher, who lives
in the same house as the nobleman, aims at no less than to
follow in the footsteps of Dr. Bartlett. Various members of
the family plot to keep the nobleman and the teacher di-

rected towards their goals. This sort of action prevails until the end. The work is a translation of the German *Grandison der Zweite* (1760–61) by J. C. A. Musaeus.[39] Probably one of the most influential imitators of Richardson in The Netherlands was Madame de Cambon, whose *De Kleine Grandison, of de gehoorzame Zoon* was translated into English as *Young Grandison* and into French as *Le petit Grandisson*. The novel was well received critically in The Netherlands at its appearance in 1782. The plot has to do with a young Dutch boy, Willem, who is sent to England to spend a year with Sir Charles Grandison. He gives an account of his stay in a series of letters to his mother; other letters in the novel are written by Willem's mother and various other people. Willem is greatly influenced by Karel, the younger son of Sir Charles. Karel's good actions are seen in an even more favorable light because of the preposterous behavior of his older brother, Eduard, who, however, eventually repents his way of life and follows Karel's example. All ends happily, with Eduard promoted in military service and Willem married to Emilia, the Grandisons' daughter. The novel's emphasis on the morals of youth is stressed in a review in *De Algemeene Vaderlandsche Letteroefeningen*: "The manner in which Madame de Cambon has carried out the situation is pleasing for youth, very well suited to keep the desire for reading alive and to enrich the spirit early with an encouraging knowledge of reasoned duty, which, by the increase of age can have nothing but a wholesome effect. And naturally the way is prepared for such wished-for results as are pictured here.

"Ending this work, our esteemed authoress therefore says with justice, 'May these examples prepare for the Dutch youth a path and teach them to be always obedient and virtuous, in order to make themselves blessed with an enduring and desirable happiness, always thinking that the temporal as well as eternal well-being is established only by invincible duty.' "[40] A father, greatly impressed by the

moral value of the work, wrote to the *Weekblad voor
Neerlands Jongelingschap*: "This story struck my little
Karel in such a way that he promised never to sing that
unvirtuous song again and always to be obedient to his
elders even though he is apart from them. . . . and in order
to prove my satisfaction to him in the strongest possible
way, I immediately bought, on the following day, a copy of
*den Kleinen Grandison* and sent it to the bookbinder to have
it bound with a beautiful French binding, with which book I
think to surprise him, so quickly have I brought it home." [41]
An abridgment of *De Kleine Grandison* appeared in Amsterdam (no date). Berquin's French adaptation was published in The Hague in 1791; a French abridgment appeared in Amsterdam in 1805 and a second edition in 1810.
A second edition of Berquin's adaptation was published in
Amsterdam in 1813.

These translations, imitations, and parodies are indica-
tive of the wide response to Richardson in The Netherlands
both during his lifetime and long after his death.

# A Note on the Text

In the text of Richardson's letters his spelling, capitalization, and punctuation are followed except in the case of his square brackets, where parentheses are substituted for clarity. Square brackets ( [ ] ) enclose conjectural readings and editorial insertions. Doubtful readings are enclosed with question marks within square brackets. Misspellings and grammatical slips are indicated by "sic." Braces ( { } ) enclose conjectural letters or words in those places where the manuscript has holes or is torn. Shaped brackets ( ⟨ ⟩ ) indicate cancelled readings where such are legible. Diagonals ( / / ) enclose Richardson's revisions, where legible. In the text of Stinstra's letters, all of which are rough drafts, his final versions are followed without revisions being indicated. The same is true for both the translations from Latin and the English letters. Square brackets and "sic" are employed, as in the Richardson letters, where necessary for clarity in the English letters. Stinstra occasionally used the Dutch vowel "ij" for the English "y" in such words as "mij" and "bij," and these remain unchanged.

In translating Stinstra's Prefaces, I have attempted to keep as close to the originals as possible, eliminating redundancies but not repetitious adjectives. I have followed his sentence structure as closely as is practicable, particularly as regards sentence length, and I have held to his use of figurative language, except in instances where the results would not be idiomatic English.

# Part One

## The Richardson-Stinstra Correspondence

# Stinstra *to* Richardson[1]

*September 14, 1752*

*To That Distinguished Man, Samuel Richardson,
Johannes Stinstra Sends Many Greetings*

Although I am indeed unknown to you, I feel that
the translation of your incomparable work, which I have
undertaken, seems to pave the way to a certain extent for
me to write to you without apology. Perhaps I shall be
regarded as troublesome for bothering you; but they will
readily excuse this boldness who have been pardoned when
they put less expert hands to the very charming *Clarissa*.
And if I can judge your mind from your writing, I am
convinced that you will not despise these evidences of my
veneration and regard.

For some time I have been looking for an opportunity to
send you as a gift the first two volumes of *Clarissa*, already
published in Dutch, since I have you especially to thank for
the first fruits of my labors. Now happily I have the opportunity to do this through a friend who has promised definitely to see that they are delivered to you. The reasons
which spur me on you will easily have gathered from my
Preface, which was sent in advance, if you understand the
Dutch language; if not, you will be able to rightly judge
whether the work has value by means of a translator who
has mastered the language. For what friend of refinement
and excellence would not desire acquaintance with such a
man? You must nevertheless not doubt that my praises
bestowed on you there, of which you scarcely have need, and

which propriety prevents my repeating here, have sprung from my heart, since I was completely uncertain whether you would ever see them. A token greater than any statement of how much I respect you is the considerable task of the translation. If I might learn that you approve it, my heart would be filled with joy. For my part, I expended all my ability and effort so that *Clarissa*, lovely in all respects, might lose as little as possible of her graceful charm. But no one can judge better than you how great are the vexations and difficulties of such a task, particularly for a man who has learned all he knows of the English language from books, and who has never had the privilege of visiting Britain itself and of becoming acquainted with idioms and expressions.

I mention this that you may excuse more readily the mistakes which I have made. Moreover, I continue actively with my translation, which has reached the end of the third volume; and next spring I hope the Dutch will receive this and the fourth volume with the same eagerness with which they have already pored over the first two volumes.

May God, most merciful and mighty, long keep you unharmed so that you may increasingly use the extraordinary talents which He has bestowed upon you to instill in the minds of men a zeal for excellence and to put your contemporaries and future generations under obligation for your favors, the memory of which time will not erase, and in which a most pleasing report announces that you are still toiling! Farewell, most distinguished Sir! And do not deny me a place among your admirers.

*dated Harlingen in Friesland*
*the 14 September, 1752*

[2]

## Richardson *to* Stinstra

*December 6, 1752*

Accept of my Excuse, Reverend Sir, for having so long delay'd acknowleging the Receipt of your kind Letter, and of the very acceptable Present which accompany'd it. My Heart thanks you for both. The true Reason/of the Delay/I will give you—It was my unhappy Ignorance of the Dutch Language; and the Difficulty I met with from the Person whom I employ'd to translate your Preface, to which in your Letter, you obligingly refer me. He has at last done it; but in such a manner, as I am informed, comes far short of the Beauty of your Style, and the Happiness of your Expression; But so, however, as to shew me, as your kind Letter also does, the great Honour you have done me, as well as the Work.

I make no Difficulty, Sir, to write to you in my Native Tongue; the only one in which I have any tolerable Knowlege (Business and Languages, Sir, interfere too much with each other in the Learning-time, to allow of a Mastery in both) ; and the less, as you have shewn in the Execution of what you have already published of this Work, that you are as much a Master of the Tongue, as of the Subject.

I see by your Preface, Sir, that the Difficulties of the Translation, which from the Nature of the Work are very great and uncommon, are not the only ones you have had to contend with. You have been obliged to justify to serious and good, tho' perhaps not enlarged-minded, Men, (and the more for being a good Man yourself) your Undertaking; as the Work you honour by it, is a Work of Imagination only, and not pretended to be grounded on a real Story. Well have you defended your self! Happy am I, in the successful Pains you have taken on that Subject. If it would strengthen your Hands, and not lay me under the Imputation of Vanity, I could give you, Sir, from the Letters of some of our gravest Divines and finest Writers, ample Testimonials of their Regard for the Work you have undertaken to give a Translation of.[2] It has brought me the Honour of a personal Acquaintance with Five of those Prelates who have done, and do, most Honour to the Bench of Bishops. One of whom declared to me in a Visit he made me on the occasion (and he scruples not to declare it to everybody) that he had read it through Eleven times, and proposed to read it over again every two Years, as long as he lived.

I hope, Sir, you will allow me the Honour of numbering you among my Correspondents: In the Course of our Correspondence, I will cause to be transcribed, if this may be admitted, such Passages, as may keep you in Heart on so arduous an Undertaking; for Clarissa has not only brought me a Multitude of personal ⟨Aquaintances⟩ /Friends/; but has been the Occasion of enlarging greatly my Correspondencies with both Sexes; in the Course of which I have been obliged to obviate Objections, and to give the Reason of my Management in particular Parts of the Work. My Correspondents, Sir, are Men and Women of Virtue and Condition. Some of them excepted to the Warmth of one Scene in the Book, in which the vile Lovelace attempts to surprize Clarissa under the Terror of a Fire. I wrote an Answer to two particular Divines on their Objections; and knowing that the Delicacy of some of my fair Correspondents, who had hinted Dissatisfaction on the Warmth of that Scene, would not permit them to speak out, I printed a few Copies of that Answer, and sent them to several of my Friends. I inclose one of them to you.[3]

Remarks were also published by a Lady, which I saw not till they were in Print. One of these I transmit likewise.[4]

And you will be pleased to accept of a little Piece ⟨I referred⟩ to /mentioned/ in the Work as Clarissa's Meditations;[5] which I have never yet published.

You will believe, Sir, that I must have had the Curiosity

to enquire after the Gentleman who has done my Work and
me so much Honour.

A learned and worthy Friend⁶ thus writes to me on the
Subject—You will judge on reading the Extracts from his
Letters, why I trouble you with them.

"I find, that your Monsieur Stinstra is the same Gentleman as wrote yᵉ Pastoral Letter against Fanaticism.⁷ It is
supposed, that the Book being originally published in
Dutch, is the Occasion of its not being known here. He has
published also in Dutch Five Sermons for Liberty of Conscience, and Toleration, and against all Imposition of
Human Authority.⁸ By his clear manner of Writing, I make
no doubt but this is an excellent Work. I am one of his
Admirers, and think he deserves a Place with Locke, &c."

The Letter from which I take the above Extract, was
followed by another from the same benevolent Hand. I will
transcribe yᵉ greatest Part of it—

"The Pastoral Letter I mentioned to you in my former,
was designed to confute the extravagant Pretensions of
Count Zinzendorf⁹ and his deluded Followers, distinguished by the Name of *Moravians*, with whom our Meth-
odists agree in many Points. This Tract is yet but little
known in England. It was written originally in Dutch, and
has been translated into French, whether by the Author
himself, or some other Hand, I know not: But the Extracts
from the Count's Sermons, and the Hymns, are printed in
Dutch only. However, it has not escaped the Notice of his
Grace of Canterbury,¹⁰ who has read, and mentioned it to
some of his Friends with the Approbation it so justly deserves; nay, more, He is endeavouring to get it translated
into English, as a very useful Work.

"To be sure, Mr. Stinstra can be no Stranger to the
Character of this excellent Prelate; yet I cannot help just
observing, that no Man in so high a Station, was ever less
elated with it, more communicative, or easier of Access. He
spends his large Revenue in Hospitality and Works of Be-
neficience; and is ready to relieve worthy Objects of every

8 THE CORRESPONDENCE

Denomination, when properly recommended. In short, he is a Friend to the Civil and Religious Rights of all Mankind. With these Qualities, it would be strange indeed if he was not esteemed and beloved by all Parties. The Lovers of Liberty abroad may justly envy the Happiness of the Church of England under his mild and prudent Direction[.]

"I should be glad to know if the Five Sermons, taken notice of in the Preface of the Pastoral Letter, have been translated into French.[11]

"P.S. The Pastoral Letter is in the Hands of the Revd. Mr. Majendie,[12] an ingenious Clergyman of the Established Church, but of French Extraction; who, I suppose, is translating it into English; since it was recommended to him by y\ue\ Archbishop. If the Author has made any Improvements since the Publication of the French Edition, I dare say, it will be taken as a Favour, if he will communicate them to that Gentleman. *Nov. 30. 1752.*"

These Particulars, I presume will not be unacceptable to you, Sir. If any thing should induce you to come to England, you will be sure of a most cordial Welcome as well to my little *Retirement*,[13] which is about 5 Miles from my Dwelling-house in Town, as ⟨well as⟩ to *that*, for your own time; and to all the Communications I can make you; either with regard to the Work you have undertaken, or to my new one.

In the mean while, your Correspondence by Letter is what I earnestly sollicitt, as a great Favour to me. I shall rejoice, if your Pains and Labour be rewarded by a kind Reception: If it answer not, I should be pained, for your Sake. How many Volumes, Sir, do you think it will make, in the very handsome manner you print it?

I am, Sir, with Prayers for your Health and Happiness,

*Your greatly obliged and faithful*
*Humble Servant*
*S. Richardson*

*London Salisbury Court, Fleet Street,*
*December 6. 1752.*

[3]

## Stinstra *to* Richardson[14]

*April 2, 1753*

*To The Very Kindly Man, Samuel Richardson, Jo-*
*hannes Stinstra Sends Many Greetings*
Without doubt you are wondering why I have not
yet answered your letter, full of all kindness and good will,
which you sent on the 6th of December of last year. A storm
which raged in midwinter and wrecked on the coast the ship
which was carrying this letter from England to Holland,
and a subsequent cold spell, because of which, for two
months, the waters stood frozen on these shores, were the
reasons that the letter was not delivered to me until the first
of this month. From that time I had to be away from home
for a few days; and finally, I had to spend quite a lot of time
in preparing the things that I have added to this letter of
mine.

I cannot say with how great delight you have refreshed,
or rather blessed me, when I finally received the letter.
Most eagerly I accept the terms you so kindly offer me, to
set up a correspondence, in which I most faithfully promise
to fulfill my share with the greatest possible care. The small
presents you sent me with your letter were very pleasing to
me. That letter, in which you successfully defended your
plan of depicting with such lively embellishment the scene
which shows Clarissa fighting against the nocturnal knavish
lusts of Lovelace, reached me opportunely, so that I can add
a Dutch translation of it to the fourth volume, which ends in
that story.[15] I indeed foresaw that certain of my countrymen
would take offense at this scene; and I thought that you sent
me this apology with the idea that these people too could be
made to think better of your plans. Meanwhile, I myself
previously approved the plan of including this scene; and I
am glad that I seem to have read your inmost thoughts

concerning this matter; for those things that are read on page 15 of my Preface concern chiefly this scene. (*But if, of course, certain scenes are drawn which in themselves would be likely to incite passion, there is a ready antidote for these*; *indignation and pity are at the same time so deeply stirred up that they check and strangle all other considerations.*) This agrees perfectly with the state of mind which you say on page 7 *of the Answer* you were in, as you were painting this scene.[16] Therefore, my hope and opinion are more strengthened that I am not an absurd translator of the admirable *Clarissa*, as it appears that in the more difficult points, I have not gone astray from the author's thought.

I was also most delighted to read the criticisms of *Clarissa* (*Remarks*, etc.),[17] which you have shown to have come from feminine hands. When the need arises to dispel similar objections, if perchance they turn up here, it will be easy to translate them into Dutch. I also return thanks for the *Meditations of Clarissa*[18] you sent me, which are exceedingly devout, sinewy, and tasteful indeed. They were the more pleasing to me because you said that they have never been published, and you distribute them only among your friends; and thus by this token you allow me to reckon myself, to a certain extent, in this number.

I am already eager for the transcriptions you promise you will furnish for my use to strengthen my mind, fatigued from the hard work. They will doubtlessly add new strength and will encourage me to finish promptly, God willing, this task, half of which I have already accomplished.

Your *Clarissa* is here, too, very deeply loved by all who are esteemed for sagacious wit and are moved by appreciation of dutifulness; for she appears not to have lost all her grace by the work I spent on her. Many people demand earnestly that haste be made in translating the other parts. Among them a certain clergyman expressed to me that he "sometimes doubted whether the angels possessed more acuteness than the author of that book." Another who, when he had reached the end of the first volume, which he read in English, complained that it was languid and produced disgust, after he had read through the other volumes, at my suggestion, confessed "that he had no doubt that if most parts of these letters occurred in the Holy Book, they would be pointed out as clear proof of divine inspiration." So it is likely enough that the bookseller [19] at whose expense it is printed will not suffer any loss from it. Most certainly, enormous praises from my countrymen will be lavished upon you; and like a real prophet, I promise myself that thanks will be returned to me.

Eight volumes, about which you asked, will be filled by this Dutch edition, just as was the third English edition, which I am using for the translation. The printers are already working on the composing of the fourth volume, and it is nearing completion. I hope to send it to you shortly, together with the third volume. I added anew the Preface, in which I took pains to instruct the readers as to how they should undertake the unfolding of ethical writings of this kind, how they must be read, to which points attention must be chiefly paid, and to what uses, moreover, they must be applied. I wove into it my observations of various kinds on the pleasures which people use to relax their minds, in order to attract them to sensible and profitable delights; I thought that this matter was germane to your writing and that it was particularly useful to procure favor for it.

Furthermore, I must examine, in some respects, what you have excerpted from the letter of your friend who is so friendly to me; [20] and since you say you long to know me, let me relate briefly the principal fortunes of my life. For though it is indecorous and silly to talk about oneself without good reason, I believe that your good will towards me demands it; thus you can see what kind of man you have judged worthy of it.

I am indeed the same person who wrote the "Letter Against the Folly of the Fanatics," who are very disturbing here. A French translation has been made by the learned de Boissy,[21] of Berne, in Switzerland, while staying at Leiden;

he has added a rather long Preface and Remarks, including a brief account of the state of my affairs. The same letter was translated into German and published at Berlin in the following year, the translator and sponsor being the Rev. Sack,[22] who is Court Chaplain to the Prussian king. And I confess to being filled with genuine delight, now that you report that it has been judged worthy by the Archbishop of Canterbury of being read by the English in their own language. It would be strange if I did not rejoice that my little work could gain the approval of such a man, whose fame had already reached me, but whose excellent goodness it is now possible to know from your letter. I would very gladly direct everything in me to the arranging of this edition; to this end, moved by the exhortations of your friend, I have gone through the French translation more carefully; and what I judged deserving of a critical remark, when the translator had not expressed my mind accurately enough, I amended and put down on paper. This I am adding to the original Dutch edition, so that if there is anyone acquainted with this language, he can compare it with the translation. Most learned friend, I pray you to see that the additions be given to the Rev. Dr. Majendie, whom your friend urged to give his attention to the translation; I shall be very much obliged to him for this labor. Perhaps they will arrive too late, after the letter has been published, since so much time has elapsed between your letter and this one of mine already; but then I shall have lost only the labor of a few hours. That letter could indeed be increased by a wealth of examples and incidents, but I have no spare time to collect and arrange them; it also seems unsuitable that a small booklet should be buried in a mass of remarks. How much would I like to have the opportunity of meeting the most illustrious translator to return my thanks for the care he has taken with the edition! On the other hand, modesty forbids my writing him.

My five discourses, which were mentioned by your friend, about the nature of the kingdom of Christ, in which I defend the freedom of the Church against all bonds of human authority, are available only in Dutch. I have sent a copy of these and also a copy of the "Apology in Favor of the Civil Freedom of Religion," [23] of which I am the author, to the states of our province, and likewise my "Suppliant Booklet" to the same states, so that from all those treatises which the French translator mentions in his Preface to the above-mentioned letter, with the help of people who are acquainted with the language, you and others can understand by what doctrine and by what kind of judgment I have been condemned. For when I had further learned the principles of a more sound theology and genuine freedom from the writings of Clarke,[24] Hoadley, Locke, and others, I considered it my duty not only to propagate them as far as I was able but also to act suitably according to their rule in all ways of life. Therefore, when I, still quite a young man, was called from here to the Amsterdam Church of the Anabaptists, as it is commonly called (I suppose you know that I am a member of their society), I refused to comply with this invitation, because in that church I would have to accept the yoke of Mennonite orthodoxy, with which I am not in complete agreement, from which rules I was exempt in this less illustrious post. The same devotion to freedom afterwards urged me to try to oppose the persecution, which was assailing our churches when this burden was laid upon me by their society, in the "Apology" mentioned just now. By this action I aroused the anger of the theologians of the Reformed Church in our country against me as a patron of dissoluteness and as an assailer not only of the church but also of the civil authority. This anger was kindled especially after I had published the five discourses, particularly when to the efforts of the theologians were added the help and patronage of the Prince of Orange.[25] It must certainly seem strange that a man of such great dignity would want to rise against such an unimportant little man as I. But it concerns the preservation of the prosperity of the Church; orthodoxy was in danger; and certain people said that the Prince had been prompted by political reasons to act vigorously as an opponent to my cause, in order to rise more easily to the summit of power by winning the esteem of the theologians, which he later held by other digressions.

Be this as it may, the Prince himself transferred the affair to the States Delegates, who, on his advice, sent my discourses to all the universities in The Netherlands for judgment and to all so-called classes of the Church in this province; the universities branded these discourses with the most offensive infamy of heresy. Without having been heard, I was condemned as suspected of Socinianism, and I was forbidden to discharge my sacred duty in my church. When I complained to the States in a "Suppliant Booklet," which you see here enclosed, I obtained nothing; neither was anything accomplished by my church, which not only at that time but frequently later asked earnestly that I be relieved of this prohibition. I myself repeated my supplication only once, when conditions of that kind were demanded of me, which I refused to obey; I did this so that the reasons for my actions could be known. I also added to this letter a copy of the *Nederlandsche Jaerboeken*,[26] which contains my complaints frankly and sincerely explained to the States Delegates. These reasons, I hold, were true and genuine, which relieved me of the promise that I would never propagate the Socinian doctrine; in reality I am not devoted to it. I gladly confess this to you. But when men try to blind us by such confessions and formulas and curtail freedom, I think it the duty of a good citizen and a true Christian not to allow these to be forced upon him. Many people accuse me of stubbornness. But I myself am aware of my innocence, and only after having weighed carefully a matter, I gratify the dictates of my conscience. If I err, I err unfortunately.

In the meantime I am living quite contented with my lot. I perform all the duties in my church except that I do not speak publicly, not abstaining even from catechetical exercises. Though I gave up my salary as soon as the church was compelled to dispense with my sermons, my means at home are not so scanty that I cannot live sufficiently on them and provide some modest library furniture, dedicated to studies, in which I delight. I enjoy the love of the whole church and the friendship of many good men, not only among our own people but also among the Reformed, who have proved faithful to me in my misfortune. Thus my condition is by no means miserable or discouraging, through the care of the most merciful God, Who, even in the midst of troubles, has kept my mind joyful and elevated. Although in the first onrush of the storm, anger at the theologians raged in me vehemently and assailed me because of their false accusations; although the sentence pronounced on me together with the votes of the theologians with whom it rested being publicly printed and published, exposed me to the reproach of all Holland; although the theologians afterwards quite often in their meetings planned, though in vain, to cheat me of the opportunity to publish my writings, that zeal seems to have cooled down now, and quietly I commit to the public light whatever I wish, as is sufficiently clear from the "Letter Against the Fanatics," in which I did not spare the common opinions of our country's theologians. Besides, I have published the following, all in Dutch editions: "Discourse Against the Defrauding of Taxes" [27] and "Reflections on the Letter of J. v.d. Honert," (a Leiden professor) in 3 volumes octavo. This man blew the war trumpet when the battle of the Churches was roused against me; I let him go after rubbing him with quite biting salt. Then I was incited by youthful ardor and the feeling of injustice; yet I did not proceed beyond what he deserved, if I am not mistaken. Very many people persuaded me that I had done a valuable thing in inserting a rather long digression in these reflections about the necessity and dignity of good works, in which I pointed out how, from the principles of sound reason and from the evidence of Holy Writ, moral virtue evidently furnishes the prow and stern of true religion. These consisted of 24 religious discourses in quarto about some principal doctrines and duties of Christians.[28] I wanted these to show with what kind of ideas I had instructed the parish committed to me. Finally, I translated all of Samuel Clarke's discourses in Dutch in 11 volumes octavo;[29] for I have always regarded this man as truly apostolic; from his golden book about the truth of natural and revealed religion, I drew faultless and certain conceptions about our most holy truth, and I shall yet get it translated into Dutch.

The hope, however, that I shall ever be restored to the free discharge of my duty has now clearly ended. In the preceding winter delegates from our parish have supplicantly addressed the Royal Princess, Governess of Holland,[30] to entreat her protection and sent a commendatory letter to the States of our province asking that they be willing to grant this restoration; but they brought back the answer that the Princess did not think it proper to intervene in this affair. When, in 1748, a furious crowd disturbed everything in this country, a seditious gang also rushed at my house and asked if I wanted to be led to the pulpit in the morning or in the afternoon of the following day; for they would see that I was no longer deprived of my freedom to preach to the people; but as I am averse to such violent measures, I dispersed them by a soothing speech, though they threatened to use violence if I did not want to go.

This then is a short sketch of my misfortunes, affairs, and treatises, as I recollect them in passing. But I also include this narrative not only with this purpose, that you would clearly come to know the man whom you allow to address you by his letters but also to confess the truth, in the hope that you can be persuaded by this example of mine to give me a greater opportunity to come to know you. May I ask you what kind of life you have led from your early youth? Whether, as the story goes, you have been continuously free of the worries of a bookshop? From whom you have acquired such accurate acquaintance of nature, the various inborn qualities and manners of mankind? What first influenced you to write? How you have produced your immortal works? Did everything flow forth from your genius; or did you have the original in real life before your eyes, which you adorned by adding embellishments? Do not take it ill of me that I am filled with desire to get to know and to admire from a distance the superb abilities of great talent. I would also like to know if other works besides *Pamela* and *Clarissa* have come from your hand. If I shall learn that there are others, I shall not permit myself to be deprived of them long. How goes that offspring which we are eagerly expecting, *The Fine Gentleman?* A certain Amsterdam bookseller [31] long ago announced publicly that he would publish a Dutch and French translation of it, from which you can judge how greatly your writings are appreciated by our countrymen. That your *Clarissa* has been translated by a Göttingen theological professor named Michaelis you undoubtedly know.[32]

From what precedes, you will easily decide that my country, like a stepmother, I do not love very much. Therefore I could without difficulty be persuaded to move my home; Britain long ago as a blessed asylum of liberty showed me its enchantments; at your most kind invitation I was delirious with joy, and I should consider it among the sweetest enjoyments of my life if I could see you personally, talk with you, and stay with you; but a strong handicap restrains me; my mother, who has deserved well of me, is still living, and I live in her house as a bachelor. I am her comfort and help in her great though robust age of 76. She would pine away with sorrow and sadness if I should permit myself such a far journey, rightly fearing (as I myself do) that I should never leave the soil of Britain when once I had set foot upon it.

Let duty therefore prevail; and while it is impossible to address each other personally, let us do so frequently by letter. I suppose it will not be inconvenient for you if I continue to use the Latin language. The use of this language is easier for me than the use of the English language; for I have not been able to find a teacher while studying it, and I am deprived of the ability of pronouncing and writing it.

Farewell, again and again farewell, most excellent Sir, and continue to love me as you have begun to.

*Written the last day of March*
*Dated April 2, 1753*

[4]

## Stinstra *to* Richardson

*April 30, 1753*

*To That Distinguished Man, Samuel Richardson, Many Greetings From Johannes Stinstra*
Although I hardly know what I can write you worthy of reading, after my scarcity of news was all but exhausted by my previous letter, sent to you at the beginning of this month, I nevertheless cannot refrain from adding a few lines to the copy of the third and fourth volumes of the Dutch translation of your *Clarissa,* which were just released from the press and which are presented to you with my greatest respect because of your very great merits. Although there are no other reasons for writing, an insignificant letter of this kind might be a sign of how eagerly I desire to keep up the correspondence with you and how much I delight in the offered permission.

I hope that you have received my previous letter, mentioned just now, which contained a short narration of my affairs, especially with regards to the "Letter Against the Fanatics," in which I had enclosed some pamphlets about which a question had been asked and which concerned the same thing; but I have not yet been notified of its delivery

by my friends in Amsterdam, to whom I committed the care
of taking it further to England.

Because other news is lacking, here you have a short
summary of the argument of my Preface to these two volumes; I have already written that I should in this way
suggest what ought to be observed by those who want to use
*Clarissa* worthily. I start from the reasons which influenced
me to handle this matter—that some friends urged me, that
youthful inexperience needs such a support, that the prejudices of others can be checked in this way. Thereafter I
divide the argument itself in three parts, taking care to
show with what mood and purpose one should undertake
reading, what is required of us while reading in order that
we may perceive the true force and virtue of this work, and
finally to what uses it ought to be applied when well read
and understood. Under the first point I establish a double
purpose for those who will read it, that they must not only
refresh their minds with pleasures but also feed them with
solid food, that they must not only pluck flowers but also
sound and lasting fruits. I show that *Clarissa* most suitably
answers this double purpose, that both of these are adapted
to each other as friends and are at the same time very
worthy of a noble man. This affords me the opportunity of
discussing the pleasures and delights of the mind in which
we commonly indulge, to refresh ourselves, as they say, with
certain points not hackneyed in our country. I furthermore
demand an attentive mind when reading it; the matter of
this book is worthy of its attention, and I observe that the
more we apply the mind, the more pleasing delights we
enjoy, and we are refreshed by them. Therefore, I urge
paying attention to the narration of events, the characters,
nature, and manners of the persons who are brought on the
stage, the ethical sayings and maxims or counsels regarding
the conduct of manners and life, and the purpose which the
author set before his eyes not only in the whole work but
also in the separate parts of it, and which it is possible to
gather from the preceding, if rightly understood. Finally I

pass on to the uses to which the acquaintance with this work, thus reduced to its bare bones, must be applied; that we indeed must discern as far as possible the manners and natural dispositions of men, which serve most of all to teach us to act more intelligently and more wisely; that we must correct in the first place our own souls and manners; that we must be frightened away from vices, and that we must pursue virtue with all eagerness; that we must accept the very many opportunities offered here to roam far and wide with our own minds through the very large field of moral sciences; and that we must cherish the little seeds repeatedly thrown out here by our contemplation that they will grow to prolific shoots; and the benefit of this work abounds in very rich fruits.

Perhaps it may have been worthwhile to have shown you this outline, because in this way you will be freed from the necessity of looking for a translator for this Preface of mine. And perhaps it will be possible by this device to turn you away from judging the quality of my little labor. I indeed fear no tribunal more than yours, though on the other hand I would commit my cause to the fairness of no one more willingly. Therefore, if you, wishing to learn further how I handled that argument, have this Preface translated in your native language, I earnestly ask that you express your thoughts on it most unrestrictedly and write plainly of what you approve in it and what you think it lacks.

I cheerfully continue the translation of Volume V. In the meantime I met with a difficulty in it: it will, I daresay, not be unsuitable to consult you about it and so adding a new impulse, thus hasten to me your letter, which I eagerly desire. There is a problem about that expression on page 175, *Such worse than Waltham disguises;* [33] it seems to be proverbial, but I do not know its origin, perhaps because I have not sufficiently studied the history of England; I cannot render it accurately; and if I translate it literally, the other readers will need an explanation just as I do.

The most merciful and most mighty God long keep you unharmed and crown you with the abundance of all good things.

*Dated at Harlingen*
*April 30, 1753*

[5]

# Richardson *to* Stinstra [34]

*June 2, 1753*

*Reverend and Dear Sir,*

I must own I was afraid that my Pacquet had miscarried, and once in the time of your Silence, I sent to Mʳ· Godin, to know if it were sent. I could not think of giving up my Hopes of a Correspondence with so worthy a Man. You have well accounted for your Silence; But cannot ⟨you⟩ /We/, Sir, since you allow of the desired Intercourse by Letter, find a speedier way, suppose by the ordinary Posts (that yet may not be expensive to you) when only a single Letter is sent?

I am glad that the Apology for the *Fire-Scene*,[35] as it is called, came so seasonably, and has your Approbation.

I have the German Translation you mention; sent me as a Present: I believe, by Direction of Dʳ· Hollar [sic],[36] who, I am told, is Vice-Chancellor of the University of Göttingen. I have also the French Edition, printed in 12 thin Volumes.[37] It is translated by Abbe Prevost, who has wrote several Pieces of the Novel Kind. This Gentleman has left out, a great deal of the Book. Belton's Despondency and Death, Miss Howe's Lamentation over the Corpse of her beloved Friend: The bringing Home to Harlowe-Place the Corpse, and the Family Grief upon it. The wicked Sinclair's Despondency and Death, and many Letters between Lovelace and Belford, all which I thought might be useful either for Warning or Instruction. He has given his Reasons for his Omissions, as he went along; one of which is, The Genius of his Countrymen; a strange one to me! He treats the Story as a true one, and says, the English Editor has in many Places, sacrificed it to Moral Instruction, &c.

Dr. Hollar, and he, have both sent to me, to request the Shts. of my new Piece as they are printed, for them to translate, into French and German:[38] But not being determined, Whether I shall publish in Parts or all together, I cannot oblige them, because, in the latter Case, they would have an Opportunity to come out in Parts, before I could publish the whole.

I have a kind Letter from a Gentleman of Amsterdam,[39] who has the Felicity of being acquainted with you. In my Answer, I have taken the Liberty of asking his Advice and yours, about the Manner of publishing; that is to say, Whether in Parts or all together. He seems to be an ingenious Man. May I ask, Sir, Whether the Gentleman be a Man of Business? And if he is, What Business? A Bookseller, perhaps.

I am glad to hear that your Bookseller [40] is not likely to be a Loser by so handsome an Edition as he gives the World of Clarissa. He is very happy in having had an Opportunity to ensure his Success by engaging so eminent an Hand in the Translation. I congratulate him and my self upon it. A very worthy and ingenious Man, who is a Judge of the Performance in both Languages, highly applauds yours. If you please to direct ⟨him⟩ /your Bookseller/ to transmit to me, in Sheets, Four Setts as they come out, with Orders to whom to pay for them, I shall have an Opportunity of obliging as many Friends with them [.]

Were I a young Man, I would endeavour to make my self Master of ye Dutch Tongue, for the Benefit I should undoubtedly reap from reading your Works, ⟨and⟩ /as well/as for the Pleasure I should have in reading your Translation of *my own* Clarissa. Pardon a kind of paternal Fondness;

which you have encreased by the Distinction you have given her.

I shall be extremely delighted, I am sure, with your Preface to the new Publication. The more there is of M<sup>r.</sup> Stinstra's in the Work, the more valuable will it be.

In what noble, what useful Works have you been employ'd! How shall I thank you enough, dear and reverend Sir, for the Account you have given me of them, and of your self and Affairs? I find in it Reason for Condolement and Congratulation: The first extends to the whole of your Countrymen; and more particularly to those of your own Church. Most heartily do I congratulate you on that noble Stand which you make for the Sake of a good Conscience against the greatest Discouragements that can happen to a good Man denied the Exercise of those Functions, and the Exertion of Talents which were given him for the Good of Hundreds.

I am sorry, that I had not sooner, your Additions and Emendations to y<sup>e</sup> Pastoral Letter.

It was advertised in English, I think on the very Day, that I recei[v]ed you[r] Pacquets, as "translated by Henry Rimius,["] [41] who states himself Aulic Counsellor to the late King of Prussia; and who had just before published a Piece intitled, A Candid Narrative of the Rise and Progress of the Herrnhuters [1753]. I send you one of each, by that Opportunity ⟨,⟩ that conveys this to your Hand.

At present your Additions and Emendations remain in my Hands.

Our excellent Archbishop has been very much indisposed. He was thought to be in Danger. But, to the Joy of every one got better. Alas! he is relapsed: And we are extremely apprehensive for him: Pray for him Sir. I have not the Honour of being personally known to him: But all good Englishmen, as well as all Foreign Protestants have an Interest in his Welfare, and Preservation. He is a man of a true Catholic Spirit.

And now, Sir, give me Leave to attend to the Questions which your Partiality for me, makes you think it worth your while to ask.

My Father was a very honest Man, descended of a Family of middling Note in the County of Surrey; but which having for several Generations a large Number of Children, the *not* large Possessions were split and divided; so that He and his Brothers were put to Trades; and the Sisters were married to Tradesmen. My Mother was also a good Woman, of a Family not ungenteel; but whose Father and Mother died in her Infancy within half an Hour of each other in the London Pestilence of 1665.[42]

My Father's Business was that of a Joiner, then more distinct from that of a Carpenter, than now it is with us. He was a good Draughtsman, and understood Architecture. His Skill and Ingenuity, and an Understanding superior to his Business, with his remarkable Integrity of Heart and Manners, made him personally beloved by several Persons of Rank, among whom were the Duke of Monmouth and the first Earl of Shaftesbury; both so noted in our English History. Their known Favour for him, having, on the Duke's Attempt on the Crown, subjected him to be looked upon with a jealous Eye, notwithstanding he was noted for a quiet and inoffensive Man, he thought proper, on the Decollation of ⟨that⟩ /the//first-named/ unhappy Nobleman, to quit his London Business and to retire to Derbyshire; tho' to his great Detriment; and there I, and three other Children out of Nine, were born.[43]

He designed me for the Cloth. I was fond of his Choice: But while I was very young, some heavy Losses having disabled him from supporting me as genteelly as he wished in an Education proper for the Function, he left me to choose at the Age of Fifteen or Sixteen, a Business; having been able to give me only common School-Learning[.] I chose that of a Printer,[44] tho' a Stranger to it, as what I thought would gratify my Thirst after Reading. I served a diligent Seven Years to it, to a Master who grudged every

Hour to me, that tended not to his Profit, even of those times of Leisure and Diversion, which the Refractoriness of my Fellow-Servants *obliged* him to allow them, and were usually allowed by other Masters to their Apprentices. I stole from the Hours of Rest and Relaxation, my Reading Times for Improvement of my Mind; and being engaged in a Correspondence with a Gentleman greatly my Superior in Degree, and /of ample/ Fortunes, who had he lived, intended high things for me; those were all the Opportunities I had /in my Apprenticeship/ to carry it on. But this little Incident I may mention; I took Care, that even my Candle was of my own purchasing, that I might not in the most trifling Instance make my Master a Sufferer (and who used to call me The Pillar of his House,) and not to disable my self by Watching, /or Sitting-up,/ to perform my Duty to him in the Day-time.

These, Sir, are little things to trouble you with: But my Circumstances were little, and your Enquiries are minute.

Multitudes of Letters passed between this Gentleman and me. He wrote well; was a Master of the Epistolary Style ⟨; our⟩ /:Our/ Subjects were various: But his Letters were mostly narrative, giving me an Account of his Proceedings, and what befell him in the different Nations thro' which he travelled. I could from them, had I been at Liberty and had I at that time thought of writing as I have since done, have drawn great Helps: But many Years ago, all the Letters that passed between us, by a particular Desire of his, (lest they should ever be published) were committed to the Flames.

I continued Five or Six Years after the Expiration of my Apprenticeship (Part of the Time, as an Overseer of a Printing-House) working as a Compositor, and correcting the Press: As I hinted, in a better Expectation. But *that* failing, I began for my self, married, and pursued Business with an Assiduity that, perhaps, has few Examples; and with the more Alacrity, as I improved a Branch of it, that interfered not with any other Person; and made me more independent of Booksellers (tho' I did much Business for them,) than any other Printer. Some of them, even thought fit to seek me, rather than I them, because of the Readiness I shewed, to oblige them, with writing Indexes, Prefaces, and sometimes for their minor Authors, *honest* Dedication[s]; abstracting, abridging, compiling, and giving my Opinion of Pieces offered them. I have been twice married; to good Women both times. My Business, Sir, has ever been my chief Concern. My Writing-time has been at such times of Leisure as have not interfered with that. From what I have written, you will gather, an Answer to your Question, "In what kind of Life I have been conversant from Youth."

You compliment me, Sir, in your next Question, with a Knowlege of the Manners of Mankind; and ask, Whence I attained this kindly-imputed Knowlege? I had greater Opportunities than I made use of, ⟨of⟩ /from/ the Correspondence I mentioned above. From my earliest Youth, I had a Love of Letter-writing. I was not Eleven Years old, when I wrote, spontaneously, a Letter to a Widow of near Fifty, who, pretending to a Zeal for Religion, and who was a constant Frequenter of Church Ordinances, was continually fomenting Quarrels and Disturbances, by Backbiting and Scandal, among all her Acquaintance. I collected from the Scripture Texts that made against her. Assuming the Style and Address of a Person in Years, I exhorted her; I expostulated with her. But my Hand-writing was known. I was challenged with it, and owned the Boldness; for she complained of it to my Mother with Tears. My Mother chid me for the Freedom taken by such a Boy with a Woman of her Years: But knowing that her Son was not of a pert or forward Nature, but on the contrary, shy and bashful, she commended my Principles, tho' she censured the Liberty taken.

As a bashful and not forward Boy, I was an early Favourite with all the young Women of Taste and Reading in the Neighbourhood. Half a Dozen of them when met to

work with their Needles, used, when they got a Book they
liked, and thought I should, to borrow me to read to them;
their Mothers sometimes with them; and both Mothers and
Daughters used to be pleased with the Observations they
put me upon making.

I was not more than Thirteen when three of these young
Women, unknown to each other, having an high Opinion of
my Taciturnity, revealed to me their Love-Secrets, in order
to induce me to give them Copies to write after, or correct,
for Answers to their Lovers['] Letters: Nor did any one of
them ever know, that I was the Secretary to the others. I
have been directed to chide, and even repulse, when an
Offence was either taken or given, at the very time that the
Heart of the Chider or Repulser was open before me,
overflowing with Esteem and Affection; and the fair Repulser dreading to be taken at her Word, directing *this*
Word, or *that* Expression, to be softened or changed. One,
highly gratify'd with her Lover's Fervor and Vows of everlasting Love, has said, when I have asked her Direction: I
cannot tell you what to write; But (her Heart on her Lips),
you cannot write too kindly; All her Fear only, that she
should incurr Slight for her Kindness.

I recollect, that I was early noted for having Invention. I
was not fond of Play, as other Boys: My Schoolfellows
used to call me *Serious* and *Gravity*: And five of them
particularly, delighted to single me out, either for a Walk,
or at their Fathers' Houses or at mine, to tell them Stories
as they phrased it. Some I told them from my Reading as
true; others from my Head, as mere Invention; of which
they would be most fond; and often were affected by them.
One of them, particularly, I remember, was for putting me
to write a History, as he called it, on the Model of Tommy
Potts; I now forget what it was; only, that it was of a
Servant-Man preferred by a fine young Lady (for his Goodness) to a Lord, who was a Libertine. All my Stories carried with them /I am bold to say/ an useful Moral.

I am ashamed of these Puerilities: But thus, Sir, when I

have been asked a like Question by others, to that you put, have I accounted for a kind of Talent; which I little thought of resuming; or thinking it worthwhile to resume. As a Proof of this, let me say, that when I had written the two first Volumes of Pamela, and was urged by a particular Friend to put it to the Press, I accepted of 20 Guineas for two Thirds of yᵉ Copy-Right; reserving to my self only one Third[.]

You ask, "If I had a Model before my Eyes, in some of my Pieces"? The Story of Pamela had some slight Foundation in Truth. Several Persons of Rank were guessed at, as having in Mind sat for the two principal Characters in that Piece: But no one Conjecture came near the Truth; nor was it likely that it should; for I my self knew no more of the Story, than what I recollected a Gentleman told me of it Fifteen Years before I sat down to write it; and as it was related to him by an Innkeeper in the Neighbourhood of the happy Pair; and which Gentleman had been at the Time, several Years dead.

The writing it then, was owing to the following Occasion: —Two Booksellers, my particular Friends, entreated me to write for them a little Volume of Letters [1741], in a common Style, on such Subjects as might be of Use to those Country Readers who were unable to indite for themselves. Will it be any Harm, said I, in a Piece you want to be written so low, if we should instruct them how they should think and act in common Cases, as well as indite? They were the more urgent with me to begin the little Volume, for this Hint. I set about it, and in the Progress of it, writing two or three Letters to instruct handsome Girls, who were obliged to go out to Service as we phrase it, how to avoid the Snares that might be laid against their Virtue; the above Story recurred to my Thought: And hence sprung Pamela. This Volume of Letters is not worthy of your Perusal. I laid aside several Letters after I had written them for this Volume as too high for the View of my two Friends. But I will send it to you.

I have been raillied on a warm Scene or two in Pamela, as well as for the Fire-Scene in Clarissa, by a few of my Friends, Lovers of Virtue; and who, knowing that my Life from Youth upwards, had not been very censurable, wondered how I came by them. To such it has been answered for me, that there were Scenes of a quite contrary Nature, to those guilty ones, and Characters too, that might be no less, the Subject of Wonder, my Situation in Life considered, and especially Female ones: But it may not misbecome me to assure my Reverend Friend M^r. Stinstra, that he may not from the Jewkes's, the Sinclair's, the M^r. B's, the Lovelace's and others of both Sexes, of like Characters, be ashamed for his Correspondent, that I never, to my Knowlege, was in a vile House, or in Company with a lewd Woman, in my Life. So I have in Pamela described, with Approbation, a Masquerade Scene; yet never was present at one.

Clarissa is a Piece from first to last, that owes its Being to Invention.

The History of my Good Man is also wholly so.

I have some little Pleasure, for the Sake of my Acquaintance and Friends, in being able to say, that no one of them can challenge either for Praise, or for Dispraise, his or her Picture in any of the three Pieces; for I am equally an Enemy to Flattery and personal Abuse. I have no Spleen to gratify, by the one, nor Interest to court by the other. Hence, Sir, you will not see a dedicatory Epistle to one of the Histories; tho' I have the Honour of being esteemed by several Persons, who by their Rank and Fortunes, as well as Merits, would be a Reputation to any Work. I will be bold to say, that never Man of a small Fortune, and obscure Birth and Station, was more independent. God and my own Diligence were ever my chief Reliance. Pardon, Sir, the Boaster.

You ask, Whether any other Pieces than Pamela and Clarissa have been written by me? None, I think worthy of your Notice. I have told you, Sir, that the little Volume of

Letters, to which Pamela owes her Being, is not. I was requested to revise the numerous Editions of Æsop's Fables in English [1739], and to give the Public one I would commend for Children. I will send you one of those: But as I have given some Acct. of it in the Preface, shall say nothing of it here; only that I choose not to set my Name to either of the little Volumes; nor indeed to any thing I have written. A few other little things of the Pamphlet kind I have written; all with a good Intention; But neither are they worthy of your Notice.

I have been engaged in Epistolary Correspondencies, chiefly with Ladies. I am envied Sir, for the Favour I stand in with near a Score of very admirable Women, some of them of Condition; all of them such as would do Credit to their Sex, and to the Commonwealth of Letters, did not their Modesty with-hold them from appearing in it. Yet with several of them, I have charming Contentions, on different Parts of what I have written. Should I ever have the Pleasure to see you in England, I would shew you Volumes of Epistolary Correspondencies; And to these, as a very agreeable Amusement, when I have attended my good Man thro' the Press, I propose to confine my Pen, should Life be spared me any time: For, Sir, I am in an advanced Age; and have by too intense Application, fallen into Nervous Maladies: In short, am almost worn out, as to my Health; tho' I bless God, my Mind, at times when not too much oppressed by bodily Disorders, is not very sensible of Decay.

Only, I should say, that I intend to give to my good Pamela, my last Hand. I find I shall correct it much; but shall leave a particular Regard to preserve ye Simplicity of the Character.

But now, Sir, to your last Question (For I think I have written to all your others, tho' not methodically) "In what Place was the good Man educated, whose History I am about to give?"—His Father is a married Lovelace, as to Gaiety and Immorality. His Mother is an excellent

Woman; who applies her self (exemplarily) to the Education of her Children and /in/ the Domestic Duties. He has
Masters in every Branch of Science, under her Inspexion,
come home to him; till he is Seventeen. About which time,
she dies. Grief for her Death being likely to impair his
Health, he is sent to travel. He behaves with so much
Prudence, tho' his Governor proves a Profligate, and with
so much Honour and Virtue, that his Father keeps him
abroad for Eight or Nine Years, much agt. his Son's
Wishes: Yet tenderly loves him, and glories in him: But,
avowedly, declares, that his Son's Goodness, were he to
allow him to come over, would be a Reproach to him, till he
had entered himself upon the Reformation Scheme; which
he long proposed to begin: But lives not to accomplish. Let
me say, Sir, that you, who have charmed me by the Instance
you give of filial Piety, will be pleased, I am sure, with that
dutiful Behaviour of this Son to both Parents; tho' one of
them was so much exceeded in Worthiness by the other. O
Sir! that we were of one Country! What Pleasure should I
have taken in consulting you, as Occasions offered!—It is
impossible but we should have been intimately acquainted.

I will not bespeak your Favour for my new Piece. I am
sure you will approve of my *Intention* when you come to
peruse it. There are of my Friends, who speak very highly
of what they have seen of it. But the Partiality of Friends
must be allowed for. This only I will say, It is entirely new
and unborrowed, even of my self; tho' I had written so
voluminously before. It is said to abound with delicate Situations. I hope it does; for what indelicate ones can a good
Man be involved in?—Yet he must have his Trials, his
Perplexities—And to have them from good Women, will
require some Management. In Clarissa, my Favourite Clarissa, there is a twofold Correspondence necessary—one between her and Miss Howe; the other between Lovelace and
Belford. The Subject of one Letter arose often out of another. It was necessary it should. In the new Work, (Except
one or two Letters of each of the Respondents, as I may call

them), the Answers to the Letters of the *Narratist* are only supposed, and really sunk; yet Seven Volumes are, to my Regret, made of it, when I have scratched out the Quantity of two, and should have been glad to have comprized the whole in Four,—/Whence/ You will judge, that this /unpublished Work/ whether it /will/ be thought equal or not, must have cost me most Pains. As indeed it has. But I designed it for my last Work; and as the Completion of my whole Plan—If a Man may be allowed to say *Plan;* who never was regular enough to write by one; and who when he ended one Letter, hardly knew what his next would be.

The Corrector of my Press is a good Latin Scholar; and being always at hand, it will /be/ no manner of Inconvenience to me, that you continue your Favours to me in that Tongue. How glad should I be, to understand Dutch as well as you do English!

What follows, are Extracts from /a few of the Letters/ sent me from different Persons, promised in my former: *Made*, as the above poor Account of my self is *written*, wholly for your own private Satisfaction, and Perusal. I will in Confidence name the Writers to you.[45]

    I. *From Mrs. Delany, Lady of Dr. Delany, Dean of Down, in Ireland.[46] The Dean is Author of the Life of David, of several other Pieces, that have been well received; and was a particular Friend of Dr. Swift.*

    *Sir,*

                             *18 June 1748.*

Having perform'd my Part as Secretary, will you excuse my taking up so much of your time, as to speak my Thoughts about your Clarissa, which I have read with great Pleasure and Satisfaction; and think myself obliged to make my best Acknowlegements to you, for such an Entertainment? And I think I may venture to say, That if all your Readers, read it with as much Attention as I have done, their Hearts must be the better for it. So much good Sense, such an Example of Virtue, such a Knowlege of Mankind, and the vicious

Samuel Richardson

Portrait by Joseph Highmore in the National Portrait Gallery, London

And now, Sir, give me Leave to attend to the Questions which your Partiality for me, makes you think it worth your while to ask.

My Father was a very honest Man, descended of a Family of middling Note in the County of Surrey; but which having for several Generations a large Number of Children, the not large Possessions were split and divided; so that He and his Brothers were put to Trades: and the Sisters were married to Tradesmen. My Mother was also a good Woman, of a Family not ungenteel; but whose Father and Mother died in her Infancy within half an Hour of each other in the London Pestilence of 1665.

My Father's Business was that of a Joiner, then more distinct from that of a Carpenter, than now it is with us. He was a good Draughtsman, and understood Architecture. His Skill and Ingenuity, and an Understanding superior to his Business, with his remarkable Integrity of Heart and Manners, made him personally beloved by several Persons of Rank, among whom were the Duke of Monmouth and the first Earl of Shaftesbury; both so noted in our English History. Their known Favour for him, having, on the Duke's Attempt on the Crown, suggested him to be looked upon with a jealous Eye, notwithstanding he was noted for a quiet and inoffensive Man, he thought proper, on the Decollation of the first-named unhappy Nobleman, to quit his London Business, and to retire to Derbyshire; this to his great Detriment; and there I, and three other Children out of Nine, were born.

He designed me for the Cloth. I was fond of his Choice: But while I was very young, some heavy Losses having disabled him from supporting me as genteelly as he wished in an Education proper for the Function, he left me to choose at the Age of Fifteen or Sixteen, a Business; having been able to give me only common School-Learning. I chose that of a Printer, tho' a Stranger to it, as what I thought would gratify my Thirst after Reading. I served a diligent Seven Years to it, to a Master who grudged every Hour to me, that tended not to his Profit, even of those hours of Leisure and Diversion, which the Refractoriness of my Fellow-Servants obliged him to allow them, and were usually allowed by other Masters to their Apprentices. I stole from the Hours of Rest and Relaxation, my Reading Times for Improvement of my Mind; and being engaged in a Correspondence with a Gentleman, greatly my Superior in Degree and of ample Fortunes, who had he lived intended large things for me; those were all the Opportunities I had to carry it on. But this little Incident I may mention; I took Care, that even my Candle was of my own purchasing, that I might not in the most trifling Instance make my Master a Sufferer (and who used to call me the Pillar of his House) and not to disable myself by Watching or Sitting-up, to perform my Duty to him in the Day-time.

The opening paragraphs of the autobiographical section of
Richardson's letter of June 2, 1753

The beginning of Stinstra's first letter in English,
December 24, 1753

Johannes Stinstra

From a photograph of the original in the rectory of the
Mennonite Congregation, Harlingen

Part of them so justly exposed, must not only be extremely entertaining, but be an excellent Lesson to those who are not harden'd so far, as *to refuse the Voice of the Charmer*. But, Sir, now you have interested me so strongly for the unhappy and deserving Clarissa, will you have the Cruelty to leave me long in the anxious State I am in for her? I have just finished the Fourth Volume, and am more delighted with the Two last Volumes than the Two first. I was so provoked by the Tyrannical Usage of the *Harlowes* to the excellent Clarissa, that I detested their Company, and was glad to run away from them. My Impatience to see her meet with a Reward to her Virtue (for surely her Disobedience hath been sufficiently chastised) is not the only Motive I have, for wishing the Publication of the Sequel; but the Hope, and Desire I have of your beginning some other Work of this Kind. The Dean bids me add, he agrees perfectly with me in all I have said, tho' he owns, that the Subject is so moving and interesting, that he could not go regularly through the Book: But by what he has read, and what I have repeated to him, he approves and admires the Work. Can you excuse the Liberty I have taken of saying so much? I am, Sir,

*Your assured Friend & obliged Humble Serv^t*

II. *From Mr. Henry Fielding,*[47] *Author of Joseph Andrewes [sic], Tom Jones, Amelia, and many other Pieces; written on Perusal of the Vth Volume. He had been a zealous Contender for the Piece ending, as it is called, happily.*

*Dear Sir,*

*October 15^th 1748.*
I have read over your Fifth Volume. In all the Accounts which Lovelace gives of the Transactions at Hamstead, you preserve the same Vein of Humour which hath run through the preceding Volumes. The new Characters you introduce are natural and entertaining; and there is much of the true Comic Force in the Widow Bevis. I have seen her often, and I promise you, you have drawn her with great Exactness.

The Character of Lovelace is heightened with great Judgment. His former Admirers must lose all Regard for him on his Perseverance, and as this Regard ceases, Compassion for Clarissa rises in the same

Proportion. Hence we are admirably prepared for what is to follow.

Shall I tell you? can I tell you, what I think of the latter Part of your Volume? Let the Overflowings of a Heart which you have filled brimful speak for me.

When Clarissa returns to her Lodgings at Sinclair's, the Alarm begins, and here my Heart begins its Narrative. I am shocked; my Terrors are raised, and I have the utmost Apprehensions for the poor betrayed Creature. But when I see her enter with a Letter in her Hand, and after some natural Effects of Despair, clasping her Arms about the Knees of the Villain, call him dear Lovelace, desirous and yet unable to implore his Protection, or rather his Mercy, I then melt into Compassion, and find what is called an effeminate Relief for my Terror. So I continue to the End of the Scene.

When I read the next Letter I am Thunderstruck; nor can many Lines explain what I feel from Two.

What shall I say of holding up the License? I will say, a finer Picture was never imagined. He must be a glorious Painter who can do it Justice on Canvas, and a most wretched one indeed who could not do much on such a Subject.

The Circumstance of the Fragments is great and terrible: But her Letter to Lovelace is beyond any thing I have ever read. God forbid that the Man who reads this with dry Eyes should be alone with my Daughter, when she hath no Assistance within call!

Here my Terror ends, and my Grief begins, which the Cause of all my tumultuous Passions soon changes into Raptures of Admiration and Astonishment, by a Behaviour the most elevated I can possibly conceive, and which is at the same time most gentle, and most natural. This Scene I have heard hath been objected to. It is well for the Critic that my Heart is now writing, and not my Head.

During the Continuance of this Volume, my Compassion is often moved, but I think my Admiration more. If I had received no Hint or Information of what is to succeed, I should perceive the paving the Way to lead our Admiration of your Heroine to the highest Pitch, as you have before with wonderful Art prepared us for both Terror and Compassion on her Account.

III. *The following is from Mr. John Channing.*[48] *Not a Public Writer: But his Letters will make out to you his Character.*

Dear Sir,

October 26th 1748.

I sat up with your Heroine till near One o'Clock this Morning; but there's no parting from *such* Company, especially in Distress. Pray favour me with a little more, if it is not too much to ask of you; for 'till I have gone through the Whole, or at least as far as I can, I shall think on no other Subject. I have visited all your Characters by turns all Night long; and shall continue with them To-day, much more than with any body else. I want Words to express what I would say—But! your Bookselling Curtailers I can never forgive. Excuse the Impatience of, Dear Sir,

Ever Yours, &c.

IV. *From the Same.*[49]

Dear Sir,

October 29. 1748

With sincere Thanks I return you the Sheets you so kindly entrusted me with Yesterday (as well as those I had forgot belonging to the Sixth Volume). Every Letter of which I have read, except Mowbray's last. This I began, but could not read three Lines of it; wholly engross'd by our departed Friend. May you and I have the same infinite Support in that Moment, when Flesh and Heart shall fail! I am, Dear Sir,

Yours, &c. &c.

V. *From the Same.*[50]

Dear Sir,

October 31. 1748.

I return'd your Paper Saturday with sincere Thanks; myself very truly affected with them. I had carefully perused every Line, and attended the last Moments of your Heroine, with such Emotions of Soul, as every unsteel'd Reader must be Witness to. But when the next Correspondent presented, I could not read Three Lines.—Who, without a much longer Pause, could leave the Company of a departing Saint, and enter that of a brutal Mowbray?—*His* Character, no doubt is as well preserved, as *I know* all the rest have been hitherto: But till I have paused, and reflected some time, I can no more be entertain'd with any thing such a Character can say, than I should have been with a Buffoon, or a Harlequin, playing Tricks over the fresh-dug Grave of my Father.

It may be accounted a selfish Partiality to my own Opinion; but to me, the Desire of having your Piece end happily (as it is call'd) will ever be the Test of a wrong Head, and a vain Mind.—Let Belton *feel*, all that Wickedness can feel; and Clarissa *enjoy* all the Serenity, which Piety, and Piety only, can bestow.—How much more instructively will these Scenes be form'd to touch the Hearts both of Good and Bad, than any which can be drawn upon the contrary Plan! Two Deaths pictured in the strongest Contrast. One filled with the gloomy Remorse created by a Life spent in wanton Impiety; the other glorious in that Peace which is the promised Conclusion of a Life devoted to Heaven and Virtue: The one like the tempestuous Sea which cannot rest, whose Waters cast forth Mire and Dirt; The other all humble Resignation, and unclouded Hope!—Who can read this, and not most heartily adopt the Wish of a very bad Man, *Let me die the Death of the Righteous; and let my latter End be like his?*

Your Reader will be shock'd forsooth! at poor Belton's horrid End: Be it so. Perhaps too at Clarissa's Coffin, and her Familiarity with an Object naturally undesirable. And yet I can assure you, my dear Friend, some Scenes I have myself been present at, very much resembling those you represent; the Memory of which I would wish never to lose. And give me Leave to say, the Reader who wou'd be most shock'd by them, has perhaps the most need of them.

My own Father was remov'd from this World, by a painful, lingering, tedious Illness. The Morning of the Day on which he died, his Pains and Oppression of Breathing were so excessive, that by the Consent of his Physicians he was blooded, with an expectation of alleviating them. It had its Effect. My Brother and self were in the Afternoon sitting by him, when bidding me feel his Pulse, he charged me on my Duty to tell him truly how long I imagined he might yet be continued. Being answered, scarce an Hour—I bless God for it, said he: Be, sure, Children, that you cultivate true Religion and Virtue. Never think hardly of God, or his Providence, from what you have seen me suffer. God has been kind and merciful to me in all this Dispensation; and I bless ⟨God⟩ /him/ for it. I can look forward with Comfort and Pleasure. I am now easy, and believe I shall *go off* without Pain[.] Then asking for a little Wine—I drink to all your Welfares: I take my last solemn Farewel [sic] of you, said he: God bless you all, and be for ever with you! I will now try to sleep; and let me not be disturb'd.—He seem'd to dose, and in a few Minutes expir'd, without any external Appearances of the least Uneasiness.

Can I remember this, can I have this Parting, awful, and, let me say too, pleasing Lesson repeated, and not take time solemnly to reflect upon it? 'Tis too solemn, too pleasing, too interesting to admit at present any other. Will God himself visit the good Man upon his Bed of Languishing? Will he make all his Bed in his Sickness? Will he put underneath him his everlasting Arms, and support him under the tottering Ruins of Morality? Have I seen this in *Picture,* and in *Reality*!

You will, I'm sure, forgive me, if the Subject engross me for some time, and I refuse to listen to Mowbray, and his detested Character.

vi. *From the Same.*[51]

*Dear Sir,*

*November 28. 1748.*

I have just finished your Clarissa; and I can't help telling you before I go to Bed how much the Whole has pleased me, and most heartily to thank you for it. Whoever accuses you of want of strict Poetical Justice, must have quite different Notions from mine; and I think will never be able to make me alter my Opinion. To tell you, or indeed endeavour to tell you, how great an Esteem I have for the Whole, would look so much like Flattery, that I shall be silent upon that Head; only give me Leave to Say, That when I had read the Whole, *I Wish'd to have that Pleasure to go over again*; or a new Work of yours of the same Length, or double if you please, to begin upon: For, tho' I doubt not many new Beauties will appear upon a Re-perusal which have hitherto escaped me, and will therefore afford a Pleasure of a different Sort; yet the pleasure arising from a Work *quite new*, can never be repeated on a Second Reading. I am ⟨very⟩ sorry Brand's other Letter was omitted; as I am likewise that *Sinclair's End*, was not *as circumstantially described*, as that Part of the horrid Scene you have inserted. Will it look like Vanity in me? I must say it notwithstanding; I think your Postscript unnecessary, and too great a Deference paid to the Opinions of many of your Friends; who, I am confident, most of them, will retract every thing they have said; and agree, that Clarissa's Apotheosis is every way a strict Poetical Justice, and a much more glorious one (due indeed to her exalted Character) as the Happiness or Unhappiness bestowed upon the other Characters.

To tell you that there are no Blemishes or Inequalities in the Whole, would be saying what could never yet be said of any Human Composition. Through the Whole, however, I can truly tell you, that no one has offer'd itself to me worth mentioning, or which I can recollect. On a second reading perhaps there may: But I have been too much pleased, and too earnestly engaged, to stop to look out for Trifles, or pick little Faults, as Subjects for dull Criticism—I ever read to be pleased, and instructed. Pleasure I am sure I have received, and I hope Instruction likewise. My Wife and her Companion went out this Evening a visiting, and gave an Opportunity of sitting down alone to read that Part of your Work which follows the Copy of the Will to the Conclusion. The deserved Distress of the Family, the solemn Scene of the Funeral, the Description of every Circumstance by Colonel Morden, the posthumous Letter to Lovelace; his wild Rage, his in vain attempted Mastery over his own torturing Reflexions: his affected outside Levity—are Pictures so drawn, as I never yet have seen; nor ever expect to see again: But must have done, or shall be suspected of the Flattery, while I mean the Friend.

In Spite of knowing the Whole a Fiction; *in Spite even of your Postscript*, every different human Passion is excited; Love, Admiration, Esteem; of the highest and most exalted Kind: Pity, Resentment, Indignation; even to Execration: In short, you carry me with you wherever you please; and enrage, calm, or transport me; and make all your Characters living and real.

VII. *From Mrs. Delany.*[52]

*Sir,*

*January 25*[th] *1748–9.*

I have just finished Clarissa. I was so eager to get the Three last Volumes that I made use of all the Art I had to prevail on Mr. Falkner [53] to let me have it before it was published: And he gratified me.

I never had so great a Mixture of Pain and Pleasure in the Reading of any Book in my Life. I was almost broken-hearted at some Passages, and raised above this World in others. It is not possible to describe the Effects it had on me and the Doctor. By Turns we read it; and many times were obliged to throw down the Book, unable to proceed: You can better imagine than I express how much we were touched. I am not only much obliged to you for the high Entertainment I have had in reading this interesting Story, but for the fine Lessons in it, which I hope to be the better for, as long as I live; and especially at those last Moments, so necessary to think of, and prepare for, before we are disabled by Age, Accidents, and Infirmities.

I own, I was surprized to find Clarissa's Distress rise to so great a Height; and flattered myself, that she would have escaped the worst of her Persecutor's Villainies. But I see plainly your excellent Design in it: Her End could not have been so exalted, so glorious, and so exemplary, had she not been the most injured of Women: Her Humiliation, and Forgiv⟨e⟩/ing/ness to all her implacable Tormentors, makes her a truly Christian Heroine. Were I to dwell on all the Beauties as they strike me; the Variety of Characters so finely supported; such Strokes of Nature, that go to the very Soul; such fine and lively Painting, that it is impossible to think it a Fiction; and the Justness of the Moral to the Whole; I should run out into too great a Length; and I am very sensible, my Approbation can do you but little Honour, tho' it does some to my own Heart. I am, Sir,

*Your most obliged Humble Servant.*

I have read this to the Doctor, who desires me to assure you, he perfectly agrees with me in every thing I have said in it, and begs you to accept his warmest and sincerest Thanks for a Work which he scruples not to declare to the whole World, that he thinks it the most valuable of any this Age has produced. He pities himself and his own Sermons, when he sees how much more nobly, and powerfully, yours touch the Heart; from the Mouth of innocent Virtue, opprest and injured, but still unconquered; and even from the Confession and Conversion of licentious Libertinism.

You have been happy in striking out two very distinct Characters of suffering Virtue: The first successful in Perserverance; the second, triumphant in Oppression: Her Fortitude unabated by Injuries, shocking to Human Nature; and her truly Christian Piety, rising still higher under them to a Sublimity, truly Angelick, I could scarce forbear wishing myself so circumstanced, in the Agonies of instant Death. God in his Mercy grant I may, when it shall please him to call me! The Character of profligate Guilt opposed to her, is, not less edifying and instructive. Confounded and appalled in the midst of insolent Success, harrassed by Remorse, distracted by Despair (Despair that heightens the Tortures of the never-dying Worm) remorseless in the Prosecution of Guilt, disappointed in the Success of it, unspeakably wretched, tormented, and abandoned to Horror in the Issue; and concluding all in a sudden, violent, and unexpected Death; pitied by his mortal Enemy; and given up to the Struggles of Pride and Rage in the very Agonies of it; but expiring (So your great Charity and Humanity would have it) in a short seeming Effort of Piety and Penitence.

God in his Goodness preserve and bless with all temporal and eternal Good, the Heart which he has so happily inspired! This is /the/ ardent Prayer of, Dear Sir,

*Your most Faithful and Affectionate*
*Patrick Delany*
(Dean of Down)

VIII. *From Dr. Young, Author of the Night Thoughts, to Mrs. Delany, who had written to him for his Opinion of Clarissa.*

*Madam,*

*February 9*th *1748–9.*

You carry your Complaisance too far, when you make an Apology for conferring a Favour; for such is your Letter. But your Request I do not well understand. If your Meaning is, only to learn the real Value of Clarissa, it is too high a Compliment to desire my Opinion, when the Doctor is so near you. However, I will give you my Opinion most sincerely. I know no Work that discovers more

Excellence of both Head and Heart together in the Writer than this. What Entertainment! What Instruction! It might perhaps sound oddly, if I should say, That the Bench of Bishops might go to School to the Writer of a Romance: And yet I think there are but few who might not be both the wiser and better for reading it. But tho' all may find their Advantage in it, yet they that have Daughters will find themselves more particularly indebted to Mr. Richardson: For I conceive, that Clarissa may not improperly be called *The Whole Duty of WOMAN*. To point all I would particularly commend, were endless. I shall therefore only /just/ touch a single Particular in the first and in the last Volume. In the First, how inexpressibly tender and affecting are the Scenes between Clarissa and her Mother! Tell me not, Madam, of any of your Friends that have read those exquisite Scenes with dry Eyes, lest, tho' they are Mrs. Delany's Friends, I should entertain but an indifferent Opinion of them: In the last Volume, my Friend (Pardon the Vanity!) *my* Friend Mr. Richardson has performed the difficult Task of making a Death-bed an Object of Envy, I think more effectually than any that have gone before him. In a Word; I look on it as a Work of true and uncommon Genius; and, like all such, the more it is read, the more it will be liked. So that as yet its Reputation, tho' great, is but in its Minority. And I verily believe it will be read with Profit and Admiration, as long as the mutable Language in which it is written is able to convey its precious Contents to our Posterity.

IX. *From the Revd. Mr. Skelton,*[54] *Author of a Piece agt. Deism and other Pieces, that have been well received, both in England and Ireland; of which last Kingdom he is.*

*Dear Sir,*

*Monaghan, June 10. 1749.*

I am almost blinded with gazing at the Sun in order to find out its Spots; and all ⟨that⟩ I could discover (if they are not /rather/ so many Motes in my own Eyes) are noted in the inclosed Paper. The Lustre and Warmth of this Object often drew such Quantities of Moisture into my Eyes, as not only hindered me from seeing its Defects (if any it hath) but even hid from me the lovely Object itself. It is happy for the Readers of Clarissa, that its Author proposed to himself so noble an End as that of rectifying the

Heart thro' its Passions; and not, like other Novel-Writers, that only of amusing its Corruptions; happy indeed! because he can do what he will with the Heart. Is it because his Heart and mine are closely united in Friendship, that every thing that comes from his, goes directly, with all its Force, and Warmth, into mine? Or shall I for this Reason have the Vanity to think my Heart is like his? No; his excites Ardours in it, and forces Impressions on it, which it had not before. And yet his tender Touches do no [sic] not with more Power and Expedition new-Model my Affections, than his just Sentiments, and excellent Precepts, improve my Understanding. Some Writers can move the Passions; others can inform the Mind; a very few can do both: Some can Please and others Shock. But who like this Writer, can please and shock, can fill us with Delight and Horror, at once? Nay, what is still more, in the midst of this Tempest (which, had it not first raged in his own Mind, could never have been propagated into ours) can steadily keep his glorious End in View; can so nicely take his Aim at our Corruptions; can with so even an Hand, point every violent Passion to his Purpose; and while the Heart is deeply pierced, and powerfully stirr'd, and laid open, as wide as it can stretch to him, can sedately form, and plentifully pour in, the most useful, the most noble Lessons of Morality and Religion? It is an ordinary thing to see an Author, who can raise, and ride in a Whirlwind; but give me the Man who can direct the Storm.

In this little Sketch, may be seen, faintly represented, what I think of Clarissa. And now give me leave, my dearest Friend, Friend of my Soul! let me call you, to return you the Thanks of an Heart, that is transported, and mended, by your Performance—

I could send you many more. But these, Sir, will be sufficient to answer ye proposed End. Some greater Names, I would not be free with, without their Leave. By the Word *greater*, I mean only in Degree.

Acquit me, dear and Reverend Sir, of Ostentation in these. I hope you would if I had the Felicity to be personally known to you.

Yet what will you think of me, if I inclose in this Pacquet a certain Copper-Plate; stimulated to it, by your Enquiries, of a minute Nature? It was done at the Command of a Great Man, tho' with some little Reluctance complied with.

I keep it entirely in my own Hands, and suffer it only to pass into those of particular Friends.

*June 1. 1753.* I kept my Letter open, in hopes to see the Friend who furnished me with the Intelligence of the Archbishop of Canterbury's Directions relating to the Translation of your Pastoral Letter; and /to know from him,/ whether Mʳ· Majendie's Translation ⟨was⟩ /were/ sunk in that of Rimius, &c. —And, behold! another choice Favour from you claims my most thankful Acknowlegements— The Third and Fourth Volumes of /your/ Clarissa! Most cordially I thank you for them, dear and reverend Sir; and for the Letter which accompanies them.

I have given out your Preface to be translated. How kindly considerate is the favouring me with the Substance of it!—The more obliging, as it gives me an Opportunity to dispatch to you my Pacquet sooner than I could have done, had I waited till it was translated. Yet, impatient to read what you have ornamented the Work with, I told the Person I Employ in the Translation that he should have his own Terms, if he made Dispatch.

As to the Enquiry you make into the meaning of the Words—"Such worse than Waltham Disguises;" they allude to the following Fact: About the Years 1722 and 1723 great Numbers of disorderly Persons associated themselves, and entered armed and in Disguise, (their Faces blacked) into several Forests and Parks (particularly into that of Waltham) in the Counties of Berks and Southampton, and killed and carried off many Deer, and frequently by menacing Letters demanded Money and Venison to be sent them to particular Places, on pain of Murdering, /the Persons sent to, or of/ burning, and destroying their Houses, Barns, &c. And to such a pitch of Audaciousness had they arrived, that assembling in large Bodies, they fired at many Persons in their own Houses, maimed their Cattle, broke down their Gates and Fences, cut down young Plantations of Trees, Avenues, and broke down the Heads of Fishponds, robbing them of /their/ Fish. Insomuch that the Legislature was obliged to Exert itself by a particular Act of Parliament making Persons appearing /armed and/ in Disguise, ⟨and⟩ to be guilty of Felony.

Our good Archbishop is better: But his numerous Friends are anxious for him still.

The Æsop's Fables is out of Print, and reprinting: A better not being to be got at Present, excuse, Sir, the dirty one I send you.

Excuse, Sir, all my Imperfections; and my bad Writing. I cannot transcribe: But if you meet with any Difficulty from my Hand-writing, I will, for the future send you my Kinsman's fair Copy.

If I am known by Name to your good Mother, Sir, Be pleased to make my Compliments acceptable to her. And believe me to be with Truth and Affection,

*Your most obliged Humble Serv<sup>t</sup>*

*S. Richardson*

*London, June 2. 1753.*

[6]

# Richardson *to* Stinstra

*June 12, 1753*

*London, June 12, 1753.*

*Reverend and Dear Sir,*

The Person I employed to translate into English your admirable Preface to the 3<sup>d</sup> and 4<sup>th</sup> Volumes, has but just now brought it to me. It is a *truly* admirable Performance. In some Places as I read, I rejoiced, (tho' I thought you did me /in it/ every where, too much Honour) that I had written a Piece, that had produced so fine and so instructive a Performance, were that to be the only Benefit to result from the Story of Clarissa, to my self.

But shall I say, good Sir, that I was not a little concerned at your mentioning the five Bishops, who honoured me with their Friendship; ⟨said⟩ /and/ that one of them had declared that he had read the History of Clarissa Eleven times, and proposed, &c? This, Sir, is true; but those Bishops will imagine that the Intelligence must come from me: And as they are known to be my Favourers, I shall not be able to see *them* with Pleasure, if they would *me*; since the public ⟨who⟩ /here, who shall/ see what you have written, will not be at a Loss to name them. Indeed, Sir, I am greatly concerned on this Occasion. And if you could procure the Leaf where that Circumstance is mentioned, to be cancelled in as many Books as possible, you would do me a very great Favour; and I will gladly pay for any Expence that shall attend it. It will not give me /much/ Pain to have what I wish to be omitted, said to your private Friends; but then I wish it not to be said *Five*, but *Several*; and to avoid naming *Eleven* by the same Word (*Several*) (And here let me beg of you, Sir, to accept of the little Account I have given of my self in the Parcel I have delivered to Mr. Godin for you, and the Extracts accompanying that Account, solely as for (*your own*), and (select Friends) Perusal, and not on any Account to be printed. I can trust my self and Character to your Candor: But as those Particulars could come from no one but my self, I must beg of you, not to expose me as the vain Creature I must appear to be to those who know me not, were the Extracts I have caused to be transcribed for you (to say nothing of my not having Leave for such an Use to be made of them) to be given to the Public[.) ]

Oblige me, dear, and reverend Sir, in this Cancelling; and let your Bookseller add the Expence of doing it to the Four Books I have requested to be sent me; and draw upon me at Sight, and I will do Honour to the Draught. What you have said, without that Passage, is greatly kind and [full ?]. But you will easily supply the Chasm made by yᵉ Omission; /for the Sake of making the Page out./

Continue to me, dear and good Sir, your Esteem. That of

so learned and worthy a Man, will be ever my Ambition to
cultivate. Yet you oppress me by your favourable Goodness
to me in a multitude of Places, in this Preface, as well as in
your former; and in the very kind Letters you have honoured me with. If I might ask another Favour of you, it
wou{ld} be, that when you mention me to the Public, you
would restrain your kind Heart, and no{t} permit it to find
so ready a Passage to your Pen.

I am, Sir, with equal Respect, and Gratitude,
*Your most faithful and*
*affectionate Humble Servt.*
*S. Richardson.*

I rejoice in the Hopes you give of a Preface to each of the
two succeeding Publications. What Labour have you
been at! What Pains! How much does that Labour,
and those Pains enhance the Value of the Work!—
What a valuable Edition will be the Dutch one!—


[7]

## Stinstra *to* Richardson

### *June 23, 1753*

*To The Very Kindly Man, Samuel Richardson, Jo-*
*hannes Stinstra Sends Many Greetings*
Yesterday, after I read your letter which was sent to
me on the 12th of this month, I was very sorry that I had
done something by which I have caused grief to your mind,
which is so very favorable to me; I forthwith decided that I
had to obey your desire and remove the sheet of my Preface
which contains the section about the five Bishops and substi-
tute another. Without hesitation I assumed responsibility of
bearing the cost which this required in order to wash away
this blame as much as I could. But after more mature
consideration of the matter and after taking common coun-

sel with my bookseller, I see a problem; and I am beginning
to fear that I increase my former lack of foresight with a
new one. For very many copies are already scattered about
throughout Holland, not only in the booksellers' shops but
also in the hands of private persons and are already much
worn and read. By putting the alteration which you want in
the smaller number of the copies which remains at the printer's, I would not satisfy the purpose you have in mind. Now
if that corrected sheet were sent around to all booksellers'
shops and handed over to private persons to exchange for
the former sheet in all copies already sold, everyone would
pay attention to this because of the strangeness of the thing,
search out the cause; and when the reason for the change
were learned, gossip would be created which would by no
means be favorable to my withholding an explanation, not
to mention the difficulty that there perhaps would be many
people who would not want to hand over their books.
Meanwhile, you so vigorously demand the alteration of me
that I am completely in the dark as to what I should do.
Therefore I decided to write you as quickly as possible in
order that, now that these circumstances have been pointed
out, you can judge what has to be done and inform me of
your wishes, which I shall most gladly obey. The interval of
time which meanwhile will elapse will make little difference
in taking care of this alteration, since very many copies have
already been circulated, as I reminded you just now.

I feel greatly distressed that I have forced you, whom I
honor with all respect, into these difficulties and that I have
brought it about that you cannot see your distinguished
friends with your usual delight. Lest you should think that I
have committed this fault very thoughtlessly, please allow
me to point out the reasons which moved me to publish
these remarks. I thought that outside the borders of these
Provinces there would be nobody who would read or seek
the Dutch edition, since our tongue is understood almost
exclusively by the inhabitants of Holland itself; I had no
idea that it would be transported to England. And I cannot

yet be convinced that any Dutchman living in London (to whom this especially would happen) who could drink in these great beauties from the fountain source would prefer to receive them from a drainage ditch. Therefore I thought that no man in England except you would ever know that I had mentioned this. Besides, you yourself had told me this truth so kindly, so sincerely, in order to encourage me (*to strengthen your hands* was your saying) in overcoming the prejudices with which I had to struggle as a theologian in dealing with matters of this kind. Finally, my eagerness to extol the praises of this very delightful and useful work easily moved me at the time to urge my countrymen to reread it more often. But if my Preface is indeed generally read in England too (as you seem to fear), I confess that my deliberation led me on the wrong path, perhaps carried away by this eagerness. But perhaps (if after committing such a fault I may speak freely), your eagerness to respect propriety renders you too delicate. For from what source, I ask, will those Bishops be able to learn that these things were written to me by you, granted that acquaintance of this affair ever reaches them? Have they not avowed to others also what they have avowed to you? Or have they perhaps concealed from others the praises of your work which they declared to you? And thus, that which I have mentioned could have been told me by others, perhaps by one of your friends to whom you had told of the affair who, also solicitious for your fame as I am, could have informed me of it. Indeed, I have come to know from elsewhere that a distinguished Bishop in England has publicly announced Clarissa as a model of living and dying rightly. This I bring forward not to diminish my fault but to reduce your anxiety as much as possible. I wish very much that I had not published this; I would wash away that fault by any atonement whatever. Most passionately I beseech you to forgive me this and not to allow that anything be taken away from the favor with which you honor me.

Please do not fear that I shall again dash against the same stone. I understand now that I am received among your more intimate friends, and I rejoice from the heart. Everything you regard proper to impart to me, especially those things about which I ventured before to ask you, will be kept in complete confidence; and I shall preserve them as a treasure committed to my very thankful heart. Finally, I am now with the greatest enthusiasm awaiting that packet which you said you have handed to Mr. Godin and which I have not yet received. And thus I do not know what these 4 books are which you said you have asked from our bookseller. As soon as they are delivered to me, I shall gladly see that they are sent to you as quickly as possible.

Some days ago I learned from the *Gentlem. Magaz.* of May that my "Letter Against the Fanatics" has already been published in English; [55] but I think this translation was done by another hand, and this was the translation for which you had raised my hope. Therefore my remarks undoubtedly have been of no use to this person. They are of little weight, for that matter.

You refresh me by your very kind request to continue with this pleasing correspondence. Because of your sense of honor for the Bishops who you think will take it ill that their favor towards you has been made known, you tell me what attitude I should take towards you; then I gladly shall accept any suggestion, and my impartial love will prevail over the feeling of shame. As for your very well-deserved praises (which my eager heart bids me to avow anew), I shall indeed try to check them as much as possible in my letters, lest they become irksome to you. But I shall not at all be able to find it in my heart to be silent about them or to suppress them when I display and recommend your works. If I should do this, I would be unjust to the cause of virtue, to the welfare of my fellow citizens, and to my own labor, by which I desire to inspire them with love for it; I shall think my work abundantly compensated if it bears this fruit.

With all glory—but remembering the promise, I take my hand from the picture. Farewell, most friendly Sir, and please continue to love me as you have begun to do.

*23 June 1753*

[8]

## Richardson *to* Stinstra

*July 4, 1753*

Let me, my good and dear M^r. Stinstra, obtain your Excuse for the Pain I gave you by the Contents of my Letter of the 12th. I hope it will be taken, if any of my Friends come to the Knowlege of the Passage I was concerned about, that the Intelligence might come from some other Person, and not from me. One of the Great Men with whom I have the Honour to be acquainted, and who might look upon himself as one of the Five, is extremely delicate. Yet has never scrupled to own his Approbation of Clarissa in very high Terms. I am sure you will forgive me, for the Pain I have given you.

The Four Books I mention in the same Letter, are so many Setts of Clarissa, as translated by you; which I will chearfully pay for to your Booksellers['] Order. I have so particularly explained my self in y^e Parcel and Letter I have sent together (and which perhaps, is by this time, come to your Hand) in relation to those, and to several other Articles, that I will take the Liberty to referr to them, and say the less here.

You are very kind, Sir, ⟨in engaging⟩ /to engage/, that none but select Friends shall see the Extracts I have actually sent you. The Authors of them would know, were they communicated to the Public, that they must come from me. But were there any thing that you thought would be of Service to your Edition, I would ask their Leave. Be free, dear and good Sir, with me; and let not this perhaps Over-Delicacy of mine, occasion any the least Reserve on your Part, to one who honours, and must always honour you.

I ask, in the Pacquet not come to your Hands, your Advice in relation to the Manner of publishing my New Piece. It becomes me to tell you, Sir, that my present Determination is, To publish the two first Volumes in October or November next; to publish two others on or about the Middle of December; the Remainder which will be three Vols. in Twelves, Two in Octavo (Six of yᵉ latter, Seven of the former, in all) about the Month of February following.⁵⁶

I forget whether I mentioned to you the Applications I had for Sheets before Publication, from Germany, France, the Hague (M. de Freval) ⁵⁷ and Ireland. I believe I shall oblige the Irish Requester soon, with Shts. of the two first Vols. He has offered me a Premium. /for the Preference./ (Let me know, I pray you, dear Sir, whether the Publication of my New Piece will affect your Undertaking any Way in relation to Clarissa. They are absolutely independent of each other.[)] I have given you, Sir, a brief Sketch of my Plan in the Letter I have committed, with yᵉ little Pacquet, to the Care of Mʳ· Godin: So shall not mention any more of it here, either.

Believe me to be, dear and reverend Sir, with yᵉ most sincere Respects,

*Your obliged and faithful*
*Humble Servant*
*S. Richardson.*

*London, July 4. 1753.*

[9]

## Stinstra *to* Richardson

*August 11, 1753*

*To Samuel Richardson, Greetings From Johannes Stinstra*

I am indeed overwhelmed with a feeling of shame when I think over your indulgence to me, by which you not only forgive my fault but even ask to be pardoned for causing me anxiety, which I deserved. When I perceive with how great conscientiousness you fulfill the rights of friendship, I cannot help declaring that my respect for you is growing daily and that I am burning with desire to render myself more and more worthy of that kind of favor of which you have given me a share.

This answer to your letter sent to me on the 4th day of this month, I have admittedly delayed for some days, in the hope that I would shortly receive the packet which you mention once more and to which you referred previously. But I am still expecting it in vain. Therefore, in order that you may not suspect me of idleness, I am sending you four copies of the Dutch *Clarissa* together with this letter. Do not be worried about the price of them, I beseech you; I shall gladly pay that to the bookseller; and, if it pleases you, when I am given the opportunity of visiting you (which hope I do not yet give up), I shall claim it back. I am especially pleased that I have found an opportunity to be of service to you, and I long to light upon it more often. I ask you to make use of my services always most freely, whenever the opportunity arises. But if, however, the means mentioned just now of paying the price is not agreeable to you for fear that the matter will be too long delayed, you will be able to satisfy me in yet another way. Please send me a copy of the work with which you are now engaged as soon

as it sees the light of day. Thus you will do me a very great
favor, and you will more than balance your debt.

Though I am eagerly expecting that edition, I still cannot
deny that the bookseller [58] who furnishes the money for
publishing *Clarissa* here fears, not without reason, that
some loss may befall this, if the Dutch translation and
publication of the new work should be hastened, as an Amsterdam publisher, Tirion,[59] has previously promised. This
difficulty would easily be removed and without public expense if this man would let himself be persuaded to show
that new work or part of it to the Dutch public only after
*Clarissa* has been entirely completed. But persuading him to
agree to this would have less success on our part, because an
enmity between this bookseller and ours interferes. If
you could approve this plan, and there were an
opportunity . . .

I had written this far when at last the long-expected
packet arrived which you sent on the 2nd [4th] of last July.
Indeed I could not at all restrain myself from reading
through the longer passages before I try to finish this letter
further. I cannot say with how much joy, admiration, love,
and longing for you it has more and more filled me after I
had read it. I am carried away as if I were beside myself.
Please tell me in what manner I have deserved that you
grant me such extraordinary tokens not only of good will
but also of friendship, confidence, and intimacy, which bind
me to you eternally in spite of separation. But these feelings
do not allow me to answer adequately today; besides, the
sending of those copies which you wished to give to your
friends would be delayed too much. I shall therefore put off
this answer until another opportunity, which I shall take
most eagerly, in order that this our communication of
friendship may flow as much as possible.

I shall only add that Dr. Noordwijk, through whom I
now dispatch your answer, is at Amsterdam, giving attention to business and trade; but I do not know what kind. He

is not a bookseller; but he is devoted to studies, a patron of humanistic studies, a courteous and kind man, a lover of virtue and sincere piety. If I am not mistaken, England is his native country, and his brother is still living in London, and by his hands our packets pass to and fro to each other. And I think this has been the reason that this packet of yours reached me rather late. I truly understood that this brother has been away from home and has stayed some time in Amsterdam. I shall send my copies this way again, because if they were sent directly by cargo ship, you would pay too much for the transport. Moreover, they are very easily transported wrapped in the heavier bundles of other merchandise. The letters only, however, will be more conveniently sent by the public couriers; I shall never reluctantly pay the price of these, with which the most learned Richardson will see fit to refresh me in the future.

I have already finished the translation of the 5th volume of *Clarissa,* and I had intended to publish it together with the 6th volume before the end of this year. But for some time past I have been distracted so much by affairs very foreign to my mind that there is hardly any hope of accomplishing this intention. For by the will of a certain rich man who died unexpectedly two or three months ago, I have been summoned to divide among his heirs the treasures he had with anxious care scraped together. And since the wife of my elder brother is among these heirs, I could not refuse this most bothersome chore as I could for the rest, lest I should involve them in prolonged lawsuits. This matter now keeps me occupied daily and will continue to do so for months; this delays very much the work I spend on the sweetest *Clarissa,* though by continuous morning work I constantly try to furnish material to the press.

Just now the bookseller left me, and he thought he had found means by which the Dutch edition of your new work promised by the man from Amsterdam [60] would cause very little damage to our Dutch *Clarissa..* To be sure I told him that I gathered from your letter that the title of that work

was not *The Fine Gentleman*, as the man from Amsterdam
had announced, but *The Good Man*. Thereupon he allowed
as how he would announce publicly that he himself intended
to publish *The Good Man* in Dutch.[61] I warned him not to
give cause for lawsuits in this way or to indulge in hostility.
But he retorted that it was not unfair to restrain a man so
greedy or at least to prevent him from causing damage to
himself by his haste and perhaps to injure the work itself.

Please continue to love me, my great friend. May the
most mighty and most merciful God keep you from harm.

*11 August 1753*
*My 46th birthday*


[10]

# Richardson *to* Stinstra

*September 11, 1753*

*London, September 11, 1753.*

I cannot, dear and reverend Sir, by any means, receive the Four printed Copies of the translated Clarissa, on
the Terms you mention. I beg of you to make me easy by
allowing me to send the Money for them. Give me Leave to
say, I insist upon it. Surely, Sir, the Copy you send me, will
intitle you to more than a Copy of my new Piece. I always
intended to count your Acceptance of it. And I now send you
Four ⟨Cop⟩ /Volumes/ of it, in half-binding, as we here call
it, as it is usual with us to do, when the whole of a Work
comes not out at once, that, when it does, they may be bound
alike. I believe, I shall publish but two or three at first: You
will be pleased therefore to keep to your self the two last,
for the present, or for about two Months to come.

M^r. Charles, the Episcopal Minister of Amsterdam has
been with me. I saw him the first time; but y^e second time he
called, he spoke to my Nephew,[62] I being on a little Tour

into the Country. He was very kindly sollicitous both times, that my new Piece, chiefly, as he said, for its own Sake, should be translated by a Hand that understood well both Languages; and he recommended, as a proper Person, M<sup>r.</sup> Tirion of Amsterdam, Bookseller; who, he said, is a learned and ingenious Man, and has translated many difficult English Pieces into Dutch; with great Approbation. M<sup>r.</sup> Charles gave high Praises to M<sup>r.</sup> Stinstra, and said, that if you had not Leisure or Inclination to translate it, nor would recommend anybody, he knew not a fitter Person than M<sup>r.</sup> Tirion. My Kinsman could give him no Answer to this. To me M<sup>r.</sup> Charles had not mentioned M<sup>r.</sup> Tirion; No Expectations therefore can these Gentlemen have upon me. And I send Four Volumes in Octavo, in Sheets, for you, Sir, to dispose of to whom you please; or to do with it as you please, as to the Translation into Dutch: For, as to the French, I think my self under an Obligation of Civility to M. Clairaut [63] of the Academy-Royal at Paris; who requests a Copy as I proceed, for a Person whose Interests he espouses.

When the Remainder of the Work is finished, two Copies, one for your self, one for your Direction, shall attend you, *before* Publication, if not delayed in the Passage; which I am sorry is so dilatory. But I am uncertain as to the time, because I have put a Stop to the Work for a while, by reason of a wicked Invasion of my Property, by a Confederacy of four Irish Booksellers; who have found means to corrupt some of my Workmen to steal Copies of as many Volumes as I had printed, and send them over to them; and they are surreptitiously, without Application, Leave, or Condition, actually printing them at Dublin, at several Presses from the Copies so basely obtained. [64]

As I have no Obligation to M<sup>r.</sup> Tirion, and never heard of his Name, but in my Kinsman's Letter to me, on M<sup>r.</sup> Charles's naming him to *him*; for he did not to *me*; only, as I said, expressing to me, his Sollicitude for the Work's Sake, without naming any-body at that time; and as I consign to you, Sir, the absolute Power of directing the Dutch Translation, which I am ready to give you in any Form you shall prescribe; I think there can be no Pretension formed by M<sup>r.</sup> Tirion on his declaring his Intention some time ago. And I should hope, that your Bookseller should make you such a Present, (if he think fit to embark in the Translation) as shall, at least, defray for time past, and to come, y<sup>e</sup> Charges you will be at in this Correspondence. For my self I ask nothing; being sufficiently rewarded, if I shall be able to serve M<sup>r.</sup> Stinstra, or his Friend.

I am sorry, Sir, that you have any Affairs on your Hands, that are irksome to you. But how do you delight me, when you give me Hope, that we may one Day be personally known to each other. May it be so!—

Be pleased, Sir, to ackno[w]lege for me to M<sup>r.</sup> Noortwijck [sic] the Receipt of his Favour of the 23<sup>d</sup> of last Month. I have been 3 Weeks absent from London, and am overwhelmed with Business and Correspondences—Make that my Excuse—Thank him for me, for the kind things he says, and his good Wishes for my Health: For his forwarding to me the Parcel you have sent me (and for which I must repeat, I *must* reimburse you) [.] And let him know, that when my New Piece is published complete, I will obey his Order.

Excuse, dear and reverend Sir, this Freedom. You are secure of my Love. May I be always worthy of the Continuance of yours—Is the Wish of, Sir,

*Your obliged, faithful, affectionate, humble Serv<sup>t.</sup>*
*S. Richardson.*

May my Dear and Reverend M<sup>r.</sup> Stinstra, see many, many, happy 11<sup>ths</sup> of August!

[11]

## Stinstra *to* Richardson [65]

*December 24, 1753*

*Harlingen December 24. 1753.*

Dear Sir:

I will try if I not can write to you in the English, your native tongue, that you may read my Letters without the assistance of any other man, and so our correspondences on both parts have the appearance of being more intimate, of which I shall always be most proud and glory. And your Kindness, I am sure, will easily pardon the faults and blunders of a novice in this writing. If by the multitude of them appears my unability and presumtion in this undertaking, my before mentioned motive to it will also excuse my rashness.

After I have acknowledged the acceptance of yours of Septemb. 11. and of the two Copies of the four Volumes of your Charles Grandison, (which to me arrived towards the middle of October) I am in the first place obliged to beg most humbly your excuse, that I not sooner have answered to those favours. With reason, Sir, admire you my so long silence, who before expressed my eager desire of frequently corresponding with you. I was of opinion, that I must first peruse these Volumes, that I could communicate to you my judgment on them, before I answered; and also take any measures relating to the publication of this your new work in our language; which my opinion perhaps was produced or greatly promoved by my greediness to enjoy your delicacies. But I was so overwhelmed with the Affairs of the Mammon, of which I have mentioned to you in my former, that I but slowly could proceed with it. I must also dayly labour in my version of your Clarissa, that the press might not cease: I assisted one of my friends in the version and publishing of S. Clarke's Treatise on the Truth of the Natural and Re-

vealed Religion,[66] which now is in the hands of our countrymen: Another friend has committed to me the publication
of Taylor's Scripture Doctrine of Atonement,[67] which he
had translated in the Dutch, and which now is printing.
Among all this business I am distracted by domestic necessi-
ties. My only Brother [68] was taken by a dangerous illness,
from which however he soon recovered. My Brother in
Law [69] is labouring under a consumtion and demands by his
weakness our visits and adsistance continually; and this sort
of demands I think that we principally are obliged to take
care of: I give moreover dayly lessons in the Hebrew
tongue to two of my Kinsmen. If this all cannot make my
excuse bij you, my dear Mr. Richardson, I know not which I
more can alledge, and must be content to be judged guilty of
an inexcusable slowness in corresponding. To your judgment
and equity I commit my cause. But subject me not, Sir, I beg
you, to your displeasure: for in your displeasure I must be
unhappy.

I feel that my long silence brings me to the necessity of
writing a more large Letter, by the excuses which I am
obliged to make. Wherefore I proceed to other matters.

I must in the first place resume your long Letter, in which
you have given me a Narrative of your life &c. to which I
have not yet sufficiently answered, as I promised in my
foregoing, if I well remember. I repeat my gratefull thanks
for that instance of your benevolence and friend ship. You
mention in the beginning my Pastoral Letter and the translation thereof by H. Rimius, which you were so good to
send me, together with his Narrative of Hernhutism. I
have readed the translated Letter, and find the version very
accurate in the main. I have not any acquaintance with this
Mr. Rimius, nor can recollect to have heard of him anywhere. Nor is he any more acquainted with me, it seems,
since I not have received a copy of this version from himself. But the German translator of the same Letter,[70] being
then in London, has sent to me a copy of the English, which
I of late have received. This gentleman, perhaps, has per-

moved the other, his country man, to follow his example, whereof he however nothing mentions in his letter. It will be an extreme pleasure for me, if this mij little treatise, may have the approbation of your worthy divines, and be of any use to stop t[h]e progress of Fanaticism among you. Then I shall have returned in any measure to your country the benefit which I have received of the eminent English Writers.

I have most heartily prayed the Almighthy for the health and welfare of your excellent Archbishop, of whom you give such a lovely and venerable character; and thanked Heaven for his happy recovery. May He yet enjoy much blessed days to the benefit of your Church and the Christian Church in general! Are there any of his works printed, Sir? I would gladly be more acquainted with his mind, while I have no occasion to know him personally.

Let me tell you, Sir, that I with much delight have read different times, and considered your particular and candid Narrative to the answering of my bold questions. Which must be the mind, that under such narrowness of time and circumstances could grow up to so much exactness and penetration of judgment and imagination, as I would attribute to you, my worthy friend, if I not remembered my engagement of abstaining from your praises. I admire your diligence and infatigable industry: and this shall I always use as an incitement for me in any fit of laziness.

Your account of your early youth, of your innate Love, as I may say, of Letter-writing, which was forwarded and cultivated by the employment, which the favour of the young women in your Neighbourhood you procured; has inexpressibly delighted me. And I cannot forbear to observe and venerate the hand and dispensation of Providence, whose footsteps we commonly not enough acknowledge in particular cases, which thus from your earliest years has instilled in your mind those happy facts, which afterwards have produced such fine and usefull fruits. However I must admire that this talent so long has laid hidden, the whole interval from your youth to your more advanced years.

By the particular of your being Secretary in Love-matters to several young women, I can perceive that you might come to the full knowledge of the woman's heart, and his deepest recesses: This has you enabled, Sir, to paint with lively colours the most internal thoughts, deliberations, and affections of a Clarissa, an Anna Howe, a Miss Biron. But by which means you have penetrated into the mysteries of unrighteousness, in the heart of a Rake, a Libertine, a wanton and sly Lovelace: This continues to me matter of astonishment! Nor produce you anything to deliver me from my wonder: On the contrary, you increase it by your professions, which I as the pledges of the truest confidence and friendship have received. Pardon me, Sir, but I was before of opinion that you in your Belford had drawn your own picture, that you had seen the world and loved her, but afterwards escaped out of her inticements. In this case I should not have been ashamed of corresponding with you: For am I not a follower of the Saviour, which declared that there were joy in Heaven on a repenting sinner? I have formerly conversed with such sinners, especially with one intimately conversed, which of a sound judgment and lively wit: having forsaken the follies of his youth, excelled in works of piety and charity: which familiarity has been to me very usefull in acquiring my knowledge however it may be of the heart and characters of men; and peculiarly enabled me to distinguish with more cognisance the natural lineaments of a Lovelace. Happy, however, threefold happy are we, my friend, and I have abundant reason to thank Heaven, which has favoured us with a virtuous education, and us preserved from the baits of corruption! What an easiness, what a serenity for a mind striving in the way to eternal happiness!

You must further have my thanks for the presents of your Volume of Familiar Letters, and the Æsop's Fables.

Both have I perused with pleasure. But I must acknowledge, that I therein not should have found the Author (I must force my self to suppress an epithet) of Pamela, of Clarissa, and Charles Grandison. The Fables of Æsop I always thought to be very usefull for children: But I should require in the reflections on them the utmost plainness and simplicity; which I suppose, you have endeavoured more and more to bring in your new edition. And, to be sure, it is not beneath the ablest writers to accommodate their pens to the fancy and capacity of the children; for I believe him the happiest Reformer of mankind, who is able to implant early in the minds of those the seeds of true knowledge and virtue. And to make a new collection of Fables, more adapted to every duty of Moral and Social virtue, and to the principal cases, of human life, than those which go by the name of Æsop, would in my judgment be a most usefull and worthy undertaking.

You are very kind to me, Sir, when you promise, that if I shall come in England, you will shew me your many volumes of Epistolary Correspondences, especially with Ladys of capacity and judgment. How very different these, as you draw their characters, from the Women of our country! That you not have strained it, I am convinced by the writings of a Mrs. Rowe,[71] a Cath. Cockburn, which I have perused, and in the last especially admired the deep penetration in the abstract Subtleties of Metaphysics. My imagination anticipates the joys, which your generous favour me would afford in the review of that valuable collection, if my wish and hope ever is to be fulfilled of seeing the happy England and your desired face. But how you damp this my hope, by telling me, that you are in an advanced Age, and almost worn out as to your health! As this is matter of astonishment to me, that such a vivacity of mind can subsist in an advanced age, and precarious health; when I presumed that you were in a vigorous age and full of spirits: So it gives me fear, that my desire of personal acquaintance perhaps not will be answered; while I am te conquer it by the

weightier duty of filial observance. Let me this commit to
the benevolent disposition of Alwise Providence! May this
give you yet many, many happy years of life! But if he not
permit me to enjoy your personal acquaintance and familiarity on earth, this loss may be more than compensated
by our hereafter consorting together in the company of
Saints in Heaven!

I am extremely astonished, Sir, by your telling me, that
you never write by a *Plan*; and when you ended one Letter,
hardly knew, what would be your next. What a happy genius, that can thus prosecute his way, through so many mazes
and labyrinths, which perplex your common readers, and
never deviate, without ever consulting a map! How prodi-
gious an accurateness of memory and imagination, which in
so much niceties and little occurrences never offends against
the foregoing, and ever preserves the same lineaments in the
numerous diverse characters! I am now not praising you,
Sir; but admire the abundant bounty of God, in granting to
mankind such egregious faculties.

You must have my thanks for the Extracts, which you
have communicated to me concerning your Clarissa, as an
unquestionable proof of your confidence and trust in me. I
have them read with pleasure, especially that of Mr. Fielding's Letter, which has given me a better opinion of that
gentleman, than I had before conceived from his writings.
These appeared to me no[t] much conducing to promote
virtue and goodness; and at them I had my view in some
reflections in my Prefaces. Now I perceive in his favour that
he could be touched by scenes, which paint the virtue lovely,
and heartily admire them.—I am charmed with the character of Mr. John Channing. His letters shew a feeling heart,
and genuine piety. You are happy, Sir, with such a friend.

You asked, what I should think of your sending to me
your Poartrait in Copper? I have received it whith the
utmost delight as a pledge of your particular friend ship and
obligingness. I am the more glad with it, as I can shew it to
every one of my friends and your admirers as such, and thus

boast in this my happiness. It adorns presently my study, and exhibits daily to my eyes the person of my Mr. Richardson, the thoughts of whom no day ever will efface out of my mind.

Now, Sir, you must allow me a little to expostulate with you on the accepting of the four printed copies of the Clarissa in Dutch. I have it considered not as a favour of my hands to lay you under obligation, but as a duty which my bookseller owed to you as the original Author. Should this pay for the fruits of his own ground, however cultivated by another, which by the cultivating reaps his profit, and nothing has retributed to the Author for the communicating of the occasion? Besides, my dear Friend, must I allow you to make my presents of your Charles Grandison, and to consign to me the power of directing the Translation, not to speak of your other favours; and may I not be allowed of declining to receive money for a little parcel of books from him, to which I am originally indebted for the power of presenting it? It is an old saying, that friendship finds or makes friends equal. Let us observe this rule, Sir. I acknowledge indeed that the case is not perfectly equal, as you have me asked for the four printed Copies; I have received your favours out of unasked generosity. But on the other hand is there a not less unequality, which I already have touched; you are the Father of Clarissa; I a stranger to Charles Grandison. However, if your superior delicateness cannot bear it, that you should accept as a present that, for which you have asked, I will submit me to your pleasure, though with much reluctance, for the foresaid reasons. If it cannot be otherwise, I beg that you will wait with remitting the price, till all the eigth volumes are published and received by you.

But indeed Sir, I cannot bear the thought of receiving money from your hands, after I have received that ever valuable present, the four volumes of the mentioned History, which far surpasses the other. I owe you the most humble thanks for them. I have perused them with the

utmost pleasure, and long to enjoy the following volumes. It
is very well, Sir, that you have me laid under a prohibition
of praising you; for I should not be able to express my
merited esteem for this your new performance, by which all
lovers of virtue and goodness are highly obliged to you.
This I will say only, that the intention of the work, the
design, the execution, in every respect is worthy of my Mr.
Richardson. If I may compare this with your former Clarissa; I should say that the most readers here will not object
any tediousness in the first volumes, because of the affecting
and dreadfull scene herein painted by you; and you have
more omitted those *minutiæ*, which I for my part much
relish in your Clarissa. The shocking levity of a Lovelace
will not here disturb the weak minds of some pious readers;
the principal characters are in the main good and virtuous.
Nevertheless I must express my regret for the suppression
of so much Letters as you have signifyed to me: not only we
miss the enjoyment of these your productions, which no
doubt merit the eyes of the publick, to say no more: But I
am of opinion, if I may have leave to offer it, Sir, that this
omission takes away a little the appearance of a veritable
History, which you have otherwise the inimitable art of
preserving. May I venture yet another remark? Charmingly, most charmingly paint you the motions and effects of
a generous Love in the heart of Miss Biron; the object is
worthy thereof: But may not this agreable sensation steal
upon the tender bosoms and minds of your readers among
the fair Sex, melt and soften them, and thus lay open more
than is convenient for the less prudent of that Sex, to the
allurements of specious Lovers? Perhaps were it more
proper that this surmise came from your female admirers,
than from me, a Batchelor. I form only those doubts, my
dear friend, that you may perceive, that I not read your
works with a prepossessed mind, nor blindly praise them;
that I read with a searching eye, yet not finding any blemishes, but meeting one or two little bright clouds, which
more accurately viewed perhaps are a collection of shining

stars. And these my doubts abate not in any manner my
highest and due esteem for your History, which I hope soon
to read again and contemplate, and then is it possible that
the second thoughts will clear them up perfectly.

I value this your work at so high a rate, that I as readily
should undertake the translation thereof, as I formerly did
that of your Clarissa; nay much more readily, as the Author
is now my dear friend. I thank you, Sir, for your good
opinion of my ability to perform this task, which merits the
most able hand. But I beg humbly your excuse, if I dare not
resolve to undergo a new this labour myself. I confide on
your equity and benevolence, that you will excuse me, when I
give you my reasons; and without these my declining would
not be pardonable. You must surely apprehend, Sir, that
translating is a very heavy work, especially of such books
which are written in a familiar style, with vulgar phrases,
and witty turns. I have yet a great deal of Clarissa to
absolve: both these together were a burden too heavy for
my shoulders: better then, than that Grandison should be
postponed, that another able translator at the same time
hereon bestows his labour. After Clarissa shall be per-
formd, think I, that I sufficiently shall have had my portion
of translating, and discharged my duty in this respect to my
countrymen. At present I am so overwhelmed with worldly
affairs, that I hardly can attend your Clarissa, as I wish.
Besides, I am bound by promise to the publick, that I should
more amply than I before have done, defend the Rights of
Liberty of Conscience and Religion; [72] from which task I am
drawn by the charms of the lovely Clarissa; but which I
think myself under obligation to resume, as soon as I shall
have ended my attendance on the Christian Heroine. Yet
have I formed a method of demonstrating the Being and
Attributes of God, a priori, different from that of Mr.
Clarke, Wollaston, [73] Rauhson, &c. which I am desirous to
perfect and evulgate, that this important foundation of all
Religion still more firmly might be established. I could illus-
trate the scripture-doctrine concerning the Death of our

blessed Saviour and the benefits of it to mankind. I have collected materials for two Moral Essays on Magnanimity and Humility, and their mutual consistency. Of all these I have given notice to some of my friends; and am thus half-obliged to bring these projects to execution, if Providence preserves my health and powers. Wherefore knowing now how long these shall be granted to me, and having thus much to perform, with a constitution of body not very strong, I dare not undertake any new work.

Notwithstanding this, Sir, I readily accept the power which you consign to me, of *directing* the Translation; and it shall be my pride and ambition, that I may perform it to your contentment, and in a manner answerable to the value of the work. And how, my dear friend, should I be of the meanness to take a present of any value from the Bookseller for transferring on him this power, when the Author himself asks nothing? Should I not strive to emulate your generosity in serving my friends and the publick? Verily, Sir, I am a little touched by your supposition, as if the charges of your correspondence must be defrayed to me by such a Reward. I should be unworthy of your notice, if the honour and pleasure of corresponding with Mr. Richardson, were not in my thoughts an ample, an infinite more worthy compensation of those little charges.—I have offered in your name this right to the Bookseller which published my translation of Clarissa, and he has accepted it with humble thanks for your kindness. He intends to associate with him in this undertaking a friend of him at Amsterdam, that he may be more secure from the opposition of Mr. Tirion; which I have approved. I have applied to the ablest Translator which I know, at Amsterdam, Mr. Verwer,[74] which has translated some pieces of Mr. Fielding and others with success. This has declared himself willing to undertake this task; if he could agree with the Booksellers for his recompence. I have reserved to myself the review of the translated sheets, that they may as accomplished come to the press, as I can procure them. I presume that the Translator will soon

begin with his work; but the Bookseller thinks fit not to
publish it, till all the volumes of Clarissa be evulgated.—I
think that I not want any other Form of your consigning to
me the aforesaid power, than you have already done. My
Bookseller has publickly announced, that he has received
this power from you; I hear not of any motions of Mr.
Tirion. He has not any right in justice to invade this work
as his property. But if he would, he should not let himself
restrain by any deed of an Author, I presume, pretending
that after the publication of a book every one has the right
of translating it, without the concession of the Author. Nor
should I in this case have reason to contradict him, as
having arrogated to myself the translation of Clarissa without this previous authority from you.

I cannot conclude this long Letter, without detesting the
enormous injustice and rapaciousness of those Irish Booksellers,[75] who have sought to defraud you of the due fruits
of your labour and property, and at the same time the
infamous perfidiousness of workmen serving so good and
generous a Master. Such instances are to me an evident
proof that we live in a state of probation. I am told, Sir,
that you have published this your *Case*,[76] and exposed their
baseness in a manner, which has the general applause. May
their villainy be the abhorrence of all honest men, that they
not purchase any of their copies, and you thus thereby not
suffer in the selling of your genuine edition.

My Mother was much pleased with the honour of your
compliments. She is an assiduous reader and admirer of
your Clarissa; and enjoins me to assure you of her respect
and welwishing. I am, dear Sir, with the sincerest love and
veneration,

*Your most humble, faithfull, and obliged*
*Servant*

*John Stinstra.*

*P.S.* Though I begun this my Letter on the superscribed
date; I must confess that it is dispatched on a much latter;
on which, I am ashamed to mention. This first specimen of

my English writing costed me more pains than I expected; I
must needs transcribe it, because of the many blots and
faults. I am diverted by much incidents. I despair almost of
excuse. May I yet hope on your favour, notwithstanding this
my unexcusable delay? Will you still love me?

[12]
## William Richardson *to* Stinstra

*March 12, 1754*

*Reverend Sir,*
     My Uncle sends you with the accompanying Books,
a complete Sett of his Sir Charles Grandison, in Sheets; the
Second Edition, in the Duodecimo Size. You will be pleased,
Sir, to give it to the Person you intend for the Translator of
it into the Dutch Tongue, several Mistakes having been
attended to in the Printing it that will render your's, when it
appears, more correct than our first was; tho', however,
most of the Alterations in the Second Edition, are Alterations of Nicety, rather than of Need—The Octavo Edition
is correct.
     I acknowledge for my Uncle the Receipt of your last kind
Favour. It came not to his Hands before last *Thursday.* He
bid me tell you, That he will take the very first Opportunity
to answer it.
     The Verses enclosed are the Production of the Pen of an
ingenious, but blind, Lady.[77]
     A few of my Uncle's Cases, on the Irish Pyracy,[78] are also
enclosed—With the Two last Volumes of Sir Charles in the
Octavo Size. They complete the Two Setts my Uncle transmitted you, and which, by your Letter, you have received,
along with the other Books.
     I am, Reverend Sir,
                    *Your most Humble Serv.ᵗ*
                    *Wᵐ. Richardson*

*London, March 12. 1754.*

My Uncle desires me to give his best Respects to you, &
Compliments to your Mother—

[13]

# Richardson *to* Stinstra [79]

*March 20, 1754*

*London, March 20. 1754*

You are extremely obliging, dear and Reverend Sir,
to write to me in my ow[n] Tongue. You tell me, that the
Attempt has cost you much time. I am grieved that it has, so
much more usefully as you can fill up your Time; and yet, by
the Propriety and Copiousness of your Language, I should
not otherwise have supposed but it was nearly as familiar to
you as your own. Rashness, Sir, do you call the Attempt? I
admire it, and gratefully acknowlege the Condescension.

Never, dear Sir, again think of apologizing (so many
great and good Works on your Hands, besides Family Concerns), for long Silence. I only wished, in all the passed long
one, that I had been favoured with three Lines, to acquaint
me of your Health; for which I could not but be in some
Pain.

Let me acquaint you, Sir, That your Pastoral Letter [80] is
considered with us as a Masterpiece. Two worthy young
Gentlemen of Cambridge, spoke to me in the highest Terms
of Approbation, within these ten Days, and of the Justice
done it in that University.

Continue, Revd. Sir, your Prayers for our good Archbishop. He is not at times so well as all good Englishmen
wish him to be. I have not the Honour to be known to him
personally: But my good Friend M[r.] Duncombe, whom I
formerly mentioned to you, a most worthy and generously
communicative Man, who is much esteemed by his Grace,

desired me to give him a Copy of Your Solicitude for His Grace's Health, and of the Works you are employed in, in order to shew both to that good Prelate; who had before so highly approved of your Pastoral Letter, as to interest himself in the Translation of it. M^r. Duncombe will endeavour to procure for you, two or three of his Grace's Sermons, formerly published.

You are very kind to me, dear Sir, to approve the trifling Narrative, that you induced so obscrue a Man to give you.

You think, Sir, you can account from my early Secretariship to young Women in my Father's Neighbourhood, for the Characters I have drawn of the Heroines of my three Works. But this Opportunity did little more for me, at so tender an Age, than point, as I may say, or lead my Enquiries, as I grew up, into the Knowlege of the Female Heart. And knowing something of that, I could not be an utter Stranger to that of Man. Men and Women are Brothers and Sisters: They are not of different Species; and what need be obtained to know both, but to allow for different Modes of Education /(or/ Situation[ )] ; and Constitution, or perhaps I should rather /say/ for Habits, whether good or bad. As to the Knowlege I seem to have had of the wicked Hearts and Actions of such Men as Lovelace, which engages your Wonder, I have been always as attentive to the Communication /I may say to the profligate Boastings/ of the one Sex, as I have been to the Disguises of the other. I will only add on this Subject, that I never was a Belford.[81] If I had been such a one, and a Penitent, I should have had no Doubts of M^r. Stinstra's Charity, had I acknowleged my Errors to him.

I am not at all surprized, Sir, at what you say of the Familiar Letters, and of Æsop.[82] They were both intended for the lower Classes of People. I omitted several Letters in the former, as too high for the Design. In the latter, the Reflexions were such, for the most part, as I found them, in one of our writers, who had some Reputation in that way, in his Day.

You wonder, Sir, that I appeared not as a writer earlier. Alas, Sir, the three Pieces you mention with Approbation, are the Products of Leisure as well as Industry. My Business till within these Ten or Twelve Years past, filled up all my Time. I had no Leisure; nor, being unable to write by a regular Plan, knew I, that I had so much Invention, till I, almost accidentally slid into the writing of Pamela. And besides, little did I imagine, that any thing I could write, would be so kindly received, as my Writings have been by y$^e$ World.

I am grieved, at times, that two Countries should separate us. How happy should I be, could I hope to entertain, my dear M$^r$· Stinstra in London! And must I give up all my flattering Hopes of this Pleasure?—And is the Advance of my Life, and Infirmities, the Bar? God's Will be done.

I think, Sir, we in England may glory in Numbers of Women of Genius. I, in particular, may—I could introduce you, Sir, to such a Circle! ⟨–⟩ /of/ my own Acquaintance! —No Man has been so honoured by the fine Spirits of the Sex, as I have been. I verily think, that the Women of the politest Regions, are not to vie with ours. And the Taste and Numbers are every Day increasing; tho' in an Age of such general Dissipation. O that we had been able to keep our Women of Condition to ourselves; that we had not given way to their crossing the narrow Seas into our Neighbouring Kingdom!—Since we have very few Instances of Ladies returning from thence improved, I may say, uncorrupted, by the Levities of the Nation I have in my Eye. Don't you think, Sir, that Women are generally more susceptible of Levity than Men? If they are, they should not be allowed to go abroad, and to Places of Public Entertainment, so often as they do.

There are many Discouragements and Inconveniencies, which attend the Man who has not Regularity enough to write by a Plan. I mentioned my Inability in this Particular, as a Defect. You, Sir, speak of it in a much nobler manner, in a manner worthy of your self.

I will only say to your Expostulation about the Four Setts of Clarissa, which I bespoke, that I will, as you propose, defer the Payment ⟨for⟩ /of/ them, till the Translation is finished. You argue, Sir, very generously on this Subject; But as I would not have sent for them but on that Condition, you must allow me, Sir, to pay your Bookseller for them.

I have sent you, Sir, by the usual Conveyance, the rest of my New Work. The Seventh Vol. Duodecimo is somewhat more perfect, than the last Vol. Octavo. I have therefore transmitted that to you also, as the most proper to be translated by.

*Do* you think, Sir, that the Letters /and Passages/ I have omitted for the Sake of Shortening, take off from the Appearance of Genuineness? May not Principals in a Story or Correspondence, be supposed to allow an Editor such Liberties?

I thank you, Sir, for your other Remark.[83] It is worthy of M^r. Stinstra's Delicacy; and worthy of the Friendship you honour me with. I repeatedly thank you for it. It comes from you, Sir, a Bachelor, with very great Propriety. From whom could it come ⟨from⟩ with greater, than from a virtuous single Man. I can only say, as to the Force of it, that I hope, no bad Consequences to the Morals of my fair Readers will result from the Descriptions I have made Miss Byron give of a tender Passion for an Object so worthy. Yet my dear M^r. Stinstra alarms me a little. Be so good, Sir, to watch me thro' the Work, in this, and in every other Instance, which may have a dangerous Tendency, and you will inexpressibly oblige me.

I have not at hand, the Copy of my former Letter—But did I any where in it, express my Solicitude for the Honour of your Translating it, on a Supposal of your Approbation of it?—If I did, excuse me, Sir. And let me beseech you, that you will not give your self any Trouble about it, that may in the least interfere with your great Avocations, and with those noble Works which you have in Design. God

Almighty preserve your Life and Health, and enable you to go through them all, for the Sake of your own Comfort, and the Benefit the World must reap from them!—Acquaint me, dear and Reverend Sir, how, from time to time, you proceed in these arduous, and glorious Tasks. How sorry am I to hear, that your Constitution of Body is not as vigorous as your Mind!

Excuse me, Sir, for every thing that appeared amiss to you, in the Article by which you say you are a little touched. I feel for you; and blush for my self, as you take and put it. I am willing to hope, that your kind Partiality for me, *allowably* blames me for my Conscious Diffidence of Worthiness in the Correspondence between us.

All that you do, with regard to the Translation, must have my entire Approbation, if you can assure me that your Cares for it, will not break in upon your more important Engagements.

You /have/ greatly obliged me, my dear and good Sir, by making mention of me to your good Mother. My most respectful Compliments attend her, accompanied with best Wishes.

"Will I still love you?" My Dear, my Excellent, my Condescending M<sup>r.</sup> Stinstra, let me be assured of your Affection, as I love you; and it will be an Happiness that will attend to my latest Hour,

*Your Ever-obliged, and faithful*
*Friend and Servant,*
S. *Richardson*

I received not your Favour till the 8<sup>th</sup> of this Month. This I mention, that I may not be thought to have too long delayed this my Reply.

M<sup>r.</sup> Duncombe, who is greatly pleased with the List of the Works you are engaged in, and have in Design, desires me to ask you, If you have the Tracts of the Rev<sup>d.</sup> M<sup>r.</sup> Balguy;[84] whom he esteems as one of the most rational Writers since the Death of D<sup>r</sup> Sam<sup>l.</sup> Clarke? If you have not, he requests your Acceptance of them from him, as a small Mark of his great Value for the Author of the Pastoral Letter; and of such Pieces as you have in View. He would be glad to know, If your Sermons on Liberty of Conscience, have been printed in French; and believes they would be well received in England.

[14]

## Stinstra *to* Richardson

*April 8, 1754*

*Harlingen, April 8, 1754.*
You are right, dear and worthy Sir: I must much sooner tho' by three or four lines have acknowledged the reception of your former favour and the transmitted Copies. I confess my fault, and am ashamed of my negligence. But how softly, how gracefully, how kindly put you this your most just reflection! I must admire your forgiving temper, and am the more ashamed.

Is there not a little of fond partiality for your friend and admirer in the praises concerning the propriety and copiousness of my English language? However, encouraged as I am, I will proceed to write in that tongue, hoping that I may acquire thereby a readier use of it, as I find already that it costs not me so much pains as in my former.

With all my heart continue I, and urge my most fervent prayers for the health and perfect recovery of your worthy Archbishop. How interesting is the welfare and life of such an eminent Prelate, eminent in the true Christian spirit, to the whole Church, to every good and reasonable lover of charity, tolerance, and virtue! His Graces Sermons, of which you mention, shall be most acceptable to me, especially offered by such a worthy hand, as that of the Rev. Mr. Duncombe. But what are you, Sir, and your worthy friend about, to communicate to that great Prelate my purposes concerning some works, that are hardly in embryo, and which perhaps I never may perform! I communicated them to you as my indulging friend, the situation of affairs between us required that I must explain them to you: But can they merit the notice, of a Man so highly distinguished? You mea[n] my honour, Sir; and I acknowledge, and thank you for it; however unmerited. Perhaps would you also by this manner lay me under stronger obligations, and add an effectual incitement to perform my purpose: By this intention I should too be honoured; and that must naturally with me be the effect of your communication. I am extremely glad that my designs have the approbation of such a Divine, which you so highly value, Mr. Duncombe. I desire my most respectfull compliments to that kind favourer of my labours, and my most gratefull thanks for his obliging goodness in offering to me the Tracts of Mr. Balguy. I have a Collection of them in 8º with which I am thoroughly acquainted, and which I very highly esteem. Never found I the Principles of Moral Rectitude so deeply and solidly laid, nor the Nature of Moral Obligation so reasonably demonstrated. Would to Heaven, that this fine genius might undertake the task of deducing from his general principles the several particular duties of men and Christians, and thus present the world with a regular and solid System of Moral Virtue, which it yet wants, for ought I know. I suppose, you see, that this Author yet lives; for I have heard of late, that several Sermons of his are published. Besides the said collection I possess a Tract of the same on Redemtion, and Five Sermons together published.

My Sermons on Liberty of Conscience are not printed in French. Much is written on this Subject in that, and in the English tongue. I have profited from such writings; and though I have the matter treated on a different Method, I cannot persuade myself that a translation would be of much service. I thought, my countrymen wanted the knowledge and practice of those principles: I would communicate them to these; but it has cost me my liberty of preaching.

I beg your excuse, Sir; I needed not your asseveration, that you never were a Belford. Never had I any doubt concerning this, since I had your candid account of your youth and way of life. Those were my former thoughts, which I in the frankness of my heart putted down to express my wonder. I am concerned, that I have given you the indelicate occasion of confirming to me the contrary. But how penetrating a Spectator must you have been of the characters of men, and manners!

Pray, Sir, pain me not with your so kindly signified desire to see me in London, which anew kindles a like desire in me to give me that honour, wherewith my filial duty and affection otherwise has enough to struggle.

I thank you, Sir, for your readiness in sending me the rest of your New Work; and your considerateness in joining with it the Seventh Vol. of the 12º edition. When I have received them, I shall acquaint you of it. The translation is not yet begun, because the Translator has some difficulty concerning my review of his work; from which condition I however not can think to recede, lest by the overhasty speed of a mercenary hand the exactness and propriety of so worthy a work might suffer; which too frequently is the case with our Dutch translations.

You had not in your former expressed your solicitude that I myself might translate this valuable work, but conferred on me the power of doing it, or transferring it to another. Your favour, your confidence on me required, thought I, that I should give my reasons for declining myself this honourable task. Such I think it; and wherefore should my dear Mr. Richardson beg my excuse on that head?

The crowding together of many very affecting and important scenes makes a story more extraordinary, and gives it more the likeness of a Romance, thought I, than if those are interspersed and separated with now little accidents and intervening reasonings, by which it gets a resemblance of the common life: This was the ground of my remark on the omissions in your work, which I mistrust, if you see not therein any reason: And I think the remark itself of very little importance.

I am sorry, that I have made so precipitantly my other remark concerning the tender, the worthy passion in the heart of Miss Byron working. A second reading has cured me of my fancy. I perceive how plainly that the pangs and uneasinesses w[h]ich attend that passion in her, and the difficulties and evils in which Clementina was involved by the same, are a sufficient counterpoise to the amiable descriptions of this passion, to secure the prudent among the fair sex from the danger, which I doubted that might attend them. For the imprudent and giddy may it be dangerous to meditate such descriptions; but these can never be secured from abusing the noblest writings. I repeat, I am most sorry to have alarmed without reason my delicate friend, the friend of my heart, and the friend of strict and nice virtue; and beg most humbly your excuse. How kindly, how generously take you my remarks! And in this respect am I benefited by my mistakes, that I am warranted by undeniable proofs to clear your character of all pride against every one who give you this aspersion. Wonder not, my dear Mr. Richardson, that the shadow of virtue attends your uncommon merits and always celebrated name.

This accompanies the Copies of the V. and VI. Volume[s] of your Clarissa. My Preface to them wish I that not may displease you, if you think fit to procure you a translation of it. It contains some reflections on the use of Invention and Imagination in promoting the study and love of virtue and piety.

How overcome you me, Sir, with all your goodness. I want words in a tongue so little used to me, to express the true sentiments of my heart. I must ever be

*Your most obliged Friend and*
*humble Servant*
*John Stinstra.*

May I request of you a Copy, Sir, of your Case published concerning the rapacity of the Irish Booksellers.[85] Your moderate temper in it against the defrauders of your right is highly applauded. The price will I deduct from that of the Clarissa's. I am so much interested in the affairs of my dear friend, that I must wish to see it.

[15]

## Stinstra *to* Richardson

*May 23, 1754*

*Dear Sir,*

I have received the two last Volumes of your Charles Grandison towards the end of the preceding month April, with a complete set of the duodecimo edition, and an accompanying Letter from your Kinsman's hand. I am extremely obliged for your kind favour. I found therein also several of your Cases,[86] of which I requested one of you in my former. I presumed that it should be a greater piece; else I should not have exposed myself by mentioning the price of it. Excuse me, Sir; I sought to revenge myself a little on your strict justice. May all spitefull revenge thus be defeated!

In this intervall I have had just leisure to read this part of your Work, which remained for me to peruse; and in every page of it almost admired the niceness and sublimity of sentiments, and the accurate justness of introducing them. How lovely paint you the native graces of manly piety and virtue! And tho' you seem exceedingly to favour the fair sex by even joining here with your Hero a Clementina and Miss Byron; our sex is as much indebted to you for Grandison, as the other is for Pamela and Clarissa. How extremely instructive this your work to moderation and equity among persons of different persuasions, and yet to a strict and faithfull adherence of our own in religion. Will you permit me to add, that whosoever will indeavour to imitate you in this kind of writing, Mr. Richardson shall be the Homer thro' all the succeeding generations. And now not more of your praises. I could have wished, that you had contrived it, that the conclusion of this History had ended in a more affecting and interesting scene; for the sake of the common readers, which love to be dimitted with strong impressions. However I am apt to think, that as the story is supposed to be so very new, this ending as it is, bears a more natural resemblance to truth.

The Translator, to which I had offered this your work, could not resolve to submit to my condition, that I should revise his translation, before it were delivered to the press; thus I am obliged to seek another; for the reasons which he did give of his unwillingness made me the more insist upon that condition. And I have already received a proposal of another by a Bookseller with praises of his ability in both languages; from which I now expect a specimen.

Now have you finished your noble Plan, Sir, and the Almighty must be blessed for sparing your health and spirits that you could happily finish it, by all those that can read your works, and have any taste of beauty, and love of virtue. May Heaven bless still you with many years to the benefit of your contemporaries and posterity! For you cannot rest idle, while power of doing good is lent you. Shall you now, according to your purpose formerly communicated to me, retouch your Pamela? Your delicate hand cannot but mend it; though I must avow, that before Clarissa surpassed her, I thought her incomparable.

My last with the v and vi. Voll. of the Dutch Clarissa suppose I that are received by you.

In what way is his Grace of Canterbury? I desist not from praying for his precious life and health.

I desire my compliments to your Nephew, and my thanks for his favour.

With you, my dearest friend, is dayly the heart of

> *Your ever obliged and faithfull*
> *John Stinstra*

*Harlingen*
*May 23, 1754*

[16]

## Richardson *to* Stinstra

*June 28, 1754*

I have before me, my dear, my truly Reverend Friend, two Letters of yours. One dated April 8. accompanying your kind and most acceptable Present of the vth and vith Vols. of the Translated Clarissa, and the Setts of the same in Quires, for which (Dear Sir, permit me to repeat my Acknowlegement!) I am your Debtor: The other May 23. But which latter came to my Hands two or three Days before the other, with ye Parcel. Think me not therefore remiss in my Return of Thanks for that Parcel and the Letter of April 8. Yet should I not have so long delayed writing to both Letters, /as/ I have done, had I not been willing to thank you for your Preface to the two Volumes of Clarissa which you favoured me with; and that I could not do with Knowlege, till I had got it translated. This took up Time.

You wish that this Preface may not displease me—Dear and good Sir, how could you imagine for one Moment, that it should? Most cordially do I give you my Thanks for the Instruction I have received by it, and by your "Reflexions on the Use of Invention and Imagination, as distinguished from sober Reason, in promoting the Love and Study of

Virtue and Piety." I have yet had time only to read it over
once; for my Business has called upon me for a greater
⟨Part⟩ /Share/ of my Attention, than heretofore, Death
having snatched from me the Corrector of my Press; a
Learned, diligent, worthy Man, to whom I had committed,
for 15 years past, the Care of that material Part of my
Business: But I shall soon, I hope, have more Leisure; and I
know I shall be improved by another attentive Perusal of it.

You ask me, Sir, "If there is not a little of fond Partiality
in the Praises I give of your English"—Indeed, there is not.
Mr. Duncombe, to whom I read your Letters before me,
admires your easy and expressive English, as much as I do. I
am glad that you write it with less Pain to your self, than
when you began with it.

My worthy Friend Mr. Duncombe is not a Clergyman.
He has a sincere Reverence for what he has seen of yours.
Be not afraid, my dear Sir, that you will suffer in the
Communications we have made to our excellent Archbishop,
of your intended Writings. May the Almighty bless you
with Health and continued Vigor of Mind to prosecute your
useful Designs, for his Glory, and the Benefit of a World
that wants such an Instructor!

The Archbishop is not neglectful of his Health; He takes
great Exercise, and enjoys the Air of his Country Palace at
Croydon; and is better than he has been for some time.
Continue, Sir, your Prayers for the Perfect Recovery of a
Health so precious[.]

Mr. Duncombe received with great Pleasure your kind
Compliments to him. I transcribe from a Paper he sent me,
on this Occasion, the following Paragraphs, as they will
answer your Sollicitude about the Archbishop's Sermons;
Your Observations on Balguy's Tracts,[87] &c.

"The present Archbishop of Canterbury, while Preacher
to the Learned Society of Lincoln's-Inn, had a Course of
excellent Sermons on the Ten Commandments and the
Lord's Prayer. It is thought he has no Intention to publish

them. His few *printed* Discourses were delivered on public Occasions; and some of these cannot now be procured.["] [88]

(a) (Allow me to add here that Mr. Duncombe still hopes to procure for you, some of the Archbishop[']s Printed Sermons.)

"Has Mr. Browne's Poem *De Animi Immortalitate* [89] reached Mr. Stinstra? It is applauded here by the best Judges.

"Mr. *Balguy* has been dead some Years. His Son, a Clergyman of Learning and Genius, was lately Fellow of St. John's College, Cambridge.

"Mr. Duncombe is of Opinion, that such a Book of Practical Morals, as Mr. Stinstra seems to desire, is not wanted in England.

"The Moral Discourses by Tillotson and Clarke, cannot, perhaps, be parallelled by any thing among the Ancients for Strength and Perspicuity.

"*The Religion of Nature delineated* [90] is an admirable Book: tho' the Author's main Pillar seems too weak to support such a Fabric.

"Dr. *Foster* on *Religious and Social Duties*,[91] must not be omitted. The Prayers at the End are rational and sublime.

"His *Defence of the Christian Revelation*,[92] in Answer to *Christianity as old as the Creation,* is worthy the Subject.

"Fordyce's *Elements of Moral Philosophy* [93] (a little Book) is a Masterpiece both for Reason and Eloquence.

"Grove's System of *Moral Philosophy*,[94] 2 Vols. 8º, is the Substance of Lectures, which he read to his Pupils; for he kept an Academy. The additional Chapters by Mr. Amory (now living) seem not inferior to the Original.

"Morality justly complains of such treacherous Friends as Swift and Bolingbroke; but smiles on these her genuine Sons; and delights to enroll with them the Name of her Stinstra[.]

"To that pious and learned Divine Mr. Duncombe wishes Health and Spirits, that he may be able to prosecute and

finish his Laudable Essays. London, 14 June, 1754. P.S. To
the Authors already mentioned, might have been added,
Cumberland['s] de Legibus Naturæ." [95]

Thus far M[r.] Duncombe. Hath a Volume of Discourses
of our present Bp. of London reached you, Sir? They are in
high Repute here. I shall be very ready to obey you in
sending you any of the above Books, or in executing any
Commissions you shall favour me with.

I am very much afraid, that the kind Care you propose to
take in overseeing the Translation of my last Piece, will be
an Invasion of, and Interruption to, your important Labours. Dear Sir, let me entreat you, not to suffer it to be
so!—

You express your self apprehensive that the Shortening I
made of it, might, by crouding [sic] the Events too close
upon the Reader, give it the Air of a Romance. But as in
many Places, I omitted some Busy Scenes, as well as the
Parts that connected them with y[e] Story, and the Sentiments
that accompanied them, I hope it will not have a great deal
of that Appearance.

Don't be sorry, my dear Sir, for the Alarm you gave me.
It was a kind Alarm. Had I made my Heroine set an
Example of an indelicate Paroxysm, and a too warm
Avowal of the Passion of Love, in the Opinion of so fine
and delicate a Judge, I should never have forgiven my self.
Harriet Byron's Part, between Frankness of Heart, and
true Female Modesty, was a difficult one; and /she/ might
fail very easily, treading a Love, as I may, and where the
least curving to the Right or Left might have overset her. I
intended that the Piece should abound with delicate Situations, in order for y[e] Trial of the Good Characters. None
of them are intended to be absolute [sic] faultless: But if
there be any great Slips that you think capable of doing
Hurt, I beseech you, Sir, to correct them in the Translation.
If I know what you do in this particular, I will amend by
your Judgment, should there be a *Fourth* Edition. You must
know, I reckon the Octavo Edition, one, as I printed 1000

of that, More than two thirds of which are sold, besides upwards of 4000 of the Twelves: [96] A great Sale considering the Damage done me by the Irish, and their Edition; [97] and that the w{ork} has been no longer published. This I mention the rather, for the Encouragement of {yours} Undertaken; and for the same Reason, that our two Eldest Princes are reading the Work {now.} But as I am told this by first rate Persons, I wish it not to be repeated as from me.

I h{ave} many Anonymous Letters sent me, urging me to write another Volume, in order to conclude the Stories of Clementina and Miss Jervois. And some /which/ blame me for suffering Sir Charles to allow the former Lady, had he married her, to educate her Daughters in the Roman Catholic Faith. I inclose two Letters that I have printed on these Subjects, [98] to give to any-body that asks for them, in order to save my self Trouble of answering. Were I to reg{ard} my Profit, I should not hesitate to oblige those who want me to write another Volume. But, that is not a Consideration most predominant with me. Give me, dear and reverend Sir, your Opinion when you have perused these two Letters, on this Subject.

I now come to your Letter of May 23. What Pleasure you give me, so good a Man your self, by your Approbation of my other good Man!

You could have wished, that the Conclusion of the Story had been more interesting. Yet are apt to think that it bears a more natural Resemblance to Truth, as it is. It would have been easy for me, (as you see by Harriet's frightful Dream, and Greville's frantic Resentm{ent} at last, as Sir Charles's Nuptials draw near), to have ended with a great deal of Bu{stle} and a great Eclat. But I thought it better to prefer Nature to the Marvellous; {the} Story, as you observe, so recent. A British Nobleman of fine Parts, has done me great Honour in comparing my Conclusion with that of the Æneid, which ends with the Death of Turnus, and includes not the Marriage of Lavinia; and even with the

Iliad, which shuts up without taking Troy, &c. And a Lady one of my choicest Correspondents, thus writes—"I am extremely pleased with Sir Charles's last Action. Comforting the dying Man, and endeavouring to speak Peace to his despairing Soul, was a fit Conclusion for Sir Charles Grandison."

I shall retouch Pamela, as I have Opportunity; [99] having gone a good way in it. What I am now e{mp}loying myself about, is, ⟨to collect⟩ /in collecting/ the Sentiments of the first and last of yᵉ th{ree} Pieces ({T}hose in Clarissa are already printed in the last Edition) and to print all containe{d} /in the/ Three i{n o}ne Pocket Volume, to serve as a kind of Vade Mecum to such as either have read, o{r}, having not read, can dispense w.ᵗʰ yᵉ Stories, for the Sake of the Instruction aimed {to b}e given in them.[100] This Design is much approved by some of my Friends; but others {rath}er wish me to go upon some new Work, or to give the World another Volume of the last. Surely I hav{e b}een already a too voluminous Writer!

Be pleased to make my {be}st Respects /acceptable/ to your good Mother. Dear, good, and reverend Sir, let me repeat my Entreaties that you will not give your self so much Trouble about the Translation of Grandison, as may interfere with your more important Cares. Receive also my repeated Thanks for your vᵗʰ and vıᵗʰ Volumes of Clarissa; and for the instructive Preface to the vᵗʰ; and believe me to be, with the truest Esteem and Affection

*Your Faithful and Obedient Humble Servant*
*S. Richardson.*

*London, June 28. 1754.*

[17]

## William Richardson *to* Stinstra

*April 7, 1755*

London, *April 7th, 1755.—*

*Reverend Sir,*

My Uncle begs your Acceptance of the accompanying Volume [101]—He has been, and is, under much Concern,
at not having heard from You for so long a Time; but
hopes You have not been prevented by ill Health, or any
other unhappy Circumstance. He earnestly entreats the Favour of a Letter from You soon. Your Friendship is dear to
him. He pours forth his sincerest Prayers for Your Health
and Welfare. I have the Honour to be,

*Reverend Sir,*
*Your most Humble Serv.*[t]
*Wm; Richardson*

[18]

## Stinstra *to* Richardson

*June 13, 1755*

*To Mr. S. Richardson.*
*Dear Sir,*

Your most acceptable present of the *Collection of
Sentiments* [102] &c. with the accompanying Letter of your
Kinsman dated April 7. have I but just received, and return
my humble thanks for this new proof of your favour to me:
acknowledging also my obligation to Mr. Wm Richardson
for his kind conveyance. Ill health was at first the occasion

of my long silence, which during the most part of the winter has kept me weak and low; and for which my business pressed very heavy upon me. After my restoration I delayed writing from week to week in hopes that I might acquaint you with the effect of my endeavours to procure an able translator to your History of Grandison; which matter is yet not brought to an issue. But of these my endeavours I wil give You an account very soon, when I shall transmit to you the two last Volumes of the Dut[c]h Clarissa, which in the following week are to come from the press. Since the beginning of the preceding month my mother has drawed to her all my attention and cares, as being then surprised with an attack of palsy whereby she losed almost all her powers, and remains since very low, spiritless, and bed-rid. The Almighty favours however her mind with the grace, that she herself can patiently submit to his depressing hand, and with ardent desire see out for her deliverance out of this decayed body.—I am very much affected with the expression of your Kinsman, *that my friendship is dear to you.* I perceive the honour therein done to me by your worthy mind; but at the same time am I ashamed, that I have given reason to you, by my slowness, of doubting my steadiness in our happily contracted friendship. I dispatch therefore this as soon as possible to assure and protest that I am, Sir, with the utmost sincerity, regard, and affection,

*Your most faithful and highly obliged Friend and Servant*

*John Stinstra*

*Harlingen*
*June 13th 1755.*

[19]

## Stinstra *to* Richardson

*June 23, 1755*

*Dear and worthy Sir,*

I hope that my letter of the 13 instant is received by you; and beg anew very earnestly your kind excuse for my preceding remis[s]ness in writing to you, whose friendship and esteem is to me (be assured of this, Sir) of the highest value.

I have now the honour to offer to you the two last volumes of your inimitable Clarissa, clothed in Dutch, for which I beg your acceptance. I have thus, I thank Heaven, finished my labour of translating this work, which however worthy my most intense labour, has cost me more pains and time, perhaps, than you in composing it. The long intervalls yet of the publication of the succe[e]ding volumes is more owing to the slowness of our press, than to my lazyness in furnishing it with materials. Never it has waited for these, and often have I diverted me with other studies. My short preface to the vii wish I that not altogether unworthy of these two last volumes may be found by you; Althoug[h] I myself must think, that my performance not satisfieth to the dignity of the subject, which surely merited a more ample and distinct elucidation. And I fear that by much aiming at brevity, for which I have my reasons mentioned in the preface itself, I have incurred sometimes the fault of obscurity. I imagined nevertheless (which I add, that you may not suspect me of a feigned modesty) that I could offer some thoughts on the subject, which I had not rencountred with others in their schemes of the State of Human Life on earth; and thus I have taken for it this, in my judgment, not improper occasion.

See here further, Sir, an account of my endeavours to procure for my countrymen a Translation of your excellent History of Charles Grandison, which might, at least in some measure, answer to the elegancies of its original. I remember, that I have mentioned to you in a former, that the Translator, which I first had chosen, made a difficulty of submitting his translation to my review and correction. This difficulty weighed so heavy with him, that he renounced to undertake this task on the said condition. And since he has declared to be glad for not having begun it, because he aknowlegded [sic] not to have been able to perform it tolerably. I have therefore sought another, and conferred me to a publick instructor of the English language at the University of Franeker; from whom I have had a specimen: But this man was so little master of the idioms and elegancies of our Dutch, that I should have had more pains from correcting his version, than from translating your work myself. A third has offered his service to my Bookseller, which on the other hand was but a novice in your language, and for this reason, after the assay of his capacity, could not be accepted. Besides these I could not think of any other in this province, to which I might commit this work with an expectation of tolerable success. A Bookseller at Amsterdam, to whom Mr. v. d. Plaats has conceded a portion in his right, wherewith you have favoured him, has a long while sought for a capable subject; but in vain. At last he thinks to have found one; he has requested of him a specimen; which he has given, with a declaration that he should not be unwilling to undertake the translation. The proof was very short, and not out of the most difficult Letters; and I have found, that it not answered the notion, which the said bookseller had given of his ability. Wherefore I dared not to commit this trust to his performing, without reserving to me the liberty of reviewing his work and, if necessary, of mending it, before it come to the press. This I have signified to the Booksellers, to be communicated to the Translator, whom I not know, before a month hence. And yet I have not an answer, if he be pleased with this condition and if he and the Booksellers can agree in others to be stipulated between them. These, Sir, are my proceedings in this affair, which I with my whole heart wish that might have had a speedier success. If this last mentioned translator again disappoints us, I should almost despare of executing this trust according to my wish and desire. This should be a very great grief to me, not so much for your sake, Sir; whose glory is illustriously established, though I would most willingly propogate it, but, principally for the sake of my countrymen, which may not profit bij your most valuable performance, and for my own sake, that I must be deprived of this highest satisfaction of procuring them a benefit by my means for which manij here ardently wish. I cannot arraign myself of a too great nicety in this affair; my immense esteem for the work permits not, that I should be less circumspect. Perhaps, Sir, had you not put this trust in me, your work should here partly be published already by the Bookseller of Amsterdam, who had first announced it,[103] before the edition of the original. But the emulation of the Booksellers works here strongly; and I have excited against me the jealousy of the common translators. Pity is it, but that your Grandison must suffer for it! Can you advise me, Sir, which methods may be taken to give him a readier success?

My Mother has, since my last, by the allwise and benign dispensation of Providence, advanced in strength of body and mind, and is presently in a very tolerable condition. The same goodness I thank for the recovering of my full health and vigour: and I pray fervently for the happy continuation of your usefull life, as

*Your most true Admirer, Friend*
*and Servant,*

*John Stinstra.*

*Harlingen*
*June 23<sup>th</sup> 1755.*

[20]

## Richardson *to* Stinstra

*July 24, 1755*

London, July 24. 1755.

*Dear, and Rev<sup>d.</sup> Sir,*

I was much too concerned at reading the Contents of your ⟨s⟩ /Letter/ of the 13th of June, which gave me an Account of yours and your Mother's heavy Illnesses, to write directly to you, as you gave me hopes in it, that you should soon write to me again, on the kindest Occasion; when, /possibly,/ you would be enabled (such were my Prayers to the Almighty) to give me a better Account of both. Thank God, that my ardent Wishes have been answered, in your perfect Recovery, and in the Amendment of the Lady so deservedly dear to your pious Heart!

You have had, Sir, an arduous Task in the Translation of the History of Clarissa. I have very great Reason to be /as/ thankful for the Honour done me by so Eminent an Hand, as you have (that so great a Labour is at an End) that you have completed it. What a Perseverance, with so many Duties and Avocations! A thousand Thanks to you for it, and for your kind Present of the Volumes so elegantly dressed. I received y<sup>e</sup> Parcel but Yesterday.

Do not be angry, dear and good Sir, that I give you the Trouble of desiring your Bookseller to draw upon me for the Setts, now completely sent me. (This was, you know, referred to the Conclusion.[)] The Work is happily perfected!—Again and again, I thank you, that it is!

How greatly do I regret the Trouble, the very great Trouble, you have had in endeavouring to procure a good Translation of the History of Sir Charles Grandison! I have 5 Volumes sent me over of it (at 3 different times, as they proceed) translated into German, undertaken by M. Weidman's of Leipsick; who have also engaged to have it translated into French, *unmutilated* (which is not the case with the Gentlemen at Paris, as I am informed; who also {c}urtailed greatly *our* Clarissa) and printed, by M. Luzac, junior [104] at Leiden. Perhaps these two Translations might be helpful to some Gentleman, who might yet be found able and willing to render it into Dutch.

M. Luzac has written to me, that 3 Copper Plates to each Volume is designed to the Edition he is engaged in, besides a Frontispiece, or Device, to the first; and requested me to give him Subjects for them. His Letter is dated 17 ultimo. My Answer bears Date the 9th of y<sup>e</sup> present Month. I have mentioned to him a /more than/ sufficient Number of Subjects for his Purpose. If you have Acquaintance with M. Luzac, he would perhaps shew you my Letter; and the rather, as he might hope for Advantage from your Judgment. If you choose to see a Copy of it, I will have it transcribed for you.

I most cordially thank you, dear and good Sir, for the very kind and acceptable Assurances of the Continuance of your Favour for me. Indeed Sir, your Friendship is very precious to me. My Kinsman could not too warmly express himself on this Subject.

I am impatient to get translated into English your Preface to the Seventh and Eighth Volumes of your laborious and generous Task. How often have I, since I have had the Honour of corresponding with my Reverend and dear M. Stinstra, wished my self a Master of the Dutch Language!

May the Almighty continue to you, that restored Vigor of Mind and Body, which will be so usefully employ'd, as it has long been, to His Honour and Glory; and perfect Recovery of your dear Mother, repeatedly prays, Reverend and dear Sir,

*Your ever-obliged, and affectionate Friend,*
*and faithful Servant,*

S. *Richardson*

[21]

## Stinstra *to* Richardson

### *September 17, 1755*

*To Mr. S. Richardson.*

*Harlingen Septemb. 17.*

*1755*

Dear Sir,

At last have I found an able hand or hands for the translation of your excellent History of Grandison into Dutch, which have engaged to undertake and perform this task. The Gentleman of whom I made mention, in my former, could not be persuaded to translate the whole work, but thought absolutely that it must be abbreviated, and many letters passed by, which not concerned the main point of the History: which mutilation I not permitting in any manner, the treatment with him has had an end. Whereon I wrote to a certain Friend of me in Amsterdam, who has a very high and just value of your works, and an uncommon knowledge of both languages, whether in that city not were to be found a company of able gentlemen, who under his eye would in community undertake this labour for the good of their countrymen. This thought has succeeded: My friend has brought together such a company; I have had an essay of their translation, which had so much my approbation, that I confidently without my reviewing could commit to them this trust. And now have the Booksellers agreed with them on the conditions by the interlocution of my mentioned Friend, for the translators themselves would not be known. The work will be printed at Amsterdam, and immediately the translation commenced.

I have spoken with my Bookseller concerning the copper plates, wherewith you have given me notice that the French edition should be adorned. He has communicated thereon with his companion, but they were of opinion that this would to much heighten the price of their book, and diminish the number of buyers. But they would fain decorate it with your portrait,[105] if this could have your approbation. Wherefore they by my means beseech you, that you would have the goodness to present them with a copy of it (as which I have informed them that not are sold) that they might let it counterfeit in a smaller form, according to that of the book, by the ablest hand in this our country. I have contracted with the Booksellers for ten or twelve sets of their edition of this your work as an small acknowledgment of your favour to them.

Mr. v. d. Plaats, (for as much you cannot be moved to accept the four setts of the Clarissa on the like condition, and he has no occasion here to draw upon you) has declared the price of them to be between 53 and 54 Dutch guldens, which amounts to almost 5 pounds of your money: but this he shall esteem to be compensated by four setts of the last edition of your Hist. of Sr. Charles Grandison which he beggs that you will transmit to me by the ordinary way. If however you might think this compensation not to be equal to the value of his setts, he concedes that you may supply the defect by a sett of your Collection of the Moral Sentiments &c. from the Pamela, Clarissa, and Grandison; and your debt with him shall be abundantly satisfied.

The edition of this your predicted Collection has me brought in the opinion, that you have laid aside the design of retouching your Pamela,[106] of which you have mentioned in a foregoing letter, which I have had the honour of receiving from you. Otherwise, I suppose, you should have expected such a new edition for this Collection. Is this my supposition right, Sir? Then fear I, that the world not shall enjoy any further fruits of your inimitable genius, from a saying in the same Letter, that you proposed this to be your last labour. Is your age so far advanced, your health impaired, that it not permits you to undertake any new work?

it would be importune for us your admirers to sollicit you further: Enjoy quietly the full-merited applause of all the virtuous and ingenious, which have already to you the utmost obligation, but cannot at once suppress the desire insatiable for further delicacies, which the taste of the former excites in them.

You have had the goodness to offer me your service in any thing which I might have need of. Should I be an abuse of this permission if I recommend to you the case of two of my Friends, if there might perhaps be occasion for you to serve them? The one is a worthy minister of the publick church in this our province, but who cannot easily accommodate his thoug[h]ts and tongue to the scheme of the Calvinist Orthodoxy, and therefore faces the persecution of his zealous brethren. He has a wife and family of children, and should be very glad, if he might honourably exit this storm. Should there not be occasion to procure him a calling from a Dutch Church in any one of your trading cities, where he might enjoy more liberty out of the reach of the synodal shackles of Dordrecht? He is master of the English tongue, and knows your country, as having been with our troops there as minister in the foregoing war, and having, no doubt, there imbibed his more reasonable sentiments. His name is H. Buma,[107] his place IJsbrechtum near Sneek in Frizeland. The reason of this my addres thereon to you is, because I from your ordering of the setts of *our* Dutch Clarissa (I am proud of the share which you concedes [sic] to me therein) concluded that you had communication with some Dutchmen of worth and condition.—Corn. Nozeman,[108] minister in the dissenting Church of Remonstrants at Harlem, is the other of my friends, which has desired my commendation to you, and by me desires your commendation to other printers in London, having undertaken, for the sustenance of his numerous family, a fabrick of letter-founding. I include here a specimen or two of his forms, which I to this purpose have received from him, and which he thinks to be most in the English taste of printing. If you might have occasion, Sir, to promote the interest of these two gentlemen, your favour should not be misapplied, and my obligation to you should thereby increase: which however already is so great, that I must begg your excuse for this trouble, if it be anywise inconvenient for you.

That the Almighty God continue to pour out upon you the fullness of his blessings is the constant and fervent prayer of
*Your humble Servant and Friend*
*John Stinstra.*

[22]

# Richardson *to* Stinstra

*November 26, 1755*

I am sorry, my dear and Reverend Sir, for the Trouble you have had in procuring Translators for the History of Sir Ch. Grandison. May the Work, when done, answer to yᵉ Benefit of the Undertakers! And the Example of the Hero of the Piece to yᵉ Good of your Public! I will send you for them the Portrait they are desirous to prefix to the Volumes. You will do me Honour, dear and good Sir, if you accept of one or two more your self.

In the same Parcel I will send for Mʳ· v. d. Plaats, Four Setts of the History of Sir C. Grandison, in Octavo, and Four Vols. of the *Sentiments,* &c.[109] which were only printed in Duodecimo; and shall think my self obliged to him, for the Easiness of the Exchange.

I have actually retouched Pamela:[110] But there being a Number of the 3ᵈ and 4ᵗʰ Volumes of that Work in hand, more than of the 1ˢᵗ and 2ᵈ. I only, printed as many of the two latter, as would make perfect Setts; and was therefore obliged to keep the two former as they were. I have also given my last Hand to Clarissa and Grandison; which, however, vary but little from yᵉ last Edition of these Works: But I was willing to amuse my self between whiles, while I

attended Workmen in their Building for me New Printing
Offices [111] (the House I live in, being in Danger, from its
Age, if I may so express my self, and the very great
Weights I had upon it) rather than to begin a new Work in
the Writing Way; for which, had I Inclination, Bricks,
Mortar, and Carpenter's Works, would have been wholly
unfit. After a very harrassing Summer, I have near finished
my Building Scheme. But to say yᵉ Truth, find not in my self
any Appelency for the Pen—And have I not written a great
deal?—A troublesome Business all the Time to attend to?
And ought I not to know when I am well off? I have long
laboured under severe Nervous Maladies; and was born in
yᵉ Year 1689. Yet how pleasing are your kind Wishes, &
those of my other Friends, that I would write something
more; as they are an Earnest of Your and their Approbation of what is already published!

　Your kind Letter before me, is dated Sept. 17. I received
it not till the last Day of October: And I should have
acknowleged the Receipt of it before now, could I have
answered as I wished the Recommendation of your Friend
Mʳ· Buma: I have for some time expected in Town, a
Gentleman, whom I intend to consult on this Subject, as
soon as he comes; for his Arrival has been delay'd by un-
foreseen Accidents. My worthy Friend Mʳ· Duncombe, who
possibly may be of Service in the Affair, has not been long in
Town. I will /also/ engage him in it; & if I can procure any
Service to be done to so worthy a Man, shall think my self
very happy; and shall give you the first Notice of it.

　I will shew to as many, occasionally, the Specimens you
have sent me, of the Types, /as I think it may be of Use./
Our Printers are engaged mostly with a Letter-founder of
our own (Caslon) [112] who gives a good deal of satisfaction;
and in Glasgow is another of the Business, who seems to
meet with Encouragement: But if the Defect in Caslon's
Metal, which falls short of its usual Hardness, hurts him
not, it will not be ea[s]y to stand against him; were it only
for this Consideration; Every Printer here, being furnished

with *his* Types, the Booksellers, in a large Work, can for Dispatch-Sake, put it to several Printers, and print on the same Type. Let me observe for the Sake of this worthy Gentleman, that in his Text Romyn, the Capital Letters are thought rather too large for the rest, and too gross; The small [w ha]s also been objected to, as not open or free enough; such a one as this w, being preferred to W, as in the Specimen. The Capitals in ye Text Cursyf are also thought to be too full and black. But on the Whole, both that and the Gar[a]mond [113] are very pretty Letters. I should be glad to see Specimens of other Sizes. If it be in my Power to encourage the Gentleman, I will. But for my self, I am greatly over-stock'd, at present with all Sorts; and want to reduce my very great Weight.

You will wonder, perhaps, my dear and reverend Friend, that while I plead my Years and Infirmities agt· writing, that I should have been all the Summer engaged in Building. But to say nothing of the different Powers required for each, I propose, God favouring! to have my Business carried on after My Decease, for the Benefit of my Wife, and four good Girls; and the Lease of my present House being near expiring, and the House having been adjudged to have stood near its time; it would not have been prudent to renew; and I must have removed while it was repairing, if I had. For these Reasons, I thought I ought not to spare my self the Trouble I have been at, for my Family's Sake; however short the Time of my enjoying the very convenient Change might be[.]

You mention not, dear Sir, the State of your good Mother's Health. My best Wishes attend her. Adieu, my dear, my Reverend Friend! Believe me to be, as I ever shall be,

*Your most Affectionate Friend,*
*and obliged Humble Servt.*
S. *Richardson*

*London, Nov. 26. 1755.*

Pray, Sir, how go you on with the noble Works you have in Design, and Operation?

[23]

# Richardson *to* Stinstra

*February 21, 1756*

.*Dear and Rev*d. *Sir*,

I have not been wanting in my Application to proper Persons in Behalf of your Reverend Friend Mr. Buma; but hitherto without Success. I am sorry for it. The Answer in general is, that there is no Vacancy, nor Prospect of one, at present. My Friend Mr. Duncombe, who is a Man of large Acquaintance among the Worthy and Intelligent thus writes to me in a Letter dated the 4th of this Month—"I did not forget the Affair you recommended to me, in relation to M. Stinstra's Friend; but see no Prospect of Success. Dr. Maty,[114] himself a Dutchman, Author of the Journal Britannique, tells me, that the Dutch and French Churches are all full; and that there are several Ministers expecting to succeed on any Vacancy that may happen. The next Kindness to the conferring a Favour is, to let a Person know, that the thing desired is not practicable."

I have not been able as yet to engage any of our Printers in Favour of the Types of your other Friend.[115] The principal Reason is, that Caslon [116] has Possession of them all; and those who are worth dealing with, are well furnished with his. It is very unhappy, that I have not been able to serve Gentlemen recommended by You, so very deserving. Is there any other Way that I can possibly be of Service to them,

Mr. Duncombe adds as follows: "When you write to M. Stinstra, pray ask, If he is acquainted with ye Writings of Mr. John Taylor of Norwich.[117] I believe they will suit his Taste."

If you have them not, I will, on M<sup>r.</sup> Duncombe's Commendation, desire your Acceptance of them.

You long ago, I make no doubt, received my Letter of Nov. 26 and the Parcel mentioned in it; containing four Setts of the History of Sir Ch. Grandison in Octavo, and four Volumes of y<sup>e</sup> Collection of Sentiments, for M. Vander Plaats; and one of the Pourtraits desired by y<sup>e</sup> Undertakers of the Dutch Translation of Sir. Ch. Grandison, and two more of which I requested your Acceptance.

I besought you, dear Sir, in that Letter, to let me know how you proceed with the noble Works you had in Design.

As also to acquaint me with the State of your good Mother's Health.

I am interested in every thing that I know will give either Pleasure or Pain to so worthy a Friend.

I am, and will be ever,

*Dear and Reverend Sir,*

*Most Affectionately Your*

*London Febr. 21. 1756.*          *S. Richardson*

# Part Two

## *Johannes Stinstra's Prefaces to* CLARISSA

# Preface to the First and Second Volumes

## of Clarissa[1]

I CAN READILY UNDERSTAND that it must appear strange and unusual to many people that I am the translator of a *novel* or adorned history about the love affairs of a young couple. One of these young people, playing the role of a libertine, must necessarily show many actions and adventures of an evil nature; moreover, the conversations and doings of such lovers are usually empty and trivial; and such histories are normally suited to bewilder and strongly excite the imagination of those young people who have a taste for such things. This role of translator does not seem to correspond with the dignity of the position I hold, nor with the gravity which people demand of a Minister of the Gospel. It appears to be neither compatible with a serious piety, which I have always advocated, nor to be in keeping with my frequent declarations of the high value I place on virtue and good morals. It also does not seem to fit my particular circumstances, since, being under oppression, I should have better and worthier pursuits with which to occupy myself.[2]

Such reasonings will certainly be made by many people, intelligent and well-meaning themselves, as well as by those who, seeking to slander my good name from a feigned zeal for their religion, will not fail to take advantage of the opportunity to bring me into disrepute with the pious, who are set on serious godliness. I believe that I have presented these considerations or objections against my present undertaking with their full force and emphasis. However, I am certain that they will lose all their force to those people who put aside their prejudice and read this excellent work with attention. Thus I have also been assured by intelligent people who have read my translation in manuscript, that they have found nothing which is improper for my ministry, my zeal for virtue and religion, and my particular circumstances. My good friends who have done me the honor (for I truly consider this an honor and a proof of noble friendship) to inform me of their uncertainties and doubts concerning my undertaking when they became aware of it, and to warn me of the possibility of the above-mentioned slander, I have especially tried to put at their ease. I shall also take pains concerning those who have not read this work and who may fall into the same doubts. This is something I owe to the impartial public, to a dispassionate desire for my good name and regard, and to the cause of pure virtue and Christian piety. The removal of the above-mentioned unfavorable considerations, the disclosure and insistence of the reasons which have moved me to undertake this translation, in spite of such prejudices, will create the opportunity for me to recommend this piece in the strongest way and to the fullest extent of my ability to all intelligent and virtue-loving readers. Everything I shall praise merits the same consideration and will provide me with suitable and ample subject matter for a Preface, without which, it seems, no book can be published. I shall, however, make it as brief as the value of the subject calls for.

I do not intend here to silence the mouths of the so called fine and serious people who put the work of their religion into a plaited and stiffly-drawn being, into a head warped like a reed, or into an affected bearing or drawling speech. My intention applies as well to those whose censoriousness cannot be quieted by even the most concise reasoning, whose prejudices condemn everything which is not to their taste, and to those to whom nothing good can come from Nazareth. I shall gladly leave such people to their peevish and fretful thoughts.

I shall not attempt to excuse myself by pleading the desire of several of my friends, who, having heard me praise this work to the skies, have long and forcefully urged me to translate it. Their desire was based on my judgment or on that of others who agreed with it; the question is whether such judgment was just and well founded. Also, I do not believe that my effort requires an excuse but rather that it merits praise. I shall not bring to my defense the fact that many other ministers have busied themselves with the publication of works either of a similar nature or which at least may be considered as having no higher value. Not to mention a Huet [3] or the Archbishop Fénelon, a great advocate of serious and modest piety, who has made himself justly famous through his *Telemachus*. To spend his diligence on a moral novel is certainly no less suitable for a preacher and Minister of the Gospel than for him to turn his efforts to literary quibblings and hagglings about writers of little or no importance. The latter effort, however, is accepted by many people. Not to speak of other writers who almost make novels out of all religion through the nourishment and gratification of bewildered imaginations. *Clarissa* does not need the cloak of the best examples taken from it; and most novels are too low even to deserve comparison with it.

I shall not request compassionate people to allow me to comfort and delight myself with a beautiful picture of an oppressed and tormented virtue as another means of consolation in my own oppression. I could enjoy this diversion for its own sake, and Heaven be thanked for giving me abundant supports to prevent my oppression from overcoming me!

I am still the same that I have always been, and have shown myself in my works to be, a patron and advocate of moral virtue and righteousness, of true, wise, and Christian piety, placing the highest value on these attributes and trying to recommend them to my fellow men in the strongest possible way. This I value as the most laudable character which can be ascribed to me, whereas all other fame of intelligence and erudition are, to my thinking, much less important. This I consider to be the true work of a Minister of the Gospel, because Christian virtue is also the spirit and the nucleus of Christian religion. This endeavor is thus proper for a minister to the highest degree, and must be of much credit to him. In this my present work, I am also compelled by this same desire to propagate the love for virtue and true piety. And I believe that this work, which I have in hand now, can be of unequalled use for that purpose. This realization moved me to accept so heavy a labor for the service of my compatriots; this conviction keeps my desire continually alive in spite of the burden and makes me continue it peacefully without the aforementioned prejudice against novels succeeding in preventing or slowing down this task.

A novel, it is true, is a fabrication, as one says. And can fabrications, one asks, can untruths also further pure truth, true virtue and religion? Far be it from me that I would agree to lying and deceiving in the service of truth. Some, perhaps, who raise their noses at novels with aversion and disdain, would have no scruples about this. But everyone judges these and similar works of fiction for what they really are; no one is deceived by them, and they serve only to make pleasanter and easier to accept for weak people the useful and necessary lessons of severe and true virtue. And if one wants to condemn all works of fiction, all adorned stories, without distinguishing between them; if one absolutely disapproves of their use for the promotion of good morals, virtue, and true godliness, where then will one be with the symbolic parables and tales of our Blessed Savior Jesus Christ Himself, which so frequently appear in the Gospels, in which He either paints the true character of His religion or describes horrible iniquities or imprints the most important lessons and recommends the loftiest virtues, and which in their own nature are nothing other than so many short sketches of novels? Because our godly Teacher Himself has not considered it unworthy to proclaim, with such adornments, His rational, His perfectly pure teachings, why should we then be too particular and too serious to use similar devices to serve our own uses? With what excuse can one pretend that it is unseemly for a Minister of the Gospel to attempt to attain by such means, among others, the high purpose which he should keep in mind in all his doings?

Everyone admits, without doubt, that examples have a strong influence on our conduct of life. We are too closely attached to flesh and blood for sober and abstract reason alone to move and affect us. But if the actions and deliberations of virtuous people are described for us and held before our eyes, they cause us to view virtue as real and personal and affect our minds much more keenly; that which previously was only reasonable and good now becomes pleasant, delightful, and lovable for us. The examples of lofty virtue in our own lives are rare; most of the best ones keep themselves hidden in silence and attract the eyes of a small number only. The examples which fiction shows us are also scarce. Among these many are unrealistic and cannot furnish most of us with anything which can be imitated. The histories, even the biographies of the most important men usually furnish us with no other stories than those of events which normally come before the eyes of the world, while the actions of common, plain, and domestic lives are passed by unnoticed. In these stories one seldom finds much else than the outer bark of events; the motives and purposes by which actions are prompted remain concealed much of the time, untouched, or are only to be traced by doubtful conjectures, because they are but the soul of an example which one sets himself to follow. A well-conceived novel can overcome these deficiencies if the author is complete master of his material and can sketch the external scenes at will and can infuse into them the most ordinary actions of human lives, whose exemplary representation is a great service for all. Such representations have a tremendous influence on the happiness of society and the author can add to his characters such purposes, such reasonings, as agree closest to the matter at hand and which perfect a beautiful and attractive example. And *Clarissa* possesses all of these advantages in the most excellent manner. The form of familiar letters especially which the author has used provides him the opportunity of putting the last touch to his picture in the most detailed and accurate way.

The truth of the events, it is true, is lacking in a novel. Yet the above-mentioned excellences, I think, can certainly be in balance with the power to affect the mind, as long as probability and naturalness in the story are observed, as long as one finds nothing but that which pleases human nature, as well as such insights and thoughts which every reasonable and honorable man in similar circumstances would want to have.

I gladly acknowledge that much misuse is made of novels, in the feeding of lustful wishes and obscene desires. Many occupy themselves with stories of all sorts of bestiality and licentiousness, of many kinds of rascalities and roguish tricks. To make these pleasant and tasteful by a comic and droll representation can bring about nothing but evil in the minds of people and in human society. Many such pictures can produce no effect except to make the brains of youth run wild with useless fancies, to foster the natural seeds of amorous passion, to expose the tender sex the more to temptations, or at best to lure minds away from useful and constructive activities. One need not or rather ought not sow that which grows without our help, because the too luxuriant growth stifles the nobler seed, which, in order to grow, does require our care and diligence. But one sees that the best things can be misused, and they then often degenerate into the most evil, most dangerous, most harmful things. If people therefore would condemn and reject the use of novels, they would have to say farewell to reason, to God's word, and to religion altogether, under the guise of which the godless and the hyprocitical wickedly conceal themselves. Then no devout soul would be allowed to raise himself in song to his God in order not to have anything in common with the obscene and unchaste songs which the world indulges in too freely. Then would the organ have to be removed from the church, because it also drones in the gaming house; then would a truly religious person shun all pleasure and delight completely, because wantonness and sensuality prey upon these pleasures excessively and too immoderately. Then, in short, would people be forced to perish from hunger and thirst, from cold and discomfort. No, to be sure! It is folly, just because a good thing is misused by many, to therefore make suspect the profitable and excellent use of it or to allow oneself to be restrained from that use.

It would be, without contradiction, scandalous and most shameful for my name and character for me to put my hand to the afore-mentioned types of novels and, by my translation of them, to disseminate them further to the public. I also admit that it would not at all be fitting to the dignity of a Minister of the Gospel to bring such books into the world, which are suited only to make readers laugh, and to help multiply them (although laughing is not useless for some people) without their having a more important use to further. Neither would I have gladly spent my time on such works which do show the wit of the author and which do portray pleasantly the manner of living and deliberations of many people nowadays and therefore meet with the applause of most people. But these works hang together only by means of many droll and comical incidents, because the observations of the author cannot stand the test of morality but scandalize modest and virtuous minds, and because the most serious happenings are presented in a light way; the most glaring sins and unvirtuous deeds are treated as play and bantering. These works in their entirety allow especially a secret purpose to shine through to paint human nature in an ugly way, as not capable of true and reasonable virtue, but in which what usually stands for virtue is merely an effect of a natural condition or disguised passions. Such writings are naturally suitable to appeal to defects and vices, to relax the bands of virtue, to dull the power of conscience, to lessen shame and mutual trust. And these writings are most dangerous in the hands of loose and impressionable youth, whose imaginations are captured the more violently in direct ratio to the lightness and wittiness of the works.

But the excellent work which I now offer and recommend to Dutch readers is an entirely different sort, not only the most beautiful and entertaining novel but also the most useful influence on the minds of those who love virtue in some degree or whose hearts are not unmoved by all incitements towards good. Clarissa shows us a beautiful and admirable, a lofty and courageous virtue, arising from the best and purest principles, prompted and undertaken by the noblest and most honest motives—not only a reasonable but a truly Christian virtue and piety which hold fast, unshakable, in the face of the most dangerous temptations, in the face of the heaviest trials. And by keeping her God and Savior and the hope of a future life continually in mind, she experiences death cheerfully. However, a virtue and piety which do not rise above human standards and although generally conducted by vigilant care in every respect are subject to some very excusable faults and errors of weakness. A Belford shows us the singular emotions and workings of an intelligent and sincere repentance, praises the glory of the virtue which enlightens him, and opposes vice with a manly power and strength of motive. A Miss Howe provides, along with her virtuous and hapless companion, the outline of a most honorable and close friendship exercised with a merry and light spirit. Even if virtue is furthered by its being portrayed charmingly and pleasantly according to its worth, it can be of no less use to present vice and godlessness in their natural, ugliest, and most abominable colors. Anyone who has any honesty left must be frightened by the conduct of a libertine, when in a Lovelace, the fourth above-mentioned person of this history, he sees this behavior painted with the most vivid strokes, although Lovelace is shown in the most advantageous circumstances of natural as well as acquired gifts of intelligence and learn-

ing, of temporal wealth and ample fortunes, having thoughtful management of his affairs and respect for outwardly refined breeding. Who would not execrate the pestilent venom
of lewdness as he considers here how it can corrupt and en-
slave the most noble abilities, pull the soul down to the most
sordid depths, and finally, how it can altogether kill the
conscience? As he finds the outward delight of the lives of
the clever libertine and his trusted friend cancelled by the
sharpest and most piercing remarks, cut to the bone and
marrow, and revealed in hideousness; as he becomes aware
of the bitter and deadly fruits thereof, in the dangers to
which such dissolute souls expose themselves, in the devour-
ing remorsefulness of a revived and most fiercely raging
conscience? And especially as he casts his eyes on the picture
of the wretched and untimely deaths of such rogues, which
are here presented in the most disagreeable and horrible
manner, especially when compared with the soft and quiet
departure of a pure and pious soul which returns peacefully
to its Creator? All feeling must be lost. No emotions in the
world can touch the person who is not touched by these
emphatic strokes.

One might here raise the question whether it is prudent
thus to show publicly the lewd life of a libertine, whether
the uncontrolled desires in lax youth might not be aroused
by his language and actions, and whether the author does
not pave the way for these desires in drawing the craftiest
devices and schemes which vice might follow in order to
achieve its purpose. Perhaps it would be of more use to stifle
these secrets of lewdness and keep them concealed in eternal
night. Lewdness, I acknowledge, has been treated by many
moral writers in an entirely imprudent way, because their
descriptions of the ways of animal lust are much more
suited to stir impure desires than their motives are to extin-
guish them. But it is an entirely different case with this
work. There is no lewd matter here which the artful rogue
can deliberately condemn and thereby make himself appear
less unvirtuous. No salacious exhibitions appear here; much

less are they dressed up with tempting adornments, so that no respectable woman, no delicate maiden would ever have occasion to blush with shame from reading this work. If some instances and circumstances are painted which in themselves would, in this respect, enrapture the imagination, the strongest antidote is immediately at hand. Indignation and compassion are at the same time set forth so powerfully that they smother and suppress all other considerations. No stupid rake with his low intelligence could ever imitate the ways which are here ascribed to Lovelace without betraying himself. A cunning rake does not need such expediencies and knows with a devilish craftiness all too well how to contrive various designs for the undoing of innocence. And even if one concedes on the one hand that some bad use could be made of a story of such roguish tricks, yet the extreme abhorrence of them is at the same time inspired throughout. How much more important is its usefulness to warn the inexperienced and therefore gullible youth of the other sex against the faithless conduct, the wicked attacks, and the infernal villainy of such rogues.

For the rest, loose and crude language in a work of this sort could not be avoided, because when a loose and wanton fellow unburdens himself to his intimate friend, his rage and frenzy must naturally bring forth from him the most dreadful curses and terms of abuse. But I have found in mentioning and translating these terms no more difficulty than in repeating the most unvirtuous sayings and propositions of the godless and hypocritical which we find recorded in the Holy Scriptures themselves, especially because in this loose and wanton style very noble lessons of wholesome intelligence and true wisdom are often put forth which perhaps penetrate deeper into the hearts of youth than when they are presented with a stately and grave mien.

An observant reader can here view as in a mirror the standards which are held by various people in the commonest and most important incidents of life and can also see the principles and deliberations which their hearts control and sway, and which of these are to be approved or disapproved. Here one can see described in a lifelike manner the most excellent thoughts, the sweetest consolations of a clear conscience under the heaviest adversities, the grim wrestling of an oppressed conscience, the futile temptations and base deceptions by which a vicious mind foolishly appeases itself and rocks itself to sleep. If a slight imprudence carries a series of difficulties and calamities after it, it teaches how necessary is a continuing vigilance together with a well-grounded trust in Providence and a faithful hope in a more lasting state of happiness. Could it ever be impressed with more insistence than is done here how much care parents must take in directing the choice of their children with respect to the important matter of marriage? Has the harm of uncontrolled and unrestrained passions ever been shown better by the experiences of a family which is so frequently disturbed and made unhappy? There never has been a description of such a situation presented more clearly. I have never found anywhere a more beautiful or lovelier picture of a serene, virtuous, Christian preparation for death. The virtues of humility and generosity, of meekness and steadfastness are here entertwined with one another by the most delicate hand, and they glitter with the most excellent luster and splendor.

Besides the four principal characters already mentioned, various other persons appear in the story, each of whom is pictured according to his particular type, character, and qualities. Obstinate willfulness, arbitrary ambition, insipid meekness, haughty pride of the wealthy, base self-interest of the common people, avarice, envy, conceited pedantry, and each of the opposite virtues take their turn or rather appear here in their natural way and do not show only their outward actions but also their inner emotions and affections and lay bare their qualities before the eye of the spectator in the finest detail. However fortunate Mr. Fielding might have been with the painting of characters, particularly in his *Foundling*, he stays more with the general, sketches more a crude and external bark. But here the persons themselves bring to light in their letters their innermost thoughts and secrets of the heart and provide the situations and dialogues with the finest details and the most delicate qualities of each character. No one should condemn these things as trifles which do not deserve to have anyone pay so much attention to them, to seek them out carefully, and to point them out in such detail. However much higher the theologians are, usually accustomed or inclined to soar with their contemplations, I cannot at all count it unworthy for me to do my work from these trifles, because I find that our godly Master Himself did not overlook trifles such as being greeted in the market places and being given the place of honor at mealtime.

To know all the particular attributes of various virtues and vices is of great service to all who fervently wish to protect themselves from the vices and to hold the virtues in esteem. For a steersman who wants to practice navigation well, it is not only necessary that he know thoroughly the steersman's art and its rules, but he must also know how to use accurate maps, which show him how far the coast extends, where reefs and banks lie, where he can anchor safely, and how the currents flow. So also, those who, safe from temptations, attempt to take their course through this world, must not only familiarize themselves with the exact rules of morality but should also learn from examples of others how and where they might possibly break them, how temptations steal upon them, and what they must avoid. Particulars of that kind cannot possibly be encompassed in a general moral philosophy. Taking all of this into consideration, I think that one can by no means doubt the excellent usefulness of this work; or, if there may be those who are still not satisfied with its usefulness in every respect, I refer them to the work itself and urge them to read it with seriousness and intelligence. And I maintain that every virtue-loving Christian will fall in love with it. Certainly not less excellent are its beauty, handsomeness, and delightfulness. An incomparable art, the liveliest imitation of nature, a perfectly controlled ingeniousness commend the work highly for the approval of everyone. The most wholesome foods are here served with the tastiest and most fragrant sauces.

A profusion of characters is here introduced, as is mentioned above, all according to original nature in every respect, each not only acting according to his special type but thinking, writing, and reasoning for himself. From each letter, sufficient in itself, from its type and style, the observant person can conclude to which character it belongs; every character preserves his own personality consistently, and each is completely the image of himself. And anyone, I think, who has had any experience with the world, will recognize the original subjects among his fellow men, after whom the likenesses in this work are so exactly struck. Clarissa's mother, it is true (for some people have something to say concerning this character), does not always reflect her own image. But how many unstable people do we not meet daily, who, swayed by other's views, abandon their own well-understood principles? How often is it that the same person, possessing great intelligence and natural judgment, does not act intelligently in every respect? And how easy is it for a soft-hearted person, for the sake of peace, to allow himself to be used by dissatisfied people for the continuation of their quarrelsome purposes? And in such a dissimilarity one will find that Mrs. Harlowe is like her own image. The circumstances and events out of which this history is woven together are very manifold, diverse, and complex. They are worked out by a superb wealth of skill, and the reader, with the greatest curiosity, longs to see the affair unfold. The events naturally stem one from the other, are suited to each other, and do not in any way run counter to probability. All of them together are joined to the one important aim of the history in the finest degree and do not cover up or conceal the aim, but each adds a special light and beauty to it. The essential idea of beauty is expressed in the work in a rich variety, exact proportion, excellent nobleness, and careful uniformity. One will find this work lacking in none of these respects; rather one must ascribe the most excellent perfection to it.

Some critics have blamed the work for its prolixity, but this and other objections were firmly answered in the Preface as well as in the Postscript, or Epilogue, by the English publisher,[4] which I shall therefore omit here. Further, no one can deny that regardless of length, all of the different occurrences are crowded together in a very short passage of time, less than a year, according to the requirements in such works of ingenuity.

If people still doubt the usefulness which a lively and orderly power of imagination can provide for us and the kind purpose with which the Almighty Creator has placed it in our nature (see *Warning Against Fanaticism,* pp. 8 ff.), then they should read and consider this work with attention; they will become clearly aware how pleasant it can make the contemplation of virtue, how abominable that of vice; how much love it can inspire in us for one person, how much hate for another; and how strongly it can cause our passions to cooperate in support of reason and true piety. The descriptions and accounts are here so wonderfully alive that the reader could imagine that he does not read the adventures and discourses of others at second hand but sees the happenings with his own eyes, hears the conversations with his own ears, and is himself present at the very scene, because the most mindful prudence is seized and transported by fright; because the purest chastity is treated in a shameful way; because virtue, by a noble courage, is made awesome; because the tenderest friendship gives itself liberally; because an unrepentant sinner wrestles with death in a mad rage and in the most dreadful agonies; because a pure soul moves out of a weak body with a joyful hope. But however lively the imagination works herein, it is arranged throughout, nevertheless, in the most orderly way, and keeps itself in every respect within the bounds of the natural, the probable, and the moral, bounds which are not often well observed in most works of this kind. Pure reason and a wholesome moral philosophy hold the reins throughout the whole work, and all the different scenes sow an abundance of the most useful and excellent lessons which are aptly applied in the most suitable circumstances and are put in the strongest light. Singular and without peer, I might say, is the author's ability here, which shines through to stir and excite the passions in the most moving way. He must be harder than stone whose heart is not softened with compassion in reading this work. He who has any tears cannot restrain himself from shedding them now and then. He who is not completely indifferent must feel his spirit rise in righteous indignation, and on other occasions feel a light joyousness transport his heart to a sweet pleasure and his mouth to a smile. Everything, clever bantering and droll witticisms not excepted, is directed towards that purpose for which the Supreme Being Himself has created in us the power of imagination and the passions for the furtherance of good morals, in order to instill in us the strongest love for pure virtue and the fiercest hatred for sin and wickedness. In earlier times Plato thought that if intelligent virtue could show its image to us in bodily form, it would excite irresistible love for it in everyone. Here, I daresay, it shows itself to the human imagination, which comes closest to the essential image with its singular and resplendent beauty; and I maintain that virtue will charm in the loveliest way every mind in which a desire for good is found and cause the mind to fall in love with it entirely and completely. I have never found in a book of devotions, no matter how well written with an understanding of piety, anything which made so great an impression on me as the actions and discourses of the languishing and dying Clarissa. And frankly I confess myself not only extremely delighted through attentive use of this book but also indeed edified—improved in wisdom and love of virtue —and encouraged to practice them steadfastly.

I need not say more to express my great esteem for this

unparalleled work, to make known the motives for it, to
justify my aim to all intelligent lovers of virtue and true
piety, and to make public to others, my compatriots, the use
and pleasure that I myself have enjoyed from it. But is my
undertaking completely justified with this explanation? And
does it not still remain reckless and bold, because of the
tremendous difficulty in properly translating a work of this
kind? This problem, I admit, cannot by any means be solved
as fully as the preceding one. Who would dare to presume
the ability to accomplish this effort according to its true
worth? Such works of ingenuity and spirit, when clothed in
another language, must of necessity lose much of their natural beauty and charming grace, which frequently depend on
words and sayings peculiar to a particular language, on
habits and customs peculiar to a particular country; and an
unconstrained grace of the original must necessarily grow
more or less stiff in a translation. Nevertheless, I feel I can
excuse and exonerate my audacity before a fair tribunal by
means of the following arguments: I did not begin this
translation until another by whom it was undertaken had let
it drop; until some time had elapsed, without anyone else's
taking it in hand; until many of my acquaintances had urged
me to take this effort upon myself. I despaired then that
there could be found anyone with more ability for this work,
which is truly difficult, who would be willing to undertake it;
and I feared that one or another of the avaricious booksellers, urged on by the praise of the work, would contract it to
a low mercenary, in the manner that many excellent works
have been wretchedly ruined. And therefore I was persuaded, by my high esteem for the value of the work, by a
zeal for the advancement of virtue and good morals, and by
love for my compatriots, from my intention to no longer use
my pen for translations,[5] and to take this task upon myself,
which is so extremely difficult and so terribly long.

I believe that I know, by diligent application, the nature
of both languages fairly well. I considered myself to have
sufficient knowledge about the matters and ideas at hand as

well as having done much work in moral philosophy, having taken a great deal of pleasure in regarding the nature and workings of different sorts of people. And I had sufficiently taken in and become completely familiar with the spirit of this work by reading and rereading it. I am not pressed by necessity to hasten myself very much with this work but am able to spend the necessary time on it. My esteem for it makes me willing to pay due diligence and attention to it. Because my own ability falls too short, I take refuge in other expediencies regarding the proper attributes of the English language: proverbs, allusions, and usages, not only by consulting helpful books but also by consulting my good friends who are accomplished in the language or who were born in England themselves, or who have been there over a long period of time. These friends have willingly assisted me.

There is one matter especially in which I must confess frankly my complete unfitness: namely, putting into verse the poems which are spread here and there throughout the work, a necessity if the translation is to satisfy the taste of the Dutch reader. But in this respect my friends, and especially one, who translated most of the verses in these volumes into Dutch poetry, have not disappointed me; and this particular friend has taken on himself the task of doing the same with the remaining poems which will follow in the other volumes. The reader will be aware from the now-published examples that this language, besides expressing itself very elegantly, is smooth and powerful enough to answer to the value of the work. I herewith pay my indebted expression of thanks to these my friends; and if I receive thanks from the public for my work, my friends shall hereby have their just part, as I would have found it impossible to accomplish the verse translations without their assistance.

Thus starting to work and making use of this assistance, I imagined that I was in a position to bring forth this excellent work in a passably good and not entirely unworthy form. And although *Clarissa* is not brought forth in Dutch

garb as elegantly and neatly as it is in English, I flatter
myself, however, that it will please and charm many by its
natural beauty. Although my transaltion cannot reach the
perfection of the original (and what reasonable man would
yet exact this of me?), I dare to presume, however, that it
will not be rejected as distasteful and loathesome by impartial people. If I had not been of this opinion, I would never
have hitched myself to this plow. All of the essential beauties which are found in the narration of events, in the
arguments between various characters, can certainly be preserved completely in a translation. The moral lessons occur-
ring herein need lose nothing of their power. Where such
works lose most in translation is in style, phrases, and idioms. I have endeavored to imitate the style of the original
as far as possible and have taken strict regard of the different personalities of the letter writers. That which I lack in
the loose style and common speech of the rakes for want of
practice, I have attempted to fulfill by effort and attentiveness in order not to spoil the naturalness of this work. This
effort has been at times not unprofitable to me. As regards
particular common sayings and expressions, whenever I
could find Dutch of like power and content, I have made use
of it; at other times I have followed the English as closely
as possible. In the meantime, I hope that the nice or delicate
lovers of the Dutch language do not take it amiss that I
have sometimes used colloquialisms along with the most
civilized style, because in my judgment they were suitable. I
thought this not to be such a great crime in familiar letters,
because the letter writer is not accustomed to take such
anxious and exact care of correctness in them. I have made,
however, no misuse of them; and if readers are not oversen-
sitive in this respect, I do not believe they will take offense
at my usage. In particular I have made no scruple of preserving the customary English titles of "Lady," "Madam,"
"Sir," etc., because the scene is in England and concerns
English people. I have also occasionally taken the liberty of
using my own coined expressions without knowing if they

were in vogue in Dutch. I think I have the right to do so as a native-born Dutchman when the words are understandable and do not conflict with grammatical rules; my original writer has given me the example in this freedom. And for that reason the translation expresses the original character of the work the more strictly. If I sometimes wanted to remain close to the familiar language of the original and occasionally seized upon a Frisian expression, which in Holland is not so familiar to the public, I gladly request to be excused by those who might be offended thereby. I yet know of no evidence, however, why the common people in one province of The Netherlands should have the privilege of prescribing to others regarding the language. If I had intended this work for Frisians alone, I would have preserved another of the fine turns of the original in my translation, which I must now eliminate entirely, in order not to appear ridiculous to most readers: to wit, that which Lovelace and Belford call in their correspondence "the Roman Style," (I, 306–7) consisting of addressing each other in what is comparable to the old informal Frisian "du" and "dij" instead of the more formal "gij" and "u," as is the custom today between all educated Dutchmen, except that the older forms are still used by the Frisians. Although it is a matter of indifference how people speak as long as they understand one another, I cannot restrain myself from being somewhat disturbed about this Gothic taste of addressing several people in one person, because I am deprived of the opportunity of expressing the witty quality of the original. Even the *polite* French can tutoyer each other; but the Dutch, except in Friesland, are too *well bred* to understand the Frisian language. These well-bred people will perhaps also wonder why they do not find these letters interlarded with the usual "Uw Eerw's," "U Wel Ed's," "Uw Hoog Wel geb's," and such niceties.[6] I have not found these in the original except in the letters of a servant or such-like, and people should not be offended if I also consider it Gothic taste to ban the second person from letters and polite language and that one

would rather be addressed as an abstract quality rather than
as oneself. But I should curb my criticism because I here
request forgiveness. I think though that I may demand this
forgiveness with reason and can be refused by no reasonable
man concerning the errors which might have crept in. Because I carry so heavy a load under which I had to yield, my
desire and spirit were not consistently aroused by the extraordinary values and beauties which, from time to time,
opened before my intellect. But this desire, I trust, will
enable me the more to accomplish the work happily to some
degree of its value.

Without doubt the reader now eagerly wants to know
just who the author or publisher of this highly-praised work
is. Here is what is known to me. The English title page
shows that the work is printed for "S. Richardson"; and
that of the second edition mentions that it is "published by
the publisher of *Pamela*." This Richardson is held to be the
author of both *Pamela* and *Clarissa*. The newspapers state
that he is a bookseller. I have received information from
England that he is a man of much learning, ability, and
skill; of a nimble and happy spirit; and that he takes great
pains with his literary occupations but has few other outside
interests. These are loose generalities, and the man deserves
without doubt to be better known to us. We can truly know
him better concerning the ability of his genius from his
published works and especially from this, his *Clarissa*, in
which he has surpassed himself. This work certainly gives
the most glorious and shining evidences of a most ingenious
and exalted spirit, which shapes and forms its material by
entering into untrodden paths and leaves nothing for its
imitators to correct.

The world has never seen, as far as we know, a writing of
this sort in which happenings were made by letters from the
very persons who played a part in the action until the publication of *Pamela* and *Clarissa* of this author.[7] Never has
there been a work which demanded a more penetrating
knowledge of human nature and in which personages of so

many diverse characters reveal the innermost secrets of the heart, not to speak of a well-founded learning and knowledge of many matters which are applied here in every respect in the most becoming and useful manner. A wonderful power of imagination and inventive skill has certainly thought these works out and shines through them in the clearest possible way. A power which with such exceeding ability to dominate the minds of readers is complete master of its passions and carries them wherever it pleases. And what is most extraordinary of all, this power of imagination is coupled here with the sharpest ingenuity and the surest judgment which directs all the parts and circumstances of this work into an exact order and polishes each in the precisest possible way. A true, sound reason has managed the power of imagination in every respect and has kept it from all superstition and fanaticism, while it raises this power to the purest and most exalted moral philosophy, to the most fiery and soul-stirring piety. Therefore, this author deserves to be numbered among the most excellent luminaries, among the greatest men of ancient and modern ages. And though England may boast of some most extraordinary minds, she will not dishonor a Newton, a Milton, or an Addison by having a Richardson henceforth sparkle in their ranks with no less luster, whether one looks at the power of his spirit or the usefulness of what he has wrought.

Several panegyrics are found in the English edition of this work, but I have not considered it necessary to translate them into Dutch. However great and just is the praise they offer the author and however well turned they are in themselves, they are too common in comparison with the work itself, and they disappoint the reader too much. I found one little verse very pretty, short, and powerful, in four lines, containing the highest praise under the appearance of blame, which I have judged precious enough to be placed on the verso side of the title page, translated into verse by my friend in the most elegant style.[8]

One should not think, though, that *Clarissa* is suitable for all readers. One cannot expect that it will satisfy everyone's taste. No one who has much knowledge of the world could imagine that it would. They who feed upon lasciviousness and who willingly keep their salacious imaginations busy with foul stories will not find here what they are looking for. He who demands of a novel that it be linked together by a multitude of comical incidents, one more marvelous then the other, as long as they are able to make the liver shake with laughter, regardless of their probability, will find this history much too tragic, no matter how many light touches it may contain. They who read novels to while away their time only or rather to kill time will also not find these pleasures suited to their insipid and turgid souls. The picture of life that is sketched herein will not please them; it will rather increase their affection for their own lazy tranquility. Those who are of sound intelligence, who at least have some love for virtue and true piety and read with the purpose of bettering their minds and morals, are alone the ones who will be able to take proper delight in these delicacies.

To these readers I now present the first two volumes of this matchless work. Although the printer and I first thought to hold publication until the first four volumes had been printed, we have, however, altered our intention upon advice of our friends in order not to stretch the patience of anxious readers too much and now present these two volumes for the satisfaction of their desirous public. Nevertheless, I must warn the reader not to judge too rashly the value of the whole from these volumes. However handsome and well conceived these may be by themselves, the excellence of the following volumes is much higher than can be guessed from these. They serve only as a preparation for the main scene of the history, and from them no complete perception can be made about the entire course of the work. The moving and pathetic elements do not yet operate here with their full power, and virtue does not yet raise itself to its unrivalled loftiness, of which I have previously spoken.

And therefore everyone who reads these volumes should realize that he receives only a feeble foretaste of the useful and pleasant which the following volumes will yield. In the meantime, these two are by no means to be rejected, because they themselves also contain the purest scenes and pictures and the wittiest conversations, in which various passions and affections play their roles very naturally and bring into view their finest traits. The critical eye which can be pleased, for example, by the plays of a Terence or a Molière, because of their natural and modest beauty, will have these volumes appear even more choice and ingenious.

Both indignation and compassion can begin to stir here with the contemplation of a grumbling willfulness, miserly avariciousness, proud ambition, spiteful envy, cunning wickedness, provoked gentleness, ensnared chastity, and anxious steadfastness; and the most outstanding lessons for various situations in life are spread throughout. One should not then hold in contempt the things brought out here as trifles and tedious tales of little concern. Besides having their own beauty, they are of very great importance in the plan of the work as a whole; they sketch exactly the characters of persons who have a part therein; they are necessary preparations and motives employed to bring about the important results of this history. And the virtue of Clarissa would not shine forth so purely, so enchantingly, so beautifully, if we did not have so minutely before our eyes all the burdensome tribulations and frequent provocations with which she is challenged. I promise that from the start she will charm and capture everyone who is intelligent and a lover of virtue, although her delightful beauty will reveal itself more irresistibly from volume to volume.

Although this work is aimed at people of all states and conditions, whether young or old, rich or poor, educated or uneducated, notable or not, wise or unwise, all of them can profit thereby and find singular delight. Nevertheless, I recommend it especially and primarily for YOUTH, who intend to set their course through this world and to end it happily and to prepare themselves thereby for an eternal state of joy and salvation. Their power of imagination is indeed at its liveliest and their passions most easily stirred. It is not just that this work would be most to their liking, but they also have the most need for their imaginations and passions to be guided in the right path, bowed to reason, and directed towards piety. Here they will find the sharpest spurs to shun the lusts of youth, to wean themselves from all fleshly desires, from all idle waste of time, and to nourish their souls with noble, rational, and truly human and spiritual pleasures. May these volumes be used much for these purposes! Then would I consider my work well paid; then would my desire double to persevere with the work untiredly. I pray that the merciful Supreme Being, Whose honor as well as the benefit of my fellow men I intend, will kindly assist me!

## Preface to the Third and Fourth Volumes

### of CLARISSA

I THINK I HAVE RECOMMENDED this work sufficiently to all who may be influenced by my commendation and praise in my Preface to the first two volumes. Therefore, I need not expand this praise further at this point or enlarge this collection of letters with repetitions of such praise. There is the less reason for it with these two volumes, which will recommend themselves to the fullest extent to those whose imaginations were not stirred enough to notice properly the beauties of the two preceding volumes. Virtue rises gradually higher in the third and fourth volumes, although not yet to its highest degree; vice removes its mask more and more; the events become continually more important, more complicated and diversified; the artifices and snares on the one side slyer and craftier; the oppression on the other side more troublesome and fearsome. So in these volumes I easily dare rely on the judgment of the intelligent and virtuous who are willing to take the trouble to read them patiently with attention.

My great esteem for this outstanding work and my aim in translating it require that I endeavor to make it of as much benefit to the reader as possible and to do my best that it be read with the most profit. I shall explain, therefore, the methods and manner of procedure which I use in the translation and which I touched on in my first Preface. Although everyone does not approve of this Preface in each particular, I do not consider such approval of all that much importance and feel that it would be going astray from the contents of the work if I detained the reader with a defense of my first Preface. Some people have judged that to this aim, the readers' benefit, it would not be amiss for me to give the readers some guidance as to how this book and others like it should be read and put to use. They made the proposal to me and found that I was not a stranger to such an idea. Most readers for whom these volumes are especially suited, namely, among the youth, certainly do not have the measure of ability to relish the right spirit and core of the matters immediately, to understand the true aim of the writer, to perceive the correct usefulness of their reading, and to determine beforehand how to achieve these abilities. Anyone who has occupied himself for a time with literature becomes aware of this after awhile, and one hears many complain that they did not begin on the right track and only now begin to understand, after much lost labor, what they had not at first observed. Such an introduction and brief comment on those important parts which they should consider can be of great service to such people, save them much effort, and make them aware at a glance of that which they would otherwise look for in vain or carelessly overlook. In addition to such readers are many others who are not yet very experienced in such moral writings, although they are familiar with literature. These instructions can also be of use to them in showing them how to add to the usefulness and pleasure which they may gain from such works. Those who read stories with a moral eye also know how they must use such moral narratives; but those who have drawn their knowledge of religion and virtue only from sermons, interpretations of the Scriptures, and essays on divinity and morals (and is this not true of most lay readers?) come here as to a strange and unknown country, in which they need a guide to point out to them immediately the right path to follow. The prejudice of many against such writings, if they do not recoil just from the word "novel," which includes many foolish, bad, lascivious, and trashy writings, is usually due to the fact that they do not follow the correct guide in the use of such works, and thus are not aware of their primary utility.

These considerations have brought me, then, to the decision of writing a second Preface to this work to precede these two volumes and for this purpose to choose from the above-mentioned material to give instructions as to how one must observe and treat such writings to receive the greatest benefits and of what, in particular, one must take notice. This material at the same time will provide me the opportunity of considering human relaxations and diversions, as well as other particulars which will not be unfit for the contents of this work and which to my mind may be of special usefulness for young readers. This decision will also have the consequence that I shall be somewhat obliged to add Prefaces to the two following publications of each two volumes, which yet remain of this work, in order for me to keep continuity in mind; and I think that I shall not be short of suitable material. This method will be quite proper, because the passage of time breaks the thread of the narrative for the reader between the publication of each two volumes. Besides, these Prefaces will not displease those who find Mr. Fielding's habit to their taste, of digressing before each book in his novels and drawing the curious reader off the track.

But to the point. I shall here then take into consideration the aim one should have in beginning such writings and this work especially, the way in which one must read or to what one must especially direct his attention, and what use one should then make to his own advantage of what he has just read. I shall strive to avoid needless prolixity on this subject to keep the reader from the work itself for as short a time as possible and to avoid enlarging this volume too much by my comments.

I suggest that there is a twofold aim which one must keep in mind in reading writings which have a moral nature yet are put in the form of an actual history: one must take them in hand for the relaxation and pleasure of the spirit but at the same time must draw from them an essential usefulness and advantage, and one will find that these parts of the aim do not conflict.

The search for pleasure and recreation is not only permitted us as agreeable with our nature and compatible with the loving intention of our Creator but is also very useful for the cultivation and fortifying of the abilities of our minds. Further, it is absolutely necessary for us to preserve the vigorous power and good condition of our minds, so that they can enable us to work steadily with liveliness, zeal, and good speed. For these reasons the use of pleasure and recreation in the employment of strictest virtue and piety is in itself not to be disapproved of and can always be distinguished from its misuse. Such a distinction is certainly not made by those who paint all happy recreations with the same black brush but who seem to be somewhat spoiled in the condition of their souls by lack of understanding and who do not know at all the nature of a religion which trains us directly to be always joyful. We should but take care that our relaxations contain nothing in themselves that is sinful and dissolute, that they provide us with no inducements to evil inclinations and crimes, nor that they fall on vain trifles which are unworthy of our rational nature. Virtuous living, carefulness, and honor make these requirements; without them, recreations will soften the spirit, make it languish, and ruin its well-being instead of refreshing and strengthening it. But the bounds of the most blameless relaxations must nonetheless be watched over, although one person by nature needs more relaxation than another and therefore there is no set measure that can be determined which would apply to everyone. However, it is beyond contradiction unseemly to allow oneself to be completely seized by one's pleasures and diversions, to waste most of one's time with them, and thus to make essential that which should be subsidiary, especially if one does not take his relaxation along the path which I shall seek to guide him. Every man, rich or poor, in high or low condition, although the former need not work by the sweat of his brow to earn a living, must consider himself obliged to do an important job which most agrees with his circumstances, to which he should apply himself with seriousness and diligence and work with the greatest effort of his abilities. These abilities themselves bring this about naturally; they show clearly the will and purpose of the Creator in this respect; and the well-being of the human society to which he belongs indisputably demands this of him. It is therefore irrational for him to roam in a continual unsteadiness and by whimsical desires be carried about through continuous changing of pleasures without determining an important and definite aim in life. The idea of relaxations itself indicates that they are of less importance and serve only to restore and refresh our powers, tired and wearied by more important work. Also, one cannot conceive by what right a person can demand any relaxation for himself who is not used to employing his powers of spirit or body or who is seldom occupied with any serious business or hard work. Effort must be the opposite of such relaxation and is the correct way to restore a person's weak powers and to encourage his faint spirits. And truly, our relaxations and pleasures function especially when we change our conditions, performances, and objectives. As much as we are refreshed by rest when we have worked ourselves tired and weary, just so much are we refreshed and cheered by a certain amount of work after a long period of rest and idleness. Our spirits, whatever may be the important objectives of their meditations, will receive new delight and life every time their objectives are changed, because they become slow, lethargic, and dull when working on the same thing, no matter how great the inducement to work. A statesman takes his relaxation in the exercise of mathematics, just as the practitioner of this science seeks his pleasure in the investigation of history and the consideration of matters of state. Desire and special inclination for such objectives certainly make these relaxations more agreeable to us, but undoubtedly, everything else being equal, the greater the diversity of objectives we find, the greater the pleasurable delight they yield us, provided that these changes are well-ordered and pursued in a correct way; for without such order, our rational intelligence can never be satisfied with whatever it deals with.

No one will dispute my praising such a work to be read as an agreeable pleasure, for the recreation of the senses, and for relaxation. Novels in general are read with such an aim; at least people pretend to use them in that way. Such writings are certainly very suitable for this purpose for most people, and when they are set forth with skill, they are eminently capable of diverting our spirits with honest pleasure. A connected series of involved and tangled adventures keeps our imagination busy and alive and draws forth our curiosity by a pleasant change of objects. If a beautiful picture of physical objects, of humans, animals, flowers, land and water scenes can draw our eyes and please us, our rational intelligence can then do nothing but find pleasure in the contemplation of a natural and well-drawn scene of the life of the world, of people's normal feelings, morals, and actions; of the various characters who make these things as much distinguished from one another as people are in the external features of their faces; of the individual workings of different kinds of passions; of the pleasant appearance of hope, which promises much, and gaiety; of the tempestuous shocks of wild and raving passions, which, like the waves of the sea, dash everything to pieces and constantly cast up mud and mire. Ingenious jokes, salted with wit, as well as pleasant puns and odd thoughts, although they by no means can be considered as proofs of truth or falsehood, yet undoubtedly serve to rejoice our spirits and loosen the stiff-set folds of an intense seriousness. They live and grow in an unusual variety of ideas, and the incongruous and droll joining together of these ideas is naturally suited to make our livers shake with laughter, as one says, and to prevent dangerous obstructions to our spirits.

This work may then be read for pleasure and relaxation by all those who labor in other endeavors, whatever they may be. Merchants who have spent the greater part of their day in their offices in the diligent care of their trades may certainly find their spirits restored by moderate refreshment. The intense concentration of philosophers and mathematicians can find a pleasant rest here, and through the consideration of human lives they may make the necessary pauses in their abstract and lofty reflections. Even Ministers of the Gospel, however much seriousness and morality can be demanded of them with reason, cannot however be denied all pleasures and relaxations from their important work. They are and remain people. The purest virtue itself is no enemy of pleasure and gaiety, and where can such be found more suitable than in spiritual and moral writings? Yes, even to those who spend most of their time reading novels and thus make them their chief occupation, I dare recommend *Clarissa* for their relaxation.

It is so very different in kind and nature from common novels that it is most suitable in this respect for such readers. They will here meet entirely different objectives and ideas than those which appear in the writings with which they normally occupy themselves. And among all exercises I know of, none by its own nature is more directed to letting the imagination run riot than the constant reading of common novels. Therefore, they who are infatuated with such novels have a special need to exchange their ideas for others. However, it should not be thought that the objectives which distinguish this work so excellently from others will be to the taste of such readers; yet this does not prevent these objectives also from producing a very pleasurable relaxation and pleasant contemplation. For what can yet more refresh our rational spirits than the contemplation of the purest virtue and the loftiest piety painted with the truest strokes and liveliest colors in an exquisite picture? In order to be truly moved by it, readers must have a certain innate taste, as I call it, for virtue, or a quality of power of the imagination which makes them receptive, just as only a person with a musical ear or with an eye for painting can truly perceive all the beauties of voice and strings or beautiful scenes. For a rational intelligence, however, the pleasure received from the contemplation of such virtuous acts and reasonings, adorned with all the beauties which wit and spirit can add to them, must be so much purer, loftier, and more piercing than all external pleasures, if the pure and healthy reason is to be considered worthier and more magnificent above all external and internal perceptions. And if the dreadful picture of the dying Niobe, when her death-like features and slowly stiffening form are well drawn, can please a discerning eye no less than can the picture of a farmer's wedding, in the same manner a healthy mind will find a rational pleasure and diversion in the natural description of a tragic tale, and thus the adversities and temporal calamities which make the warp of this work do not deprive it of the temper and power of correct relaxation. Pity and compassion, suited to reason, are not disagreeable passions for a true soul, and they can be a well of various pleasurable thoughts and affections. It is not necessary to say that virtue in such circumstances shines forth most gloriously and shows its noblest, most soul-rending power.

This leads me by the hand, as it were, to the second chief purpose which I have mentioned, that should be the aim in one's reading moral novels, especially *Clarissa*, namely, for him to draw from it a substantial usefulness and benefit for the betterment of his frame of mind, morals, and actions. With such an aim, to advance in virtue and true piety, we must indeed read not only the Holy Scriptures but also any other books which lead to virtue and piety. To this purpose we should direct our exercises in history, natural philosophy, and other sciences, and especially in moral writings; we shall be able to enjoy the right savor and profit from the latter if they are written in an instructive way or by means of a story and adorned events. This is the primary purpose for which moral works are written: to instill in us the strongest virtue and a strict piety in the most pleasant and graceful way. Those who overlook and neglect this purpose in reading must of necessity be deprived of the correct use of it. Those who take *Clarissa* in hand for a pleasant diversion only or to cheer up peevish humors and to drive away the vapors of their brains without aiming to advance in true wisdom and to find an inducement for the bettering of their own hearts and actions—it is no wonder that it cannot please them, that they do not discover its noble beauty and toss it aside even before they know the meaning of what they read. Without a virtue-loving nature, one can taste only half the pleasures which I have pointed out as relaxations and diversions; one will not be aware of the meaning of many adventures, conversations, and sayings, and thus will find them insipid and tasteless and naturally fall into the complaint about tediousness. Are not steadfast usefulness and benefit to be valued infinitely above passing pleasures and precarious relaxations; a benefit whose enjoyment not only can remain with us through our entire lives but can stretch itself forth after death to an endless eternity? (Thus, I may confidently state, is the benefit of advancing in wisdom, virtue, and piety.) How unreasonable and foolish would it then be to apply oneself exclusively to pleasure without troubling oneself with a useful advantage.

But how has this man become so serious here, who just a moment ago recommended gay pleasure and light relaxation? What strange and odd thoughts of pleasure and gaiety has he who endeavors to talk us into believing that while we seek to enjoy ourselves with relaxations, we also ought to be prepared at the same time for essential usefulness and to direct ourselves to the progress of moral virtue and godliness? The lovers of diversions will probably think this, and wrinkle their noses. But a little patience, I pray! Before you judge me unheard and, despising me, run from me, read but yet a little further. You are truly mistaken when you imagine that seriousness and gaiety cannot exist together. Joy and sorrow are two extremes that are hardly capable of being mixed, although they may still be brought together to a pleasant sadness or a sad pleasantness when one appeases both these passions. As I have already observed, our spirits are able to enjoy themselves in commiseration. But seriousness is not sadness, gloominess, or melancholy; seriousness and vanity are really opposites, the first consisting of well thought out deliberations about useful and important matters, while the latter loiters about trifles of no value. A pleasant gaiety, a refreshing enjoyment match themselves just as fittingly with the former as with the latter. It then becomes a reasonable man not to be vain and dissolute but serious and deliberate even in the middle of his gay relaxations; you must admit this if you have not completely lost your reason and healthy mind. Also do not imagine that the aims of usefulness and benefit and your purpose of passing the time pleasurably are incompatible, or that  your sweet pleasure would be curtailed in aiming towards such a goal. I believe I shall be able to convince you clearly of the contrary from your own experience. At least one of your most cheerful masters who has ever lived, who was intent on skimming the cream from all earthly pleasures, witnessed resolutely that such writings, written for enjoyment, can command all honor and respect only if usefulness and sweetness are mixed together. Would the nicest delicacies of a rich table stroke your tongue more pleasantly if you had no hunger or thirst to appease, if you realized that your body did not need food or drink for nourishment? If you dance, if you take a pleasant walk for relaxation or enjoyment, you would not say that the enjoyment loses something of its power to refresh you because at the same time you have in mind protecting or promoting the fresh and well-kept health of your body. It is true that some people go to such extravagant lengths that they delight themselves with useless activities, and because they are useless, neglect in their pleasures all thoughts of usefulness and gain: those, for instance, who break windows with sixpence pieces to save bricks.

But I cannot suppose that my reasons are directed towards such people or that it would occur to them, while reading pleasant books, to satisfy themselves with an enjoyment based on reason. They who have surrendered themselves to recreations which in themselves are not bad but at the same time not useful in any respect strive by all sorts of pretenses to attach some value to them as clear proof that they do not willingly want to be regarded as occupying themselves with idle pleasures only. Smoking a pipe not only clears up their brains but also their eyes; the smoke protects them or frees them from a sharp toothache, but a spiritual minister meditates in the clouds of smoke surrounding him on the emblematical nothingness of earthly life. And are not relaxation and pleasure taken in themselves really regarded as essential usefulness and gain? And must not they be regarded as such by those who seek them with any insight? And do they not have as their purpose our enjoyment, the refreshment of our spirits, and the restoration of our powers? How then can one imagine that they cannot combine with the aim of usefulness and wholesome intent? Why then can we not see other advantages in them at the same time? Or why should the enjoyment and pleasure of a matter be cut short because it furnishes us or others more happiness and has the influence of improving and perfecting our condition more and more? We must clearly realize that by pursuing relaxation and usefulness at the same time, we shall be able to make our happiness, our enjoyment, our relaxation, our diversion and pleasure consistently steadfast rather than briefly stimulating.

I may then justly recommend to my readers that they add to their recreations and diversions the aim of an essential usefulness and advantage. I well know that we mean creatures are not always able to occupy ourselves with important matters; my opinion then is not that we must treat every trifle with a strict seriousness. But gravity matched with gaiety shows our nature to the greatest advantage in every circumstance, and a great usefulness can often evolve from the suitable treatment of light affairs. I acknowledge that there are many indifferent recreations in which there are no other advantages or aims than the restoration of our wearied powers through pauses in our work. Many of them are used as refreshments which derive all their power of enjoyment and pleasantness from habit, after one had first more or less forced his nature to get used to them from a blind and whimsical desire to imitate. I am not in favor of positively condemning all such recreations and diversions if we do not busy ourselves too much with them and if they do not have a harmful influence on us through misuse. The imaginations of most people must be able to play with the idea of following freedom of choice, which, if it is disputed, may lead to something worse. But if we do not consider our freedom impaired by directing our choices towards reason and sound intelligence (and what reasonable man would not think that this is the noblest exercise of honest freedom?), I think that we ought to attach ourselves as little as possible to such recreations and enjoyments which yield no other usefulness than merely a change of objectives; which furnish pastimes, but other than these offer no other advantage; that those recreations are to be preferred which contain more essential usefulness and gain as well as enjoyment and whose pleasure remains with us thus steadier; and that we should allow our choice to fall on and fasten itself especially to such recreations which, while they cheer up our rational spirits, also most improve their well-being, which is of utmost importance to us, as well as improve our frame of mind, and also serve to shape our morals towards the rules of pure virtue, honesty, and piety. Indeed, it goes against wisdom and sound intelligence for us to do something without knowing why and with what aim. The more reasonable usefulness we intend in any matter, the more we are able to guard ourselves against foolishness, which we certainly must avoid both in our recreations and other actions. It is absolutely unworthy of a reasonable man to make recreation itself only a pastime or diversion, or, to express it stronger, to kill and murder time, which is here so short, so dear, and so valuable. It is unworthy of him even though he seeks to divert himself by reading useful books, if he reads just to be reading, in order to guard himself against a burdensome emptiness and rusting of his spirit. It will not even suffice for him to have the aim of feeding only his curiosity and loading his memory with the knowledge of things which do not concern him. But if he wants to divert his spirit according to its rational nature, then he must also steadily keep in mind its continual welfare and direct everything in this respect towards essential usefulness.

From these observations I may now reasonably draw the rule that each of us should choose such objectives especially for his recreation and pleasure which have the most in common and have the closest connection with his chief work, the important occupation which each in his state, profession, and circumstances must perform. In this way our diversions will interrupt and divert us the least; and therefore we shall not lose sight of our objectives, although we do interrupt our work; but our pleasure itself will be a help for us to continue them the more happily and speedily and for us to increase our ability in the practise of our professions. If a minister sometimes must pause in his work through exercise, it is more proper that he seek it by taking a walk or working in his garden than by dancing or fencing, because the former serve as inducements for seeing and contemplating the works of his great Creator. What use will it serve a physician to spend his spare time rummaging among Greek and Roman commemorative coins or investigating the nature and origin of Gothic, Runic, Anglo-Saxon, Kalmuck, and other such languages? And is not the examination of natural science, of the nature and characteristics of plants and vegetation a much worthier recreation? And to consider the histories of ancient and foreign peoples is a much apter means by which a monarch or government official may refresh himself from the burdens of his duties than for him to attempt to penetrate the secrets of chemistry in the dust and

ashes of a philosophical retort. Our spirits are not of such
broad abilities that they can keep themselves occupied with
many different and squarely converging objectives without
one of them working to the detriment of the others. In
order to succeed well in our professions, we will do best if
all our efforts, exercises, and actions, from whatever side we
may begin them, whether we occupy ourselves with them in
work or in recreation, are ordered as much as possible and
made to cooperate and concur in one principal aim. However different may be the occupations of particular people,
in which they perform their chief work in this world, they
are suited to the individuals' different circumstances and
inclinations, and thus there is a clear field for free choice,
not only as regards serious activities but also as regards the
diverse pleasures which surround every vocation.

There is yet another matter which each rational human
being must consider his chief work and to which he must
apply himself in every respect; there is an important aim
which is the great end of each of us in his total life, however
different our circumstances may be from one another's,
which we should keep firmly in mind, especially if we want
to be regarded as Christians, that must prevail above all
else and to which we must apply everything we do, whether
directly or indirectly. This aim is our utmost blessedness in
the favor of the all-sufficient Supreme Being, the enjoyment
of which stretches out Christian hope to an eternity. It is
achieved by the zealous and firm practice of pure virtue and
righteousness, of unfeigned and manly piety; by true repentance, through which we erase the stains and faults which
adhere to us through education, examples, and habits, bring
to order our unregulated passions and lusts, and by the
steadfast exercise of holy, honorable morals, more and
more perfect the condition of our souls and complete our
sanctification. This is the most important activity for all of
us, for every Christian, no matter how different our particular conditions and tendencies may be. This is the one way to
attain that great end of our entire lives, to obtain God's

favor in time and eternity. To advance, therefore, in virtue and piety is the greatest and most essential usefulness which we can aim at in anything we do. If we keep this in mind not only in all our serious activities but also in our recreations and enjoyments, remain as close to it as possible and direct everything towards it, we shall then find more and more pleasure in virtue and piety themselves and become aware of their charms, which create the noblest and purest comfort of soul for their true lovers. Therefore, we shall not find the chief work a burden, but we shall always delight ourselves in the discharge of our most important duties, and in the diversity of our work enjoy an unbroken pleasure during our entire lives. On the other hand, they who seek their pleasure in things which have absolutely nothing in common with virtue and good morals divide and scatter their aims, make duty and pleasure clash, are often at odds with themselves, and can never truly and completely experience either the usefulness of the one or the sweetness of the other.

*Clarissa* is excellently conducive to this great and essential use. Everything in it is designed to instill in us a love and desire for virtue, to give us a feeling of abhorrence and abomination for vice, although set in such advantageous circumstances, and to put the most powerful light on our various duties in the most important events in life. I shall say no more about this now, as I have already discussed it at length in my first Preface; perhaps I shall press the point again in my next. They, then, who take this book in hand with such a wise and intelligent purpose may be assured that they will in no way be disappointed with it. I have already cited that which can convince them that they will not receive any the less pleasure and enjoyment from it. With this aim in mind, they will find in these letters correct taste and become attracted to and relish the nourishment that is served here. Those who are devoid of a love of virtue should not touch these relics with their unclean hands.

In order that we may satisfy this twofold aim, to draw both pleasure and usefulness from this work and others of its kind, we must take the next step, to deliberate how we must read such moral writings and the excellent *Clarissa* especially, and to what particulars we must pay special attention. I shall, to be brief, reduce everything into one requirement which this work may justly demand of all its readers and to which they should commit themselves if they are to draw from it the right pleasure, fruit, and usefulness. And this is no other than the usual one which we should follow in reading all useful books concerning all worthy matters: an exact attention and regard concerning everything we meet in it. To read without attention is but an empty occupation for people who are at a loss with their time; it is the work of one single machine by which the intellect passes over ideas which appear, as the hands of a clock move over the hours. Or is this a too realistic image for these time killers? Things which occur go one after the other through their brains, as in a dark room the images of passersby are projected on a white wall or paper, leaving no marks behind. With the closing of the book they no longer know what they have read, just as these images disappear altogether as soon as the window through which they appeared is covered. If we want to make a reasonable, pleasurable, and useful exercise of our reading, then we must without doubt take notice of what we read, concentrate our thoughts thereon, make our judgment of it, separate the wholesome from the unprofitable, and especially dwell on that which is of particular importance. And the great and excellent use which can be drawn from *Clarissa* and which we have seen we must aim at in reading it certainly requires that one should not run through it lightly and without thought but should consider everything closely, contemplate attentively, and with one's intellect apply oneself to obtain a perfect realization of all that is noteworthy in it. If one considers one's attention and observation not ill spent when searching into the sense of old writers, the feelings of ancient philosophers, the lofty fine points and flights of mathematicians, how much worthier an objective for us is the discovery of the power, nature, and beauty of virtue, of the means and urgent reasons to improve our morals and thus to assure ourselves of a pure and steadfast happiness here and in the hereafter?

But although this in itself may be true, it will nevertheless sound strange to many that so much thought and attentiveness are required in reading a *novel*. One may perhaps at first glance imagine that I contradict myself when I prescribe that one must exert the power of one's mind in taking a pleasurable and useful recreation and must spend exact and careful attention on it. Must one not work and expend energy instead of resting and refreshing oneself? I confess that very little effort need be spent on novels in general, as they indeed usually merit very little effort. If they are of no worse influence, most of them certainly belong to those recreations the power of which exists primarily in killing time. We are usually able to read them when we are half asleep without our losing much of importance through such carelessness. Most readers of novels, I can understand very easily, are not accustomed to such an effort and close attention; their souls are so accustomed to ease and idleness that all their powers have become weakened and useless. And it truly cannot be demanded of them to read a book on which they must spend any effort, any exactness.

*Clarissa* is certainly a work of an entirely different nature from those writings which normally come under the heading of novels. Those pious people should have thought of this when they took it amiss that in my first Preface I praised a *novel* so highly and even applied the name "novel" to some parts of the Holy Scriptures. In general I used that term for an adorned story, and it is unreasonable, because most such writings are either useless or harmful, to fasten that odious epithet to all others, as I clearly indicated what benefit and wholesome use can be made of *Clarissa*. I had no other aim in comparing the parables of our Savior and the nature of a novel than to attack the prejudice which can tolerate no adornments at all. The difference between good and bad or

useless novels should also be taken into account here; we
should not deny our attention to a book which delivers to us
in every respect useful ideas and wise observations simply
because they are not needed for unsavory and drawn out
stories, which are really of no consequence to us at all. One
should not exaggerate my opinion. I do not demand here
such a strenuous effort of mind which would weary and tire
people greatly. To discover the beauties and benefits of
*Clarissa* requires less work and effort than what is required
to gain an exact knowledge of the attributes of a language,
to discern the fine subtleties of a scholastic philosophy and
divinity, or to penetrate into the secrets of abstract mathematics. Events happen in *Clarissa* which are more natural to
us, with which we are more familiar, and which therefore
are much easier for us to comprehend if we pay but decent
attention to them. Yet I demand attention and effort; and
thus will not they, who look for their relaxation and enjoyment in *Clarissa*, be deterred from it? At first glance it may
well seem that relaxation and effort are incompatible; but if
one investigates further the nature of matters, one will
notice that attention and the ability to observe do not clash
with pleasure and enjoyment, but that they themselves are
needed and are definitely demanded for proper enjoyment.
Who can truly taste and become aware of the noble savor of
delicious food and drink who rashly gulps them down his
throat? No man can draw a soul-refreshing enjoyment from
the observance of pleasant and beautiful pictures of nature
if he does not observe them attentively but carelessly passes
over them with scattered thoughts. And if one wants to
consult experience, it will show one clearly that people in
general have not banned attention and effort of spirit from
their diversions. How many are there who make their hobby
(a prevailing and strongly-loved recreation) the exercise of
letters; in the investigation, for instance, of the errors
which have crept into ancient Greek and Latin authors and
in the correcting and straightening out of these errors by
clever conjectures? But this pleasure is surely reserved only

for those who take the trouble to observe and trace with great accuracy the nature of languages, the style of the writers, and the geographical context. If this pleasure seems too little to the taste of the common world, suitable only for scholars, who can lock themselves in their rooms and bury themselves in books, one may then take music as an example. This certainly may be included among the normal sweet-nesses of life, among the most pleasant delights which ca-ress our senses and enliven our spirits; no one who has a good ear will dispute me this. But how can we get any pleasure from music if we do not listen carefully to it? How can we enjoy ourselves with it at all if we do not carefully observe the rhythm, the tone, the proportions of sounds, the runs, the intervals and pauses? And although a farmer often receives more enjoyment from the clumsy and tire-some scraping of a fiddler at a fair than from an artistically performed concert, no true lover of music will judge that the latter is less refreshing because varying degrees of effort are required to perceive its pleasing beauties. And they who see men and women at modern parties in modern society in deep silence, in steady and rigid thought, their features stretched taut, their eyes glued to their cards, indeed cannot doubt that attention and effort accompany an enjoyable di-version and an exercise undertaken for pleasure only.

I must here accuse myself that I have not earlier men-tioned this noble and exalted amusement, card playing, by whose timely and untimely use the civilized and well bred world today shows its fine and choice taste. Although I cannot praise those who play for high stakes or cleverly pick the pockets of ignorant people and make half their liveli-hood from this undertaking, because it would be too much to expect that I would defend the practice, seen as a relaxa-tion and pastime, I must confess that I could have found it handy in my deliberations all along, and I must ask forgive-ness of card lovers for having neglected them. I could have indeed praised the attractive sweetness of the game, which can often capture its true lovers so that they often spend half their days and nights in play without thinking at all of home, bed, office, store, affairs, wife or husband, or children. I could have searched for the great and essential use which this hobby combines with its pleasure and shown with what highest right it should be honored by the name of recrea-. tion. I could have considered how suitable a recreation it may be for persons of all states and stations of life and how close a relationship it may have with everyone's principal job and important activities; how suited it is to enlarge the ideas of a minister or philosopher, to sharpen the clever ingenuity of a politician, to make a merchant skillful and experienced in his trade, and to help parents educate their children thoughtfully; in short, how worthy and decent it is in general for the rational and wise natures of people. But I assure myself that the lovers of cards will forgive me for this omission. To tell the truth, I know of no higher praise for this habit, now so universally and strongly in vogue, than that it refrains us from worse while we spend our time at it, and it excludes slander, foul language, and evil motives during that time. I say "during that time" because I have sometimes noticed that card lovers, although defending themselves principally with this argument, for the sake of a change, also pass their time with such conversations. And perhaps those people would rather have played cards with me during the time in which I wrote these few words. I shall therefore drop the subject and return to the business at hand.

My purpose was to show that even the common pastimes, recreations of much less importance, and useless diversions do not exclude a certain amount of intense concentration and attentiveness; and I may therefore with justice require them for a work which can yield a very dear usefulness, besides the most rational pleasures. All such pleasures themselves cannot refresh us if we allow them to pass by unobserved; the same is even more true for rational pleasures, which may serve as diversions for our intellects. The more attention we pay to this usefulness, the more pleasure and enjoyment we discover in it, and the better we shall answer the purpose of our relaxation. If one goes into a garden replete with a wealth of all kinds of plants and the most beautiful and fragrant flowers, one will indeed enjoy oneself more by looking attentively at the great variety, manifold shapes, gorgeous colors, and exact and artistic products than by regarding everything only in a general and superficial way. Attention and attentiveness do not of their own nature conflict with enjoyment and relaxation. They will never be difficult or hard for us if we spend them on matters which suit our nature and for which we feel a true desire and satisfaction. Thus they will not bore us when we contemplate the frequent beauties and charms of the matchless *Clarissa* if we but approach it with such a virtue-loving heart as I have previously demanded. When the body is tired and overworked through long or difficult labors, certainly no other relaxation can be given it but soft rest and inactivity. But it is entirely different, I believe, with the diversions and enjoyments of our rational minds, regarded by themselves. Their nature, differing so much from that of the lazy body, consists of activity. By work and exercise they become steadily livelier, quicker, and gayer. Attentiveness and careful thoughtfulness never bother a person except when he is enslaved by animal lusts and overpowered by bodily laziness. In order not to tire himself by his attentiveness, he seems to need nothing else but a pleasant variety of materials and objects; and when he has thought himself out on a certain matter, he can whet himself much quicker and much better by trying another one than by allowing himself to be rusted in lazy idleness. One should then not hesitate to apply some effort in reading these volumes and to spend one's undivided attention on them. Such effort will be richly rewarded not only by the dear usefulness gained thereby but also by the pleasure and enjoyment.

Next, let us now consider what we must especially take notice of in reading this and similar works and on which particulars we must fasten our attention. In these letters a connected story is given of a remarkable history in which the principal aim of teaching and an inducement to goodness are wrapped up. We should first accurately trace the thread of this history, the wrappings, observing the particular occurrences from which the whole is woven together, and by which ties, incidents, or intentions the one is connected with the next. These appear in a well-organized novel which delights us by reawakening our attention constantly through various and unexpected sudden thoughts and by keeping our curiosity steadily alive through many involved detours and precarious circumstances. The thread of this requires our attention even more because it exists primarily of small and common happenings which every household of any importance can experience and which can happen in the daily life of any man. Although this normality of happenings is necessary for the purpose of the author, to make his scene of human lives more generally useful; although his painting is therefore more natural and more suitable for the common course of the world; and although the art and spirit of the writer excel even more because he knows how to arrange and present seemingly unimportant incidents and conversations in such a way that the attention of each intelligent and observant reader is eagerly kept aroused; nevertheless, there are many people who are less struck by such common subjects than by marvelous productions, strange and unusual meetings, and strong flourishes and colors; and these readers would need to pay even more attention regarding the happenings so as not to overlook carelessly the direction and wittiness of them. One can hear the complaints of some about the tediousness of the first two volumes because everything is so usual and natural in them and they lack the strong flourishes mentioned above. If such readers would pay proper attention, they would discover more easily the beautiful order of the common happenings and perceive the author's marvelous art of painting the circumstances of daily incidents. It is this attention alone which enables us to comprehend the purpose of the history, to realize what kernel is enclosed in the least important circumstance or the most trifling saying, because otherwise we often miss the basis and cannot place it; thus the reading bores us and we reject it as being insipid and trifling. Indeed, it makes much difference in what kind of circumstances something is said or done, to what the speaker or doer always directs his aim; and thus we cannot judge his intention accurately if we are not acquainted with the circumstances surrounding it. And by "history" I do not mean merely that which is committed and carried out but also the purposes and intentions of the most important characters, who play their parts in this history and who reveal their roles in their own letters. In order for the reader to get a complete idea of this context of the history, it would be most useful for him to read the whole work of a piece when publication is completed, even though it of necessity appears in parts. He will then be able to judge better how exactly and suitably all the particular parts lock together in the whole system and perceive its perfection, which does not show itself so clearly at first glance when one considers the volumes one by one. And if any of the particulars in one volume may slip our memory, the short "Contents of the Letters" following each volume can be of great help in reminding us of them and can bring everything before our eyes again in a compendious sketch for the enlivening of our thoughts.

Further, the manifold and diverse characters of the people who play their special roles in this history must be principal objects of our attention. Through the personalities of the characters we perceive their different moral conditions, according to which their deliberations, conversations, undertakings, and actions are so very different from each other just as the differences in countenance, features, shape, and bearing are clearly discernible among thousands of people, each from all the others. These are not composed of morally good or bad qualities only but are also mingled with different natural attributes, whether these be innate or acquired passively through education, conversation, and habit.

A virtuous character is not always of the same kind but different in different people, according as one is of a livelier and quicker, the other of a duller and more melancholy nature; according as the passions in the one are fiercer and more explosive, in the other more composed and subdued to a clear intelligence. Each inclination, profession, way of life, and opportunity, carries with it a different practice of virtue and the exercise of various particular duties. And this diversity holds good not only for such characters in whom vice is superior, for there are different degrees of vice; and since virtue is regulated uniformly, according to a set rule, the shortcomings which control men are endlessly different and are linked together in an infinite number of different combinations and can show themselves in an infinite number of different shapes because of their inconsistency.

Such different characters now appear here in great numbers, all painted lifelike; and each, as long as he remains on the scene, keeps his own nature from the beginning to the end. To observe them closely makes the reading of stories truly pleasurable and useful; they appear in such moral novels as are suited to describe the conduct of people, and to show these portraits as either charming or abominable; they make up the soul of the occurrence which is narrated; and without considering this fact well, we cannot properly perceive the great usefulness to which everything is directed in reading such works nor make a wise application of it. We must especially mention here that it is necessary when reading these letters to observe the nature of each different character in order to truly realize the value and the power of the sayings and opinions which appear to us in them, and not to misunderstand the purpose which the author meant by them. Although indeed the same words are spoken, all do not use them alike. A testimony to the disadvantage of dissoluteness, by a libertine, although disclosed in his loose manner, contains a special power and emphasis, more than does the abhorrence of a serious and sedate person against the same thing. And one would wrong the author to attribute to him the disesteem for the honor of the pure sex, which Lovelace so often blurts out, while in fact the author makes Lovelace speak as a libertine, and shows his own thoughts the clearest in the unbending steadfastness of a Clarissa. In order to get to know these different characters precisely, one must observe by what principles or passions they are primarily managed and swayed, and to which stirrings or desires and lusts they are most subject; in what ways they reveal themselves most; how they act in common and special occurrences; which thoughts and deliberations usually suggest themselves to them; and to conclude it all in one word, which are their natural and different marks and characteristics. These now show themselves frequently in small matters and trifling circumstances, not only in the words and expressions, but even in the gestures, the bearing, and the tone in which they are spoken. "Speak, so that I shall see and know you" is an old saying by a wise expert of human nature; and a conversation over the tea table concerning things, as one thinks, of little importance, depicted in all their circumstances, is capable of painting for us several characters with their subtlest features and their clearest colors. Those who find such descriptions, created from life and nature, tedious, and judge all these trifles superfluous, show that they consider only the outermost bark of the matters and do not penetrate to the core. The clever Lovelace knew better how much importance there is in minutiae, to know people basically and to take his measures accordingly; for this reason he paid the strictest attention to this in his own behavior (III, 294). The transparent Clarissa would have taught this earlier to those who complain about it in her history, if they had read her letters with sufficient attention (I, 6, 10). For those who are really inclined to penetrate human nature, and to profit by it, such pictures yield the most charming spectacles, with which we can delight ourselves with the greatest taste. And if experiments are of very much usefulness in the physical sciences to teach us thoroughly the nature and attributes of the physical world and to use this knowledge carefully to the advantage of human life, in these pictures in which is given to us the experience of the moral world are thus included many experiments concerning the human spirit and mind, the annotations and consideration of which are no less wholesome for the regulation of our own condition of mind and for our associations in society. Meanwhile, it is thus evident that these trivialities, these fine features, these choice and often interwoven characteristics demand a close attentiveness for us to understand them accurately and well, and that they are not too trivial or of too little value to deserve this attentiveness by wise and judicious readers.

Furthermore, such readers will also attentively observe that the moral sayings or proverbs which occur often in these letters are used very aptly and are interspersed everywhere as warnings against failings and mistakes and as guides for us to follow in managing our conduct carefully in the most important circumstances of our lives. Such sayings and proverbs here are of two kinds: either those which point out directly the stated aim and are presented in a serious manner, or those which consist of witty jokes or puns which reprimand slighter failings no less strongly, make the follies of the world ridiculous, and point out the truth to us with easy grace. We must observe the latter carefully so as not to take seriously that which is meant only jokingly and to turn such a saying into its right meaning, and to separate that which is essentially enclosed from its outer binding in order for us to appreciate its proper wit and refreshing ingeniousness. And for this purpose our attention is the more necessary because these jokes often contain short words, sometimes interrupt most unexpectedly, and frequently allude to some small particulars, the true savor of which we fail to taste if we pass them by unnoticed. As to the serious sayings and moral lessons, the warnings against mistakes and failings and the incitements to virtue and piety, with which especially the letters from Clarissa, Miss Howe, and Belford are interspersed, these are of the greatest importance, based in every respect on reason and truth and worthy of our closest attention. Although their meaning is usually completely revealed and no effort on our part is required to trace it, our attention for it is even helped and aroused, because, by their being worked in ingeniously, they appear in the strongest light and the most soul-stirring circumstances. So that no warnings may slip by the lover of truth and virtue, it is certainly of great service that they are gathered together in the third English edition from the letters, divided into different headings, and are added at the end of the work,[9] where one can thus find everything that is related to special virtues or vices and to the most important circumstances of life in this work and can see them at a glance. This is why I have intended to spare no pains in the translating and rearranging (because these are related) of the sentiments.

Finally, we should trace and deliberate the aims of the author with all our attention: what he wants to represent and show regarding human behavior and way of acting by his work in general and in its particular parts and what he wants to teach and point out to us in these revelations regarding our morals and actions. These moral aims of the writer must be clearly distinguished from the aims of the characters whom he introduces through speaking or writing. As indeed a historian does not make all the aims his own which inspire those whose deeds he relates or whose conversations and speeches he brings up; as Homer certainly meant something different by making his heroes speak in this way or that from the aims which shine through in their own reasons, thus should this difference certainly be taken into account here. A Lovelace, for instance, writes elaborately and openheartedly everything which he has in his heart and brain to his friend, with no other aim than to while the time away, to give his friend pleasure, and to boast about his cunning discoveries. The author's aim is surely much worthier and more exalted than merely to paint in a natural and striking manner the innermost secrets of a clever libertine, the treacheries of sin by which he deludes himself, and the manner in which he violates his own conscience. Although we should also well consider the aims of the characters who appear here on the scene, we shall properly realize the inner course of the history and receive a perfect idea of the particular natures of these characters, although something else is required of us to comprehend fully the moral aim of the author.

It is this last matter, however, that I especially aim at here as the subject of our attentive investigation and deliberation and which is here the principal point: this is the spiritual sense of the work, as the divines put it, and without it, all the rest is but dead words. And after well comprehending this purpose, we need only prepare ourselves to extract the true fruit and usefulness from reading and using it. To this end it is not enough for us to know the general purpose of the entire story, but we must also trace it through all its particular parts and consider carefully what is meant, essentially and in particular, by the different scenes, by the painting of the various characters, and by each moral saying and remark. A few examples will best serve here to unfold my opinion clearly. The general purpose of this book is certainly the improvement of virtue and good morals, which includes drawing us towards piety and nobility of mind, and especially in deterring us from all the vice and lasciviousness of this century and in teaching parents how much prudence is required in the choice of a mate for their children; and in the management of their choice a firm basis will be laid for their children's happiness in the marriage bonds. All the particular parts of the story are subordinated to the improvement of virtue and good morals and related to it. The events of the first two volumes especially show us how wrong tempers and unbridled passions can disturb and confuse the peace of an otherwise happy household; how they are the toys of cunning people and how they frustrate and upset the intentions of thoughtful, wise people. The two following volumes, which are now presented to the Dutch reader, primarily present to us the consideration of the fraudulent tricks and elaborate snares of a wicked libertine and the unshakable and vigilant prudence of an honorable young lady; we thus see in the clearest light the dangers to which daughters expose themselves when they put themselves under the power of such people and also the noblest example of strict chastity: the character of Clarissa is suited to show us the lovely beauty of steadfast virtue and piety. And although the character of her generous friend may be more pleasing to many, because in her character virtue is joined with a livelier and gayer nature, it exposes her, nevertheless, to more frequent mistakes; and she would by no means excel as charmingly in the same precarious circumstances in which Clarissa is entangled. A single letter, number 42 of volume IV, reveals to us basically the character of the loose and crafty Lovelace as a desperate villain, who cares for neither honor nor shame.[10] The letter contains vice seen in the most favorable circumstances but nevertheless shows it in its most shocking and hateful form so that anyone who has any conscience and feeling must abhor it. It also teaches us how pitifully a noble mind can be spoiled by the indulgence of desires and how a neglected and wrong education can open a wide and disastrous door. The moral reflections themselves can also be subject to grave misunderstandings if we do not pay attention to their aims. Medical doctors would no doubt be insulted if they attributed the cutting remark of Lovelace (IV, 433), which applies to all of them without exception, to the account of the author; the meaning of it must rather be explained and cleared up by the remark of Clarissa (p. 436). And if this virtuous young lady falls, perplexed by trouble and sorrow, accusing herself in the eyes of some ministers (IV, 307), that man can sin even in his best deeds, one must not therefore imagine that the author himself approves of these opinions in every instance and wants to make them pass as strict truth, but rather that he wants to make it clear that such thoughts come forth naturally from a frightful anguish of mind. For the rest, a virtue-loving Christian should attempt to search his heart with close attention and not allow himself to be swayed by deceitful designs. It is sufficiently evident from these examples that in order to obtain a true realization of this moral aim of the author in every respect, one should well observe all of the aforementioned particulars of plot, of characters, of sayings and moral remarks, and should compare them with one another. To this purpose a closer consideration and a more judicious deliberation are required than are expected from those who want to hurry through this work with a skipping, running, or flying eye, just as they would through ordinary novels.

In order to discover and become aware of all the beauties which lie locked within this elaborate and incomparable work, and not to let any of the particulars which I have suggested for attentive consideration slip by, it is truly necessary that most readers not be satisfied with *one* reading but must repeat it once and more than once. I can easily recommend this effort to anyone who has a taste for such rational diversions, which I have shown to be found in this history, and I submit that no one will regret such effort. The work will not disappoint in any way through rereading, unlike others which please only by their newness, but will continually in itself reveal new proofs of art and magnificence. My own experience and the testimony of others fully convince me of this. Among many wise and virtue-loving people who have read the first two volumes with much pleasure, I have met more than one who have testified to be no more than normally satisfied at the first reading and only after further readings have enjoyed the true savor and taste of it. What more convincing proof can there be of this than what I hear from a trustworthy source in England, that Mr. Richardson has had the pleasure of learning that among five eminent and highly esteemed bishops of the Church of England, whose knowledge and friendship *Clarissa* has brought him, one of them was heard to declare that he had read the whole history eleven times, and had resolved to read it again every two years as long as he lived?[11]

Now it yet remains for me to show at the end of my Preface what further use readers must make of such moral writings and of this most worthy *Clarissa* in particular, after they have read and considered it properly, in order for them to make it be of such useful influence in serving themselves from the nature of the book. My thoughts concerning the purpose and manner of the readers' approach point this out sufficiently and thus permit me to further shorten this last part of my Preface, which again is becoming too long.

I think primarily, then, that a sincere reader can make wholesome use of this work in three respects. First of all, one should usefully contemplate the characters and the conduct of the persons who appear on the scene here, in order to get to know the world, as one says; in order to fathom the nature, qualities, and aims of one's fellowmen as much as possible and then to make a correct and just judgment as far as is permitted one. One should compare the pictures which are given here with the living examples one meets in daily society; and one will acknowledge from the latter not only the skillful elegance and nicety of the former, but by means of this comparison one will be able to obtain an accurate knowledge of the people whose traits are sketched here. One should compare the outward behavior, the reasons and actions of persons, with their deliberations and intentions revealed here; and this will give one reason to judge with more solid bases the acts and conversations of one's fellow men, the depth of their hearts, their inner frames of mind, and their prevailing opinions. For this purpose I dare to recommend this work confidently, because it is not just a satire against the whole human race, as is the case with some works, which portray none but unvirtuous or foolish characters, as if there could be found no other subjects among mankind than those who, through passion, tend towards excessiveness, or reveal only false virtue, or who are too slow and dull to undertake anything evil. However general such depravity may be, this vision of human nature is altogether unnatural and unjust; and they who praise such writings and make much of them must either not notice this aim or, with the help of this aim, and following their own hearts, be eager to treat all mankind alike. The virtuous and pious example of Clarissa is here opposed to the unvirtuous example of Lovelace; and although the former may not be completely infallible, in the latter, rational nature makes its bitter reproaches from time to time. The gay and passionate Anna Howe yet rises on principles of sound reason to a noble practice of virtue and can well counterbalance a multitude of low, insipid, and sordid souls, who here crawl about her feet, and of which the world, alas, is only too full. Although Belford in his repentance is urged and helped by several outward circumstances, the example of a pure virtue and its sound reasonings in particular persuades him to complete his conversion. And the pompous and ridiculous pedantry of a young clergyman,[12] who makes his appearance in the last volumes, does not serve to mock the order in general, but to put into finer relief the laudable character of the pious, wise, and prudent Dr. Lewen. To try the condition and inclination of people from such ability of the heart is the work of a laudable prudence and can be of great use in society. Indeed, no one can deny that it is very important to know such people, with whom we have dealings and with whom we daily come in contact, and in whom we always have to place trust, more or less. This ability enables us usually to choose for ourselves the best and most useful company, to study them in the most wholesome and advantageous way, and to have the most influence on our fellow beings, to remedy their failings, to avoid their displeasure, and to teach us to beware of the malice and wicked craftiness of others. These additional uses are too clearly and lucidly knit together with the recommended use for me to dwell on them any longer.

However much benefit this use may be in society, we must

make another use of the things we read and think about so that they can be of even greater value to us, by which we not only achieve a quiet and secure life but can assure ourselves steady happiness to an endless eternity. While we strive to get to know our fellowmen, we should not pass by and forget ourselves. To be really aware of our own hearts and frames of mind, in which lies a principal foundation of true wisdom; to add to this knowledge the improvement of our own failings and mistakes, the sanctification of our hearts, and the well-ordered rules of our conduct and morals: for these purposes the contents of this novel can be an outstanding influence and therefore should be used and applied by us in that way. We shall be inclined towards and willing to make such use if we have but read the work with the correct and designated purpose; and if we have paid the required attention to it, we shall find ourselves sufficiently able to make this use of it. Then *Clarissa* will provide us a very pleasant and enjoyable teacher of virtue. Certainly for this purpose the moral standards, remarks, and lessons which are spread throughout this work in great abundance are directly practical; we should therefore imprint them deep into our memories and make them our own, as rules suitable for our own deliberations and actions. The admonitions and incitements for good, the warnings and dissuasions from mistakes and sins which are given here on occasion to this or that person, should be regarded by every reader as concerning him and applying to him. What do you think is the important reason why the hearing of good lessons and warnings, the reading of the Holy Scriptures and other good books usually have so little effect on otherwise not evil and irreligious people, as one usually indeed discovers? One does listen attentively, understands the matter, and is even convinced of its importance and rational basis; but what is lacking is that one does not think about oneself; one leaves oneself completely outside any consideration and neglects therefore to test one's own heart against the matter presented and neglects to bring home the lessons and warnings to one's own condition and morals which one so eagerly knows how to apply to others. If we thus also treat *Clarissa,* it too will be of little advantage to us; and however wholesome the books are which we take in hand, although an angel from heaven spoke to us, they naturally will and must then be of little influence. Then one should turn the mirror of good and evil towards oneself, and by the sincere use of it, attempt to know one's own visage accurately, to improve one's deformities, and to accustom oneself to true virtue.

If ridiculous exhibitions appear to us here of people who, infatuated with their failings, disregard that which is proper and harmonious, or want to imitate rudely, we should not be satisfied with laughing about them or even finding other originals for such paintings. I have thus truly heard someone label another person with the name of Solmes, and not unjustly, someone who himself ran the danger of being honored with that name by others. But we should observe ourselves, each himself, to see if we also lapse into similar follies and indiscretions, and to try and avoid carefully that which appears so foolish and extravagant in a painting. By the sharp mockeries of a Lovelace, with which he justly chides many failings, we may, although we are much more pious and virtuous, well scrub ourselves and clean up our own failings, in order to show thus our virtue and piety in a more pleasant and agreeable form. If his example leans so far towards evil that our lives and hearts cannot be compared with it (which I hope and presume of most readers; how deplorable otherwise would the condition of the human race be), we should not therefore fancy that the example does not touch us at all, but should let it rather instill in us an abhorrence for even the slightest beginnings of lewdness and dissoluteness, to which we can yield so easily and thoughtlessly in our youth. If this scene shows us most vividly the awesome confusions which the unbridled passions and furious tempers can cause in society and the disastrous results they can carry with them, it will compel us to curb them thoughtfully and strongly, in order for us not to provide ourselves such an example in reality, which shows itself to us here in such an abominable way and not to plunge our innocent fellowmen recklessly in sorrow and suffering; it will caution us never to play the role of an ambitious father, covetous brother, malicious sister, or cautious mother or female friend. If we often find it difficult to penetrate the inner secrets of our own hearts, the accurate observation of the characters and the comparison of their conversations and actions with their innermost thoughts and emotions revealed in these letters must give us cause to observe our own reasons and deeds and to surmise, according to this guide, what lies hidden within us. If we are presented here with many precarious incidents, similar to those which we may easily meet in daily life, we should place ourselves in such circumstances in our imaginations and seriously decide to follow the good which is presented to us here and to avoid the mistakes made (in these incidents); and such a deliberation and foresight will make us preeminently capable of holding to the right track if ever we may be placed in any of these situations. An intense meditation of the excellent example of Clarissa must cause in us a strong desire and love for pure and unswerving honor, virtue, and piety. But I shall not elaborate further on these, because I believe that the consideration of them will provide me with sufficient material for another Preface, as I have already indicated.

To all this, I now add lastly a third use which we must make of this noble book, after its contents have been understood and considered by us: namely, that we take the opportunity of widening our thinking and enlarging our deliberations to the matters at hand. Many important lessons, sayings, and thoughts we shall here find presented with only a few words, brief and concise, as if just touched with the finger, as the style of familiar letters naturally entails, which encourage us to this use. They are replete with a rich surplus of worthy thoughts which, if we breed them and care for them properly, can be uncovered and spread out far

and wide. As a small seed kernel in fertile ground, display-
ing each of its parts gradually, grows into a large plant,
shoots out broad leaves and strong stalks and produces a
fruit of a much larger circumference than the very beginning of it all, thus it is the work of a thoughtful soul to
penetrate the heart of such proverbs and short sayings, to
be active in them, to enlarge in every direction the rich
materials which are locked in them, and to cultivate fruit-
fully many other similar wholesome thoughts. This exercise
is excellently suited to enlarge our understanding, to enliven
our wit, and to sharpen our judgment. If we only acquiesce
with the reading, it is primarily our memory we exercise
when we make ourselves familiar with the matters therein.
But those thoughts and deliberations which we ourselves
foster and breed further will please us for this reason so
much the more and will give to our rational minds new
courage and life. And because the seeds which are spread
here, naturally cannot bring forth anything but healthy,
pure, and lovely fruits, thus it is apparent that this exercise
must be of a powerful influence in order to make a healthy
soul improve in true virtue and piety in every way. I realize
that the intelligence of all people is not equally capable of
this; some are much more able to fly with their own wings
than are others; and they will, once they have gained the
air, fly higher and further. Nevertheless, all those who
possess any measure of judgment and wit can make their
work from this exercise to a greater or lesser extent; and
the more diligence they apply towards it, the more skillful
they will become and the further they will enlarge their
abilities. Even those who are accustomed to this the least
will find in this book a choice guide to help them succeed in
this exercise; the concise lessons are not only put in such a
light as shows the attentive reader how to continue to think
further, but we also find abundant examples in which a
slight inducement causes a whole series of moral thoughts to
appear. Truly, in former times, Socrates might have cor-
rectly imagined himself as a midwife who delivered the

human intellect of the rational ideas with which it was pregnant. This ability, I think, may be attributed with just as much reason to Mr. Richardson; and his actions may be praised even higher than those of the ancient philosopher, insofar as it is easier to be made to think insensibly than to be forced to it by questioning. But as for those who are void of all judgment and intelligence, I consider that we should not only excuse them from this effort but also that we should exempt them from the reading and the using of a *Clarissa*.

Thus I have here finished the task which I set for myself. Before I close this Preface, however, I must inform the reader with a word that the translation of the verses which are found on pages 73 and 194 of the fourth volume are not from the same hand which has favored me with most of the other ones, although the reader would perhaps have noticed this for himself. I have also decided to add to the fourth volume the translation of an answer from Mr. Richardson to several objections which were made against the last letter of that volume and the description of the incident therein mentioned,[13] because I foresaw that some Dutch readers might also be shocked at it, who, I imagine, will now be satisfied with the author's defense. This answer, although printed, has not been made generally known and openly published in England, but has been sent to me by Mr. Richardson himself, in whose favorable correspondence with me I can now justly glory, and whose courtesy and friendliness need not yield to his intelligence and wit, to the support of the work which I have undertaken, so that the Dutch edition in this respect even has an advantage over the original.

## Preface to the Fifth and Sixth Volumes
## of CLARISSA

To HOLD TO MY PROMISE made in my Preface to the third
and fourth volumes of this history, and in order to keep the
publication of two volumes consistent, I shall here preface
these volumes with a short treatment of the use of such
writings in which wit and invention have the greatest part,
in which the imagination primarily is struck in a lively way
and the passions strongly acted on to the advancement of
the practice of pure virtue and unfeigned piety. How much
*Clarissa* has been conducive to this aim, I have already
generally indicated in my first Preface in defense of my
purpose in translating the novel. But I thought it right to
declare in my second Preface that a yet more particular and
exact consideration could be so expected from me about this
subject, because since then I have collected several thoughts
about that subject which I considered to be not unpleasant
for the public and especially for the lovers of *Clarissa*. And
at the same time I could reply to an observation which I
have heard made concerning my ardent defense of such
writings. For some people this desire in me was an object of
astonishment, since I had indicated on several occasions my
high regard for pure and sound reason and had asserted in
every way that reason is the only basis for all virtue and
true religion, which should be practiced and put into effect
by the rational mind; and I had given very strong warnings
agains the disadvantage of submitting oneself too much to
one's imagination and passions in matters of religion.[14] It is
strange, one reader said, that the same man is now so
zealous for a work which is so passionate, and in which the

imagination is primarily affected by the ingenious pictures of all kinds of emotions, adventures, and meetings.

Although my high esteem for pure and sound reason has not decreased at all, on the other hand I acknowledge that the principal power by which this work will advance the exercise of virtue and piety has as its object the imagination and passions of people. But yet I am of the opinion that reason itself teaches that its most excellent goal, the practice of virtue, can and must be attained through imagination and passions in an especially fortunate way, and that therefore such writings, in which an orderly imagination reigns, are to be considered very conducive to such a goal. I have never stated anything to the detriment of imagination and passions which is contrary to this. And my present suggestion, I think, will be justified sufficiently by the following considerations, and can be completely reconciled with my former statements.

The practice of virtue and the exercise of pure religion are so important to human society and to each person in particular for his temporal and eternal well-being that these should be nourished and strengthened from all sides and no means neglected which are capable of serving the advancement and cultivation of them. Many defenders of them, it is true, occupy themselves only by applying these or those special means to achieve this purpose and by neglecting and condemning all others as useless and unworthy, according to whether this or that is to their taste, or whether they are averse to the other, or whether other reasons may cause their particular choices. These people, observing only the excellent magnificence of sound reason, give little or no concern to the Holy Scriptures. What matters to them is a shrewd and succinct discourse, and they consider it beneath themselves to investigate the sense of any phrase, and they leave it to the fanatics to stir the passions of people. No one who justly regards the Bible as God's word works only with its unfailing authority and considers it dangerous to go outside of its simplicity, thereby mistrusting reason, if he

does not already consider reason depraved. Others, noticing
that many free spirits boast about subtle reasonings and
that the majority of people is not very amenable to accurate
and dry discourses, are somewhat apprehensive of them,
and they assert that the only way to instill religion strongly
into people is to strike at their hearts and consciences—that
is, to move their imagination in a lively way and to excite
their passions. But such a particular choice I considered
more the work of a one-sided and unthinking imagination
than of a calm and healthy discourse, to whichever side this
might lean. Reason and Scriptures both must be held by us
as valuable; and to enlighten the intelligence by firm proofs
is by no means incompatible with a powerful and moving
stirring of the heart. A wise and knowledgeable lover of
virtue and religion ought to take care not to fall into the
weakness of such narrow-minded spirits who have exercised
themselves in one science alone, raising it as the only necessary one, while they presumptuously consider all others, of
which they know nothing and which do not fall within their
compass, as unworthy of their attention and pursuit.

Reason is certainly the basis of all religion, of all obligations; and if we neglect it, all means to procreate religion
are very uncertain and unstable. I have made this plea on
more than one occasion against those people who doubt its
value; and formerly having set forth the same statements
concerning reason, I still hold them unshaken, although
now, aiming at others, I shall defend the correct use of
imagination and passions especially. By reasoning and
proofs our intellects must be convinced and a foundation
laid for a steady belief in our souls. To neglect the use of
the Scriptures, not to concern ourselves with their sense and
not to investigate carefully their meaning, not to urge at
every suitable occasion their serious and powerful admonitions and reproofs, cannot be justified by us, who embrace
them as the true monuments of a godly revelation. Their
power is more sharply cutting than a twice-tempered sword
and continues to the separation of the soul and of the spirit,

of the joints and of the marrows. One will find considerable proofs of this in these volumes of *Clarissa*. And although the human imagination and passions cannot be the touchstone of truth and falsehood, and in this respect must give way to reason, is it, however, wise and thoughtful to allow them to be untouched? Can they not be taken in by good as well as by evil? Can we not promote virtue as well as vice with their help? Or must we leave this effort to the actions of those who try to cultivate lasciviousness and sensual delight by idle mockery and unchaste stories? This, to my mind, would be just as imprudent as to relinquish careful and well organized discourses to those presumptuous people who undertake to fight religion and virtue under the pretense of being profound philosophers. From no side must we give up to the unbelieving and the dissolute, and as we make clear the truth by the firmest reasonings, thus also we make virtue appear lovely and graceful through beautiful representations and soul-stirring conversations, and attach to it our imagination and passions. Then eloquence, ingeniousness, skill, and wit can easily be used to the advantage of good as well as evil. Yes, they have the correct value only in the first case, because in the last case they carry a false stamp; and if tested more closely, they are found to be vain, unsavory, and unseasoned. Why then should not these weapons of vice be wrung from their hands and used to fight for virtue?

This, I acknowledge, would not be necessary if people were rational beings only, who have nothing to do with imagination and passions. But we did not come from the hand of the wise Creator in such a way; we can never be advanced to such a perfect spiritual state, at least not in this world, however it may go with the righteous in their glorification in the hereafter. Yes, they themselves, who have tried in this life to get rid of all emotions and passions, have rather lost themselves in the meteors of a soaring imagination instead of walking the paths of pure reason. Man must be treated as man in every respect and must also be drawn towards virtue and piety by human bonds—that is, moved towards them by all such means which agree with his human nature and with his various attributes and qualities, whether they be of a nobler or a less exalted nature. Among these now, it has also pleased the Almighty to grant us imagination and passions, which we must in no way view in their basic natures as unworthy of man, but on the contrary, as perfections in man's low and fragile state, as qualities very suitable to make him enjoy as much happiness as can fall to him.

By imagination, or if one will, power of imagination, I understand that quality of our souls by which we do not judge something good or evil, right or wrong, after rational procedure (for this is the work of our reason), but by which something pleases or displeases us or is enjoyable or not enjoyable at first sight or sensation. This power does not merely receive its ideas from external objects, but also creates them from word descriptions, yes, shapes them from things that it has never encountered or received. It preserves the received ideas in the memory and knows how to exchange, separate, and add them in an endlessly varied way, in which ability lies the wit of an ingenious intellect. It is the mother of passions, so to speak, or rather is knit together with them in the closest possible way; it feeds them and again receives from them its deep impressions. In it lives wonderment, and because it separates at a glance the pleasing from the displeasing, the enjoyable from the unenjoyable, it also immediately creates in our souls an affection for the one thing, an aversion for the other. I shall not expand this further in order not to make a philosophic treatise, which would be unsuitable in this Preface. I have had to say the little that precedes here in order to make the reader understand clearly my ideas and to make him see that I do not continually add imagination and passions together without purpose, which will perhaps become further evident from my following observations. But what I must not let pass by unmentioned is that this, our imagination, if it possesses its original and innate power, is not only capable of distinguishing the pleasant from the unpleasant in external objects, but also in the moral sense with respect to human deeds, words, deliberations, and conditions. It is the innate moral taste, to express it thus, which makes us discern between the decent and the indecent, which makes us realize immediately at the first sensation the beauty of virtue and the ugliness of sin, in which some wise moral writers (Hutcheson,[15] Fordyce) have placed the principal basis of virtue and moral obligations. And in this respect it also holds our passions by nature to its will and service. It makes us love immediately the decent and the honorable and take up an immediate aversion against the opposite; it makes us, if we view somebody in need, fly to his aid without looking back, without arguing about our duty; and if we are conscious of something unworthy, it stirs our consciences with shame and makes the blood rise to our faces. Now from this it is evident that the all-wise Creator gave us this talent not only for the use and advantage of our animal life, but also to cooperate with our reason for the creation and confirmation of a truly moral and virtuous emotional state, in order for us to meditate on and love our reason by being helpful to its ideas in everything that is honest, pure, lovely, and euphonious. And, consequently, we keep the aim of the Supreme Being Himself worthily in mind if we try to advance the practice of virtue and true piety by means which primarily act on the imagination and passions. However strong advocates of reason we may be, although we can never use reason too much, it would, though, be unreasonable for us to want to pass by the highest wisdom and to neglect contemptibly other arguments for which it has made us susceptible and which can be employed for this purpose with usefulness. It is true that our rational intelligence also has its influence on our imagination and passions, and we therefore keep it in order if we enlighten and strengthen it. I myself acknowledge that this must be the principal care and diligence of a wise lover of virtue, without which he often exposes himself to delusions. But who, then, can dispute my claim that by other means, outside of strict reasoning, by singular happenings, by remarkable examples, by natural demonstrations, by beautiful similarities, by suitable eloquence and impressive language, by savory jests, and whatever else, our imagination can be struck in a lively way, even in a very lively way, and our passions stirred? It is also true that we should take care not to go outside the path of reason in the use of such means and actions. But the thoughtful readers of *Clarissa* run in no danger of this, as I have already pointed out. I now plead only for the use of such writings, and I want this to be assumed in all my observations without my needing to reiterate it.

The godly revelation itself makes a beneficient use of such means. God's prophets and apostles, yes, our blessed Savior Himself, have not judged it unworthy to direct themselves to the natural state of man, to act on our imagination and passions for the attainment of the great aim which can never be praised enough, and for which they were sent: the improvement of the human heart and morals and man's inheritance of an endless happiness. Does not that excellent example of exalted eloquence, which could gain the admiration and praise even of a heathenish Longinus himself— God said: "Let there be light," and there was light—strike us as much more forcible than if it simply had been written: "God created light in a moment"? How moving and soulstirring are the writings of many ancient holy men, whose expressions of their innermost emotions are capable of enrapturing us in love for God and piety, and instilling in us an irreconcilable hatred against sin and godlessness? To this can also be added the unequalled power of language, the exalted expressions, the strong strokes, parables, and symbols, with which the prophets conveyed their messages, thundered against the injustice of the people, and lured them towards the practice of religion, which in every respect was becoming to the gravity and the majesty of the spirit which inspired them. The unreasonableness of our not wanting to forgive our enemies because we have such need for all of God's forgiveness is absolutely obvious; but how much more easily shall someone, not inclined thereto, realize this unreasonableness, how much livelier will be the impression of it, if it is brought before his eyes through the example of a servant, who, relieved of a debt of ten thousand gold pieces by his master, is not willing to do the same for his fellow servant to the extent of a hundred pennies. The eternal blissfulness to which we are called is described for us as a repast and wedding, as a glorious and imperishable crown, as a treasure which does not perish or can be spoiled by moths or rust, for the purpose that our inclination for enjoyment and recreation, our desire for honor and wish for gain, would be drawn away from everything earthly and transitory and carried over to worthier goods. I could explain this with more particulars which one normally does not consider sufficiently and which could add some light, if I did not fear touching matters too far removed from the purpose at which I now aim. I shall only add this, that the outward rites established in religion by the highest wisdom act primarily on our imagination and receive their unusual power from it for the furthering of the practice of virtue. Is not baptism a portrayal of our obligation to purify ourselves from the habits of sin, and of the assurance that God will cleanse us of the same debt? And does not Holy Communion present to us a forceful image of the sufferings of our Savior, in order to confirm our belief and to encourage us to walk the same way ourselves as He has walked? And who can doubt that it is our imagination which is particularly active when through sacred music and hymns we glorify God's name and rejoice and exalt our minds?

Furthermore, in order to make man truly virtuous and pious, it is necessary that all his powers and faculties be impelled in the right order, and that these simultaneously cooperate to this purpose, as one obviously has to acknowledge. And revelation shows us clearly that if man will be completely sanctified, not only his perfect spirit but also his

soul and body must be immaculately preserved. It is not
sufficient that our minds clearly apprehend the bases and
obligations of rational religion and are most strongly convinced of this, if our imagination and passions gallop unrestrained and untamed to the other side; because our wills
are not only ruled by our rational minds, but also the imagination and passions have their influence on the mind and run
away with it. And if this is what is meant by the statement
that our religion must not only reside in our heads but must
also inspire our hearts, then this is indeed correct. Truly,
although our reason prevails so much over our will that our
outward deeds and conversations are proportioned to the
precepts of our reason, one cannot, in a moral and religious
sense, be considered suitably holy and virtuous as long as
one inwardly relishes sordid ideas, cultivates these with
pleasure, and permits vicious lusts to inflame and gnaw him.
It is also necessary that we work on our imagination; that
we preserve this natural taste for virtue, which I have
mentioned, pure and alive in our imagination; that we make
virtue appear pleasant and appealing to it in every way and
vice hateful and detestable; and that we fill it with such
thoughts as can impel us to follow reason steadily, in order
that the very path of our passions tending in the right
direction, reason may reign unimpeded over all our
thoughts and deliberations, words and works. If we neglect
this obligation, our reason runs the greatest danger of get-
ting entangled with our desires and sometimes being lifted
out of the saddle, and it will be ten to one against its always
being able to keep hold of the bridle of our outward actions.
Then we shall be (how could it be otherwise?) double-
hearted people and unstable in all our ways. We must then
continuously suffer the struggle between flesh and spirit of
which the Scriptures speak, to often do that which we hate
and not to do what we want to, and to find a law in our
bodies which opposes the law of our consciences, because if
our imagination is not taken with good ideas and occupied
with them all the time, it of course preys on evil ones,

because it has an active nature and cannot remain idle; and the outward objects generally control it much more, and a host of allurements entice it. Experience teaches us that it can go so far that the passions also change into violent tempers and fleshly covetousness, the natural taste for virtue itself is completely lost, and the quiet voice of reason is heard no more. But about this, more presently.

If, through the above-stated reasons, it has generally been proved sufficiently that to instill the love of virtue in people, we should not omit, among other means, using the help of their imagination and passions, it will be worth the trouble to add here some thoughts which can convince us that we should work on these especially to the afore-mentioned purpose.

I have already made it known that I consider the imagination and passions as the true origin of human failings and sins, through which we diverge from the instructions of pure reason and jump to unreasonable notions and actions. Although the whole human being from his birth is no clean sheet of paper, as one says, on which all kinds of notions and principles can be imprinted indifferently, as the doubters and freethinkers would gladly have it (because the principles of reason are completely inflexible and unchangeable, although education makes man unequally skilled or unskilled to be able to become clearly aware of this fact); if this, however, is said only of our imagination in particular, one must acknowledge the truth of it to a certain extent. This imagination, although ordered by nature and supplied with a taste for moral virtue, can, however, almost completely lose this taste through habit and amuse itself with truly discrepant objectives. Habit is here indeed second nature, especially if it is implanted and rooted from a very young age onward. Then our imagination is very tender and impressionable and can easily receive all kinds of ideas (while reason is still too weak to test them properly), and so deeply, that afterwards they can hardly be completely erased.

How the beginning of errors hides in our imagination is not now my job to indicate more closely, but it will here be suitable for me to clear up and confirm through some particulars how sin and vice sprout forth from it. Everyone will acknowledge that our passions, desires, and covetousness are the instruments of sin and iniquity; and the principal exercise of a virtuous human being, without contradiction, exists in the correct direction and restraint of them. As we trace the actions of the imagination to their beginning, we will perceive clearly that they receive their power from the imagination and are continuously fed and incited by it. Does not the basis of our pride lie in our all-too-great image of ourselves, or in a misconception concerning the nature of our worthiness and greatness? Does a minister in his pulpit consider himself elevated above the public because he alone speaks and all others listen to him with willing ears? An idea of excellence easily steals upon him, a fancy of his being God's servant in particular, and he considers the others only as his people to whom he speaks in God's name and the words of God Himself. This attitude causes the greetings of "Rabbi," of "Dominie," to sound so pleasant to his ears; and finally it instills in him a desire to rule over the Master's heritage. The outward luster of a monarch or statesman, the pestilent flatteries of slavish courtiers, the experience of his power, which seldom finds resistance—yes, the exalted titles of honor with which it is adorned, make his imagination first dizzy and make him forget that he is essentially a servant of the people, if this has ever occurred to him. Gradually he comes to the idea that he is a more exalted creature than his subjects, and that they are created only for his benefit, just as the flock is for the shepherd; he assumes for that reason an undeniable power, cannot stand the constraint of laws, and regulates his greatness to rule so for pleasure only, which then becomes the origin of all sorts of oppression, tyranny, and injustice.

And why else does the strong desire for earthly greatness and respect in the world originate in people of lower rank except that these people have been taken in by such a delusion and become idly infatuated with external pomp, beauty, and splendor? It is pleasing to our imagination that we get our ways and our wishes; if people have always given in to us, or if we, when contradicted, win by means of a more violent temper, no wonder that we then become intolerant and are subject to angry irascibility, rancor, and spite. Even a child in a cradle must become wantonly naughty when it learns that it can win more from its mother with loud screaming than with friendly smiles. It is especially the imagination which makes us explode in raging fits of anger and vengeance and which cankers our spirit with sordid hatred and wrath. It makes us regard as insults remarks which mean nothing and usually paints the real insults blacker than they are; and thus, struck much deeper by its own fancies than it ought to be, it cannot rid itself of them, but carries them around alive constantly. The animal pleasures naturally cause a strong emotion which in our imagination, hanging on to it and pampering it, fires our desire more and more and makes us into slaves of fleshly lusts and desires. That these temptations receive their principal power from our imagination can be discovered clearly by experience, because the real enjoyment of all these pleasures and luxuries appears to us far less pleasant than the idea by which we had formerly been taken in. Is it not the imagination which, feeding on the deliberations of unbridled acts and animal enjoyments and showing them constantly and in many ways to the spirit, makes the libertine burn in a fire of wanton lusts, a fire which is also kindled by the viewing, hearing, and reading of dirty pictures, stories, and writings? The sluggard has his head full of obstacles and mice-nests which make him shy away from work and fatigue and keep him chained to his laziness. He says, "There is a lion outside; I might be killed in the middle of the street."

If we consider next the nature of avarice, we shall find matters just the same. Earthly goods are really of service to us; one can see the desire to own something even in young

children. He who is supplied with some goods usually has
more to say, is able to do more, and can have greater
enjoyment. All this starts our imagination going; we seek to
increase our goods with a view to use them, but our imagination, blinded by this increase, gradually loses this view. The
general fancy of happiness and prosperity tickles the imagination with the gains obtained, and because of this, desire
too increases from time to time. Is it not the imagination
which lifts up the melancholy miser and makes him receive
pleasure in hearing his money clank, in the consideration of
his thousands and hundred-thousands in his accounts lent
out at usurious rates to other people, who make a liberal use
of it, while he himself scarcely dares to supply himself with
necessaries from it? Or does he gather and scrape in order
to cut a figure in the world, to make a great flourish, and
thereby to excel in outward appearance? Oh, vanity of vani-
ties with which his empty soul feeds itself!—a wind and a
fancy which cannot give any satisfaction. It is just the same
imagination which enables children, when they are showing
off, to amuse themselves and which stirs them so restlessly.
As I have already discussed this, I do not need to point out
what unrighteousness and oppression, deceit and villainy,
also among common people, are indebted to for their origin,
when they are but results of the afore-mentioned lusts and
desires. And if these are even advanced and nourished because one allows free play to his imagination and is tanta-
lized by such ideas, then these lusts and desires are to be
considered proofs of singular ingenuity, a quick brain, and
clever invention. And how many neglects of our duty, how
many real misdemeanors even, does a false shame bring
forth, which certainly is also resident and active in the
human imagination!

This now, I think, will be sufficient to convince everyone
of the justness of my observations: that sin receives its
primary power from our imagination, that this imagination
exposes us particularly to temptations and seductions, fires
the passions and with their help transports us, in spite of

our reason. Must not each wise defender of virtue and
piety, then, consider it good and serviceable, useful and
necessary, that one pay special attention to entertain the
imagination with worthy, healthful, and noble ideas; in
order thus to safeguard it against the penetration of the
other ones, or in case these have already penetrated, to
drive them out; in order thus to attack vice on its own
grounds, on its own footing? We can indeed, if it is not
completely spoiled, imprint good as well as evil ideas on our
imagination. Yes, in the first instance, one gives an advantage to its natural taste for virtue, with which vice usually
more or less struggles. How much benefit must it give to our
love for virtue and the practice of it so that we do not
become infatuated with worldly greatness, external flourishes, luster, and pomp, but are filled with ideas of the noble
worthiness of a reasonable behavior, of the excellent magnificence of a virtuous person, and of the inestimable value
of godly honor and approval, so that we are filled with the
greatest desire to give service and advantage to others,
instead of flattering ourselves by ruling over them? Instead
of throwing oneself away to earthly pleasures, one should
keep busy with the imagination of the beauties of a quiet
conscience, of a charitable and liberal soul, and of a truly
grateful heart; these are offered to us here in a soul-stirring
manner. Why can we not contemplate as well the examples
of chastity and excellent honor in a Joseph, in a P. Scipio,
and others, as the unchaste feed their lusts by staring at the
lascivious and sensual examples which ravish their imagination? Can it not be just as enchanting in the cause of goodness for us to consider a Pamela, a Clarissa, a Charles
Grandison, and instill in ourselves a pure and soul-refreshing pleasure, as it is for the lascivious and lewd to prey on
scandalous and shameful stories, worthy to be buried in
eternal night? How can any desire for such unruly ideas
endure in us, if our imagination is moved in a lively way by
the shocking tyranny with which a libertine ravishes his own
conscience by his wretched self-deceit, by the self-condemna-

tions and awful regrets which tear his heart apart, the ideas of which are painted for us here so naturally according to life? The aversion to poverty and a low state, which appear so abominable to the worldly minded, cannot drive us to the desire for money if our imagination keeps itself continually busy with the consideration of the enjoyment of a contented spirit which has the best advantages in common with the very richest, which is satisfied with its modest part, and which, for the smallest gifts, cheerfully thanks God, Who did not owe it anything. Is this consideration not just as pleasant and enjoyable for an upright soul as it is for an earthly-minded man who stands gaping at the tinsel of flourish, pomp, and luxury? Why is it that the shepherds' songs, the descriptions of low and simple country life, usually yield so much enchantment for our spirit? We are naturally afraid of death and of the hardships of this life. When we can imagine how a Christian can face them calmly, how he owns his soul in patience, and how he can have confidence even on his death bed and cheerfully rejoice in his well-grounded hope, this fear loses its greatest power, if it does not disappear altogether. And if some people assert that one can best conquer one passion by another, although I do not quite disapprove of this, I still consider it at the same time advisable for one to cure the illness in its beginning, to let whatever passion it may be take its natural course by turning one's imagination to the right direction. In short, if we can persuade our imagination and passions to the interest of virtue and piety, we certainly shall have won much. We shall then cut off the artery of sin, so to speak, and safeguard ourselves in the strongest possible way against all temptations and seductions from outside, from the world, and from our own flesh, which otherwise come upon us so easily and through which our imagination often betrays us so wretchedly, notwithstanding the fact that our intellect still has such a clear apprehension of our duty.

For this purpose we must also be especially incited by the thought that in the greatest number of us weak people, if not in all of us, the imagination has a greater power than the rational intellect and usually imprints itself much deeper and more forcibly upon our spirits than the principles of sound reason, taken separately, can do. One may think that human nature thus entails this concept as well as its being much improved by education and habit. Imagination already exercises its power in a person when reason does not show itself at all or only vaguely. The angry face of a father or master will win more from a child than the clearest and firmest reasons, even when he is already capable of understanding them. But one should also acknowledge that these reasons are often neglected in education much more when their use is apt and can be applied with effect, and that most parents would rather settle everything quickly by their authority and tempt their children with something beautiful or sweet or make them fear the rod rather than to convince them by calm reasonings as well of the justice of their commands and treat them as reasonable creatures. Through these uses and through endless external objects, our imagination is awakened, nourished, and strengthened from our youth on; and our passions are kept in continuous movement and start up at every opportunity and work unhindered, while the principles of reason, if not smothered by unreasonable ideas, are cultivated but little and are oftentimes faint and weak and unavailable for our use. This, among others, is the reason why we are influenced so strongly by examples more than we are enticed by lessons and admonitions. These examples act especially on our imagination, which, finding them to its taste, increases our desire to imitate. For this reason one finds this action chiefly in children and young people in whom the imagination has yet more power than in older people. And because it is unstable, as we have seen, and can be brought over to the side of evil, it is this that makes habit follow evil as well as good examples. This greater power of imagination and passions is the reason that fanaticism usually wins more ground and succeeds more happily among the majority of people than a sedate and sober reasoning, no matter how concise and keen. Must, then, wisdom and prudence not advise us in these imitations to apply everything under the guidance of sound reason for the shaping of the imagination and the passions and thus to give our attempts for the improvement of virtue and right religion their just power and success? Thereby we shall recognize our duties as not just reasonable but also loved as agreeable, pure, and beautiful; and sin is not just disapproved of as unreasonable but also hated and abhorred as shameful and detestable. These resources will make us aware of the principles of reason themselves much more clearly and will imprint them much more forcefully and more deeply in us.

Even though we are convinced by reason and God's word that the Supreme Being is present with us always and everywhere, nevertheless, in order for us to be moved powerfully, so that we will walk with fear and modesty before His all-seeing eye, it is necessary that we always be impregnated with such an idea and imagine that He indeed is with us at every moment and in every place and sees and hears what we do, wherever we are. Yes, such an imagination, imprinted with emphasis and painted with strong strokes, will strike us with greater strength and sensitivity than the most indisputable argument concerning it, considered in cold logic. This natural taste for virtue thus being awakened and truly active in us and steadily strengthened by honest, pure, and beautiful ideas, will make the perception of our duty immediate in every case without our needing much deliberation about it and make us practice our duty thus much more easily, quickly, and smoothly. Our imagination itself will then become prolific in supplying all kinds of reasons which can be applied to this or that occasion, which are borrowed from this or that circumstance, which make the justice of this practice increasingly clearer, and give us a stronger impulse to it. Or do we fancy that the imagination and passions are of less power when they are used for good than when they are used for evil? I admit, the action of the imagination should not be allowed to go higher here than reason demands. But can one also have a too high idea of God and his service? Can our love for Him and virtue also be too ardent? Can vice also be painted too sordid and abominable? Will the living memory, "I am in the fearful presence of the Most Holy Supreme Being, before Whom my soul lies exposed; how will He judge my deeds and thoughts?" move us less than, "What will the world say about it?"—fill us less with shame and awe than our viewing a group of people whose examples force us to accompany them to the same pouring out of anger? Shall we find less joy in nobly handing out our bread to the poor than in tasting the delicacies of an exquisite and excessively-loaded table? Only those can doubt this who are unfortunate enough never to have made a test of it. And because the imagination is usually the liveliest in youth and the passions quickest and strongest, how advantageous must it then be for them for us to hand them writings in which virtue and good morals are described in the choicest and most beautiful way for the imagination and in which the passions are stirred with abhorrence for sin and iniquity.

To all of this, I now finally add that we, in our practice of virtue and piety, need the help of the imagination and passions in order for us to promote them with true zeal and to surmount the difficulties which we meet therein with courage and to perform this work with eagerness. It is evident from the afore-mentioned remarks that the imagination and the passions often are much stronger and more active in people than the principles of pure and sound reason taken by themselves. Reason must then in every respect hold the reins of our zeal, to keep it from running wild. It is especially necessary and powerful to make us steadfast in our efforts for good and to serve as that which teaches us to build everything we think and do on unshakable bases. But it usually works slowly, coolly, and sedately. It is the imagination, added to it, which makes us ardent of spirit, afire with desire for justice and truth, passionate to love God above all and our neighbors as ourselves, and to hate sin with our whole hearts. These passions, then, for their part, continually give the mind a more lively impression of those ideas by which they are moved. This, one may think, may be a reason why one usually finds more zeal in fanatic or superstitious people than among the defenders of a purified and reformed religion, why one puts up with more indefatigable work to obtain the benefits of this life and to avoid its disadvantages than to assure one's eternal interest. In the first instance, the imagination and passions are acted upon most strongly, and in the latter, the ideas of worldly success and adversity usually strike much stronger than those of a future happiness and misery.

If we then truly act zealously for the good and exert our powers with desire and diligence for it, we must not only enlighten our intelligence but must also act on our imagination with powerful and impressive means and stir and inflame our passions in such a way that in their actions they will follow wherever our reason leads us. The soul, burdened with the gross body, is usually beset by an indolence from which reason by itself is too weak to awaken it. A greater power is required to make it function with industrious vigor. A lively imagination is by nature very suitable for that purpose, and one sees those who are most gifted with it working in their professions with the greatest speed and zeal. Therefore, the more powerfully one works to enliven it for good, to create for it deep impressions of virtue and piety, the more fire and vigor one's spirit will feel kindled for the practice of them. And one should not imagine that in such instances reason steals from the imagination and passions its strongest power. If the examples of a Miltiades and an Alexander had so much effect on a Themistocles and a Caesar that they burst in tears from regret and could neither sleep nor rest at viewing their monuments and the memory of their deeds, how, then, must the excellent examples of virtue and piety, if we properly accustom ourselves to mirror them with our imagination, ignite a sacred glow in our bosoms to pursue them, to strive for the ulti-

mate perfection of which our nature is capable, and with
indefatigable efforts to work, wake, and tire ourselves to
advance the welfare and true benefit of our fellowmen?
Will the luster of a worldly crown charm man so much that
he endures all kinds of trouble and discomfort for it? He
can also, if he wants to, be moved to constrain his body and
bring it to service, if he steadily keeps in mind the idea of an
infinitely more beautiful crown. How necessary to us is this
zeal to lead in this world a truly honest and virtuous life?
How unworthy of our calling if we miss this opportunity?
How useful, then, to paint in the most lively way the beauty
of virtue and the horrors of vice through such writings?
Surely, one does not want to contend that such awakenings
are not now necessary and that contemporary Christianity
has no lack of zeal. Experience, alas, teaches everyone
clearly how faintly virtue and religion are often treated by
those who usually take great pains over them. But to complain about this is not presently my work. It is sufficient for
me thus to have defended my undertaking briefly in this
respect.

I cannot close this Preface without informing the reader
that the *History of Charles Grandison*, to which I have
made reference in passing, is a new work by Mr. Richardson, lately published, in which he, in his own words in its
Preface "offers the public an example of a man who behaves
himself uniformly well in many different instances, in which
his virtue is brought to the test, because he lets all his deeds
be ruled by one steadfast principle: a man of religion and
virtue, of a lively and courageous spirit, polite and pleasant
in company, happy in himself and a blessing for others."
Truly a charming picture, which must attract every honorable heart! To its praise I cannot say more except that it
shows in every respect the fine hand of the publisher of
*Clarissa*. This gentleman has done me the honor and has put
his trust in me by recommending to me the care of a Dutch
translation and publication of this History and has left it to
me to dedicate it to whomever I should choose.[16] Although

my great respect for Mr. Richardson, added to the excellence of this work in which ingeniousness, judgment, and love of virtue contend with one another, could easily move me to endure again the work of translating, I have, however, for other important reasons found myself obliged to excuse myself from it. But I shall use all possible care and exactness in order to deliver to my compatriots a translation from a capable hand, in keeping with the worth of this work, and to answer suitably the trust which its most illustrious writer has so favorably put in me; and the bookseller F. van der Plaats has already promised responsibility for the publication.

# Preface to the Seventh and Eighth Volumes
## of CLARISSA

THUS THE HISTORY of *Clarissa* comes to its end. It is closed with sad, dismal, and frightful scenes which can strongly stir with a moving sadness a heart which is not altogether unfeeling or fill it with fear and trembling and cause the tears of compassion to flow from the eyes. Dreadful is the scene of the sensual Belton on his deathbed, suffering the results of his sins in a defeated despondency and inconsolable despair. Fearful are the anger and rage with which the godless Sinclair rants and roars in the midst of pain and danger, which were brought on herself by her own dissoluteness and which hasten her wretched death. Miserable is the condition of Lovelace, who now and then runs wild in a loose and unrestrained wantonness and thereby tries to drown his suffering, affording the reader a sufficient variety of scenes. But most of the time he is sharply bitten, tormented, and harassed by his remorseful conscience; and finally he suddenly meets his doom because of his rage and his unbridled arrogance. Clarissa dies an untimely death, in the bloom of her years. She dies simple and innocent, forsaken by her closest friends, by some persecuted through envy and covetousness, mistreated and tortured by rogues almost to the end. Although essentially she dies happily, her death is an object of compassion; and although her noble preparation, coupled with the steadily increasing reform of Belford, pleases a truly Christian mind, this pleasure is sad and somber and consists of a series of mournful thoughts.

These sad subjects are not to the taste of many in this country as well as in the fatherland of *Clarissa,* and the author has defended his choice here and there in the history itself, as well as especially in the Postscript [to the third edition], to answer the remarks of his compatriots. Various objections concerning this course and the sad end of the history have occurred to me also. I shall here bring up two of them and answer them with the hope that my observations will yield suitable material for a Preface to these last two volumes.

Someone now withdrawn from this life by death once said to me that human life is beset by so many cares, by so much grief and sorrow, and by the real discomforts and tortures which so assault man from all sides, that one need not make this burden greater by sad descriptions which depress man's spirit still more, but one should rather cheer man up and divert him through cheerful subjects.

This thought is like the scoffing reason which Lovelace once gives for his aversion to tragedies; (IV, 220–21) [17] but it originated from an entirely different source and from a serious thought of the changeability and the manifold misfortunes of this life; and because this aversion can be felt by others, I shall seriously present what remarks I have to make about both this objection and the principle.

If this idea of human life is just and in accordance with our condition here on earth, then I cannot perceive how it can be brought as a fair objection against this work. Indeed, it paints human life with its particular colors because, on the contrary, an unnatural picture of it must be regarded as the greatest deformity in a work of this nature. This latter idea being taken for granted, the objection can be considered of no great value. One must not think that this work is adapted only to diversion and pastime but also, and indeed especially, to usefulness and wholesome teaching. Indeed, we live here in a state fraught with so many disasters, dangers, and pains, that what is more useful to us, what education and learning can be considered of more value than how we should behave ourselves under these circumstances, how we can avoid this one, ease that one, and which qualities can enable us to bear the heaviest with courage? A living scene, in which these examples are shown to us, must then be considered of the greatest service by every human being. Instead of making our spirits dejected and cowardly, it will, if it is well used, strengthen them considerably. If we are surrounded in this world by so many adversities and objects of sadness, we indeed cannot become happier, nor improve our state, by avoiding thinking about them or by turning our eyes away. To do so is to run the greater risk of falling suddenly into the same circumstance and consequently receiving a greater hurt from it. It is also a foolish joy, I think, in the midst of disaster and danger, to divert ourselves with forced pleasures and enjoyments. "Even in laughter the heart is sorrowful; and the end of that mirth is heaviness" (Proverbs 14:13).

But is the state of human life, taken in general, so awful and ghastly as we picture it? Is this world so full of sadness and misery that it must be counted as merciless or imprudent to darken our spirits still more with sad imaginings? Letting my eyes go over mankind as far as my ability reaches, I cannot find this to be true. Most people I see, for the greatest part of their lives, rejoice and are cheered in them either with real or imagined benefits. For many, it seems to me, who let themselves be carried away in immodest joy, it is not inexpedient that their spirits be kept in balance by the contemplation of sad ideas so that they will not forget their dependency and frailty and be safeguarded against greater dangers.

I admit that no one lives in this world who has not undergone his share of stress, pain, and adversity at some time or other, that there is no household which does not bear a cross. But I believe that one expresses it too strongly if one describes this world in general as a valley of tears unless one speaks comparatively with respect to the future state of the truly pious in which all tears will be wiped away. Also, I cannot reconcile the philosopher's judgment with experience, who attempts to indicate in a mathematical manner that a greater amount of unhappiness than happiness has befallen man here on earth. This is not the place for me to investigate this supposition fully; I shall only make these few remarks about it.

Most people, by far the most, enjoy the pure and essential happiness which true virtue yields and which can be enjoyed here on earth itself—a very small part, because they neglect the exercise of it, and they themselves disturb their rest by uncontrolled passions and misdemeanors. In this respect, one may truthfully say that the measure of happiness in this world is very small and is not to be compared with that of misfortune. But it is not the particular nature of our state of living, but the people's own guilt, that is to be blamed. And in this respect Clarissa much better shows us the way to increase our happiness rather than for us to lose something from our virtuous pleasures by meditating on her adventures.

But as far as external happiness and the present pleasures of the human spirit are concerned—in this regard it is certain that human life is beset with many misfortunes and adversities. Anyone would have to be a complete stranger to the world if he doubted this. And although we bring much pain on ourselves by our folly, it is also no less certain that this life itself yields many pleasures, benefits, and diversions for our present enjoyment. The world is, in part, dreadful and ghastly, but it also has its beautiful and heavenly scenes. Good and evil, joy and sadness are mingled in them and interwoven in various ways. Not only are some people gay and happy, while others are unhappy and filled with distress, but also the same people experience life differently at different times; joy and sadness follow the one after the other. Some people, it is true, are assaulted by misfortunes and discomforts which follow each other continually; and they usually lead sad lives. But this number is not great compared with those who experience both fates alternately, and I do not believe that these are in greater number than those for whom the wind of good fortune continually blows

into their sails and who are seen to spend their days in
undisturbed rest, healthy and carefree. And if one considers
the common mass of people, among great and little, rich
and poor, I find, even among the virtuous and the unvirtuous, according to my experience, more enjoyment and
desire in this life than sorrow and pain. In order for me to
elaborate accurately about every kind of person would be to
go too far afield from the scope of this Preface. I admit
that one cannot make a just and firm decision about this
because our experience is too limited, and it is impossible to
be able to know the constitution and condition of all people.
This, however, is no reason to make us lean more towards
the unfavorable side. If there is much sorrow and pain
which is stifled and does not show itself outwardly except in
an exuberant joy, there are also many pleasures, in particular the most steadfast and sweetest, which make no sound,
but which are enjoyed, unnoticed, in silence. It is certain that
nature in general yields to people many more advantages
than disadvantages, creates many common and daily enjoyments which are neglected by the common majority of mortals, overlooked unattentively, or made unfit to use, but
which, however, must prevent us, it seems to me, from
regarding the condition of human life in its normal course
as a condition of disaster and misery.

But what then is the reason that both religious and irreligious people so often make such an abominable showing of
this life? The latter, although they seek all their pleasure in
this life but must frequently fail of success, easily become
peevish and grumble about the direction of the Almighty,
for Whom they have little respect; or they sometimes try,
by this pretense, to weaken the principles of the belief in a
merciful and wise Providence. With others, a melancholy
and heavy-hearted frame of mind has much influence on this
attitude, which is insensitive to enjoyments which please
others. This attitude makes them lift each straw as if it
were a beam and sigh faintheartedly over the least struggle
they meet with on their way and thereby collapse. But their

ideas are of no more value in the true appreciation of the
matter than those of the gay and superficial souls who are
always well pleased with themselves, know no difficulties,
walk over everything lightly, see no danger anywhere, and
would leave heaven to God if He left them the earth. Both
of these judgments are based more on imagination than on
well-organized and sound reason. Differences in years and
other circumstances also may bring about a great variety of
thoughts. Young people, whose abilities are quick and alive,
whose constitutions and powers are strong, healthy, and
fresh, and who have not yet been able to learn about the
vicissitudes of the world by experience, communicate their
own gaiety to all of nature, which seems to smile on them
from all sides; and on their present pleasures they pile with
an undaunted hope an abundance of future ones. Old people, on the contrary, having seen their happiness disturbed
by so many adversities, having become naturally duller and
more fearful by the decay of their powers, and, indeed,
feeling the discomforts of old age, take a truly contradic-
tory attitude towards this life. But because the number of
the latter surely is much smaller than that of the former, it
is evident, even in passing, that in this respect there is a
marked abatement coming in the misfortune of mankind in
general. One can easily understand that someone plunged in
sorrow, laden with pain and injury, assaulted with disasters,
oppressions, and persecutions, and therefore tired of life,
will be so struck by his own particular feelings that he will
hardly consult the general condition of the world outside of
himself. He therefore concludes that "man is born unto
trouble, as the sparks fly upward" (Job 5:7). It is then no
wonder that a philosopher (as such are called today), tired
of studies and travels or dissipated by too strong recreations whereby he does not have money to pay the servants
who trouble him for it, greatly exaggerates with a grumbling mood the adversities and miseries of life. And others
just imitate these words without considering the matter
accurately themselves and make this or that declaration of

the Holy Scriptures, produced in particular circumstances, cover the condition of mankind in its entirety, without foundation. This is the best that one can think of such people, who have plenty of everything and look fat and satisfied, but who nevertheless picture this life as an awful, horrid, and wretched state; one does meet such people now and then. In the mouths of these people this language is as little suitable as the promise to make gold is in the mouth of a poor vagabond.

But no matter how it may be, it is certain that our life here on earth is changeable, that we are enough exposed to adversities and misfortunes to make us admit that it is of much service to us to be warned against them, to learn to avoid them as much as possible and to know the means to make the inevitable nevertheless tolerable for us, yes, even useful and beneficial. Death is certainly the fate of all mortals; to put this thought out of his head, in order not to disturb his pleasure, is foolish for such a person who does not fancy that everything will be over for him at death. It is infinitely better to banish the fear of death from us by the meditation of a glorious scene in which a blessed hope triumphs over death altogether. The dread with which the wretched end of rogues and the godless moves our spirit is wholesome and beneficial to the utmost, because this must move us naturally to escape from the paths of iniquity and thus protect us from the many misfortunes which such people cause for themselves. And if we consider the troubles and tortures, the awful regrets and inconsolable griefs, which corrosive envy, foul malice, immovable stubbornness, arbitrary ambition, blind temper, or unsavory weakness, drag after themselves, what must be the natural result of them other than that we learn to be on our guard against these wretched causes and thus in fact decrease the wretchednesses of human life? And if the sad adventures of Clarissa are the most sorrowful which we come across in this entire history, if they were not pictured as so abominable and wretched and undeserved, her behavior in the same adventures could not create such powerful thoughts in a virtuous mind as to dissolve fear of the disasters of this life and to comfort and console it under this burden.

But this brings me to the second objection, which I would take into consideration briefly. Not only the idea of poetic justice, which is treated in [Richardson's] Postscript to this work, but also other thoughts oppose its sad outcome: for one may believe that it is not suitable to encourage youth to the practice of virtue and to commend piety to them as being beautiful, because virtue and piety, in the person of Clarissa, are so cruelly persecuted there and exposed to unremitting tortures and the basest abuses, which are concluded only by an untimely death. Most of them, one may think, might rather be frightened away from virtue than coming to love it.

But I note first of all, that the death of Clarissa is unjustly included in these objections. For one would surely not assert that a virtuous and pious person should be pictured as delivered from the common fate of mortals. And as a human being can die happy, the death of Clarissa must be regarded in the same way. As it is pictured here, and as she observes it herself, she is happy to come to the end of her sad adventures, which constitute only seven months of her otherwise continually pleasant life. She is thereby withdrawn from all the vicissitudes of this frail state in the firm hope of transferring to a state of pure salvation and happiness, endlessly more desirable than all the pleasures which the longest life here on earth could afford her. The more ghastly and dreadful the adversities and disasters described for us by this excellent work, the more abominable the contrasted godlessness, the fierce and unmerciful vices of hate, envy, covetousness, and wanton debauchery are shown to us; and the more powerful is the horror each reasonable conscience, which is not altogether hardened, must receive from them. The compassion itself, with which such a mind must be moved concerning the torment and oppression, naturally will incite respect and love for Clarissa's virtue and piety. The greater the disasters which her unshaken steadfastness has to fight, the harder the abuses are which her noble patience and Christian forgiveness can overcome; the more exalted, the more glorious and beautiful they must show themselves to a truly noble-minded soul.

I gladly admit that temporal happiness has very much influence on human nature and can move most of us in the most powerful way to take that direction which people have tried to encourage us to take. And I have no objection if one applies these arguments to the advantage of virtue and piety, if a careful use is made of them. But to depict virtue always as prosperous and blessed in the world I do not find in accordance with the true condition of sublunary things and therefore not prudent, because a person, surrendering himself to virtue on this basis, must naturally succumb in his efforts, if he does not find his opinion answered, but besides his mutinous temper also must face external disasters and misfortunes, which I think not seldom happens. Virtue and godliness are depicted by many moralists to be so beneficial in this life that they, except during times of persecution, make man certainly happy even here on earth and yield to him a peaceful and joyous life, riches and honor, blessings and prosperity. But I would think that this view, being so general and mechanistic, is taken in too wide a sense, and that there are more exceptions than one to be made to it. The purest, the noblest happiness, a peaceful conscience, the true peace and satisfaction of the spirit, and the realization of the inestimable favor of the Almighty, are inseparable from an upright and wise practice of virtue. And if this is supported by the well-grounded hope of eternal life, it can make most, yes, even the cruelest misfortunes of this life lose their most painful sharpness. And there are for each pious Christian sufficient reasons for him to rejoice at all times, although not always in the same measure, but to rejoice more in the happiness which he expects in the hereafter than in that which he always enjoys here. And this happiness shows itself with the most brilliant luster in the frame of mind of the unfortunate Clarissa.

But I cannot observe that the external and physical happiness of the world, even in the usual course of matters, is so firmly knit together with virtue, and that its lovers usually receive in this life an abundance of goods, honor, and respect among their fellowmen, as well as peace and enjoyment, strength and health. I know very well that an honest mind in ordinary circumstances, unseen and unknown, can enjoy much more essential pleasure than the greatest monarch in the world who is hurled about by his passions. But this is not generally understood by the world; and such a virtuous person, if he is beset by a melancholy mind, if he is laden with a weak, ailing, and painful body, if he has sorrow from the behavior of his next of kin, if he is assailed by others with tortures and injustices, cannot, according to my thinking, be considered happy with respect to his present state. And that an honest heart and a pious mind can exist here on earth in these circumstances is taught us not only by the Holy Scriptures by example and testimony but also by human nature itself and by common experience.

I do not want to say that virtue and piety have by their own nature less chance of receiving and enjoying the external benefits of this life than do sin and vice. By their own nature the former are much more suitable; and even in the present state of mankind, which weakens their influence and often disappoints us, they still have, in some respects, a notable advantage over vice. A moderate and modest life is more beneficial for the health of our bodies than are insobriety, dissoluteness, and ungovernable temper. Diligence and industriousness coupled with it serves naturally to make us exist honorably, to improve our conditions, and to increase our means, because laziness, thoughtlessness, and unconcern waste these, decay those, and in time produce want and poverty. A pious and honorable person will also obtain honor and respect from those fellowmen who possess any desire for virtue at all and enough intelligence to know his good qualities well in their nature and worth.

But in other respects I maintain that vice and injustice in the present condition of the world have at least as much advantage in the pursuit of external happiness, ease, pleasure, and abundance, that is, if vice does not run on to the most extreme excesses but is moderated by intelligence and does not really concern itself with the rules of honesty and piety but only regards temporal happiness. He who seeks his ease and enjoyment in this life will preserve easily a clear and fresh health as well as he who thinks himself obligated to tire himself in effort and work for the benefit of others. Hypocrisy often knows better how to appease and captivate people with no deep understanding (and are most people not like that?) and to obtain their ardent favor for itself, while a strict honesty and unfeigned sincerity trail behind and are treated but coolly and weakly. By breaking the rules of righteousness from time to time, selfishness can often succeed to a point which cannot at all be reached with the utmost diligence and frugality. Who does not know that to speak the truth directly usually provokes hatred, while sly flattery and friendly and obliging hypocrisy pave the way for the ambitious to become great and distinguished in the world and thereby receive everything to the fullest? A virtuous person, a God-fearing Christian especially, who expects his highest good in another life, has not as strong an inclination for the goods and benefits of this present state and thus easily overlooks the opportunities to provide himself with these, while a worldly-minded person, keeping his heart here by his treasure, does not let anything slip past him through which he can obtain a considerable benefit. And how many opportunities to make his fortune in this world show themselves, which his strict conscience must give up, because he cannot use the opportunity without hurting justice, truth, or love to some extent, no matter how little, about which scruples others, who are not so particular, step very easily? Not to mention how much external benefit a

lavish generosity, a true noble mindedness, and a little-un-
derstood humility often reject and leave for others; on the
other hand, they who are bolder and pull everything greed-
ily to themselves will lose nothing of that which they catch
in their nets.

One regards society; in a world where the virtuous and
pious constitute the smallest number and where those who
*do* mean well make many mistakes because of narrowness of
understanding and rash passions, it is most probable that
these people receive more disadvantages than benefits from
such errors. Profligate and unjust people, although they do
not spare their own kind, if they have the opportunity,
would rather first cool their lusts and desires on those people whom they fear the least, that is, those who they are
assured have nothing evil in mind towards them. These
people, usually not easily suspecting something evil in
others, according to the condition of their own honest
hearts, are therefore more susceptible of being trapped and
duped by rogues and cheaters. And although people preserve a considerable amount of awe and respect for true and
wise virtue, they themselves do not bother much with prac-
ticing it. That practice takes place only in those people who
have a lesser degree of vice and who have no particular
interest which incites them to oppress the pious. The latter
work much harder, more restlessly, and more untiringly
than others, who are stirred only by a weak approval of
virtue for the protection and defense of it. Such people even
find frequent pleasure in attacking and slandering an outstanding piety, shining too brightly in their eyes, and thus
rob it of an immense part of its benefit, which it otherwise
would still have for those who are not altogether hardened.
How often is virtue also the subject of scorn and mockery
for dissolute and desperate souls! Yes, there is not even a
lack of such hellish rogues who hate virtue for its purity's
sake and who, because it serves their godlessness with a
steady reproach or stands in the way of their shameful
efforts, make virtue into the subject of their most evil mis-

treatments. In such a world, true Christians are really stran-
gers, and it must not appear odd to them that they are more
or less oppressed. If they are not persecuted because of their
creed, the normal course of the world frequently makes
them subject to similar discomforts, if they are not safeguarded by unusually beneficial circumstances and attributes.

The less one thinks that temporal happiness and prosperity are the definite fate and part of virtue, the less one is
disappointed to learn that, on the contrary, one must often
struggle with cruel disasters and long-lasting adversities.
One observes that this life is not immediately rewarding but
is, instead, a trial and preparation for another life in which
the pious will receive the real reward for their good works.
That we must regard it as such is taught to us explicitly in
the Christian revelation and consistently confirmed by all
parts of it; and the consideration of our present state of
living and human nature itself can instruct us about it rather
clearly. We cannot, it is true, judge perfectly and infallibly
the measure of virtue or vice in our fellowmen and thus
cannot determine exactly which measure of happiness each
must be allotted so that each would get his just reward. Nor
do we know exactly all the pleasures and displeasures which
fall to the lot of each particular person, in order to indicate
how much the pious lack in the former and the impious lack
in the latter. But we nevertheless are able to make sufficient
definite comparisons and distinctions between excellent and
steadfast practitioners of virtue and others who do not at
all obey the laws of righteousness and piety, and between a
life consisting of prosperity, pleasures, and delights and one
burdened by sorrow, pain, and oppression.

To conclude: people in this life are not allotted a proportionate fate of happiness or misfortune according to their
virtues or vices, yet what a proportionate reward rational
creatures may reasonably expect from the relationship
which they have with their Creator and Supreme Lord and
from a just idea of godly righteousness. Often one sees that

they who show by their work that their hearts house no
virtue or piety live undisturbed in peace, joy, and gaiety.
Others, on the contrary, who cannot be accused of great
vices, have everything running against them: their tender-
heartedness is tormented with continual sorrow; they are
objects of the hate and disfavor of the foolish and the
powerful, or they live in afflicted and pain-filled bodies. And
how weak would be the relief from this misery which a
peaceful conscience could give, if those affected could expect
no salvation outside of this present condition? Even though
it yields the purest and noblest pleasures, the soul would
become insensitive to the taste of it through the fierceness of
the other displeasures.

How then can this, our present state, be regarded as a
life in which good is rewarded with virtue and a proportionate happiness is inseparably knit together with it? On the
one hand, a strict practice of virtue and an exalted and
noble-minded righteousness often cause man the greatest
disasters; and by helping some unjustly oppressed person,
through a pure and immediate love, one must suffer the
disfavor, hatred, and vengeance of one's more powerful
oppressors. Ingratitude for good deeds is the expected base
reward of the world. On the other hand, a high measure of
happiness and prosperity endangers the virtue of most people who enjoy them and naturally has many enticements in
itself to make their minds swell with haughtiness and pride
and weaken through thoughtlessness, wantonness, and sensuality, because this happiness is not only surrounded by a
host of external temptations but also attracts many tempters
and hypocritical friends, who basely try to disturb and spoil
their virtue and happiness at the same time.

The human intellect is not equal to the dangers to which
we are subject in this life. It is not extensive enough, not
intelligent enough, not penetrating enough to know accurately everything that threatens us with harm, and therefore, to avoid carefully such dangers. A great prudence
about any feared disaster and an intensified effort for a

specific happiness decrease our care concerning other dangers which may meet us unexpectedly. It is not from a culpable ignorance, even for the most virtuous person, that he takes a poisonous plant and eats it as wholesome food. Even if the whole world were virtuous and pious, who would yet be in a position to foresee when he would have to protect himself against storms and thunder in order not to drown in the wild waves and not to leave a sad widow and orphans behind? And who, in the mixed multitude of people, good and bad together, can distinguish definitely one kind from the other and see through the hearts of shrewd villains sufficiently to be always on his guard for the snares which they set? Rogues are often not capable of this, let alone honest and upright people. And although by observation and experience one can learn to know all these dangers much better, although one could acquire all the ability to avoid finally all of them, how many dangers, however, can hurt us before our minds would be brought to that maturity?

A slight imprudence, hardly to be counted as a fault in a fallible person, is frequently seen as carrying in this life a series of misfortunes with it and can cause much pain and sadness, which perhaps do not end before death, and which, however, cannot at all be thought as deserved by such a slight imprudence. But such could not be the case if each person were to fare well or badly in this life according to his virtue. A virtuous and pious person can, for example, advised by parents and friends and deceived by outward appearance, commence an unhappy marriage. And even though she herself cannot be completely acquitted of passionate rashness or instability, who would dare to state that she receives nothing but her just reward for her entire life, having to swallow the sorrow of a wicked husband, of loveless and cruel treatment, of the poverty and neglect of her children, all of this being, nevertheless, the natural result of this one step? Many children who were produced by the Creator with fresh and healthy bodies and thus by nature are more suited to a better state in this world can, through no fault of their own, be so hurt and spoiled in their systems by the temper, carelessness, or ignorance of their parents or those to whom they are entrusted, that for many years they have to endure ailing and painful bodies.

I do not at all raise these observations with the idea that the lot of the pious in general, all the internal and external advantages and disadvantages taken together, is worse in this world than that of the godless. I am of a very different opinion, especially if the former have the fortune of living under the light of Christian revelation. But this conclusion, I think, can be clearly made from this: that virtue here does not always receive an equal reward and that the nature of our present condition of life itself reveals that we are put here on earth for trial. Because this now is the purpose of our wise Creator, it is also evident that they who adhere to Him cannot always depend on his temporal blessings and that this fact must considerably weaken the power of arguments for the present advantage of virtue and piety, derived from God's immediate favor, aid, and protection. The happiness and unhappiness of this world are indeed both suitable to make the man who behaves himself properly under both of them more virtuous and thus to make him progress more and more in the most noble perfection for which the rational nature is capable and to prepare him for the enjoyment of the highest good, for which the merciful God really intended us. And His all-wise Providence, although saddening nobody without reason, nevertheless distributes that unequal lot in unequal measure among the good as well as among the evil, by His infallible knowledge of which experiences, according to the particular state, kind, and qualities of each, can serve best to obtain that great purpose. To some, who can safely enjoy the advantages of this life without weakening in the practice of virtue, who rather reap benefits from good deeds, he gives these advantages in a proportionate measure. But others, whom a continued prosperity would make careless and inattentive and whose legs are not strong enough to carry the luxury, He deprives wisely and mercifully, in order to protect them from their temptations. Misfortunes and disasters bring forth virtues in the pious, the exercise of which cannot be brought about by continuous prosperity; and the realization of having acquitted himself well of his duties in all respects and having passed the test without weakening in all cases must notably increase the rational and spiritual happiness of a peaceful conscience and must strengthen the assurance of the ardent favor of the Almighty.

One might observe here that if this life is suitable to prepare us for a better state, this purpose cannot be reached so easily, perhaps, by misfortunes and adversities, because those particular virtues whose exercise they bring about, such as patience, submission, and the like, certainly do not fit in a condition of uninterrupted and eternal blessings. But this doubt is of no importance when one realizes that the highest happiness of the future life will be created from a perfectly pure practice of virtue and justice, in which those glorified will be immovably confirmed and that therefore a conscience, provided with virtue in general, is most capable of the enjoyment of it. And who should be acknowledged to have a greater virtue—he who has withstood uncorruptedly all sorts of trials, or he who, in one kind of trial, has found and shown only his steadfastness? Not only for the enjoyment of the purely rational and spiritual pleasures but also for all external salvations which the state of heaven will yield to its happy inhabitants, and which, whatever they may be, certainly differ to the utmost in nature and quality from the external advantages of the present world, it is very beneficial that our taste for virtue in this life already be cultivated and that we learn to wean ourselves from the pleasures of this earth, for which certainly misfortunes and oppressions are naturally very helpful to us. Deprived of external benefits, we automatically, if there are any seeds of virtue in us, pay more attention to internal pleasures which are created from pure piety. Our desire for a better life

becomes the stronger and doubles our diligence to put to
work the means which are conducive to the acquisition of
this better life. A virtuous mind becomes stronger and
firmer in adversities, and by repeatedly conquering them,
increases steadily in moral perfection. When everything
goes his way, the best man does not control his actions and
thoughts so carefully and often overlooks some hidden defects which misfortune, attracting his attention, uncovers
before his view and teaches him to improve. Although patience is not really useful if one has nothing to endure, it
does instill qualities in one's soul of contentment, of joyous
confidence in God, which indeed essentially belong to a state
of perfect happiness for rational and dependent creatures,
as we shall always be. The more pressure and sorrow one
has undergone, the more desirable the change and deliverance from them will be, and the more lively feeling the subsequent enjoyment of salvation must naturally bring one.
And who knows in how many other respects the dangers of
this life make the pious capable and prepare them for that
state of the highest good, the nature of which we can now
view in no other way than in a faint dimness.

With these loosely-strewn thoughts about the state of
human life, I conclude my work on the excellent history of
*Clarissa,* thinking that such thoughts will not fit badly with
these last two volumes. Anyone will easily observe that
these could have been stretched out much further. But I
have had to shorten them in order not to burden this volume
with too long a Preface. What is contained here is enough, I
imagine, to make us see that a truly religious person does
not have to seek his true happiness in this life; to give him
courage and to comfort him in all of life's changeable circumstances; to keep him from begrudging the foolish
worldly person his vain and short-lasting pleasures; to justify completely godly Providence in exposing His favorites
to disasters and oppressions; to instill a courageous and
manly piety in him in spite of all these difficulties; and to
cleanse the subject of this work, Clarissa, tortured by anger

and godlessness, and dragged finally to her death by sorrow, of all reproaches in this respect. May it please the merciful God that all the readers of this work, by the viewing of this beautiful picture in the cruelest of her disasters and misfortunes, might be moved also to prepare themselves for death, according to their circumstances, and might be enabled to undergo that unavoidable fate with contented souls and well-founded hopes!

*Notes / Index*

# Notes

## Introduction

*1.* de Clercq Family Archives, file Nos. 932*a* and 932*b*, Gemeentelijke Archiefdienst, Amsterdam. Parts of this Introduction appeared in my article, "Samuel Richardson and The Netherlands: Early Reception of His Work," *Papers on Language and Literature*, 1 (1965), 20–30.

*2.* From the genealogical diagram of the descendants of Johannes Stinstra's father, Simon Johannes Stinstra (1673–1743), de Clercq Family Archives, file No. 920.

*3.* The correspondence, as part of the de Clercq Family Archives, was placed for safekeeping in the Algemeen Rijksarchief, The Hague, by the late Mr. S. de Clercq, the last private owner of the letters. Mr. de Clercq stipulated in his will that the archives be transferred at his death to the Gemeentelijke Archiefdienst, Amsterdam, their present location.

*4.* Stinstra's letter of August 11, 1753 (Letter No. 9), gives this date as his date of birth, as does the *Mennonite Encyclopedia*, IV (Scottdale, Pa., 1959), 634; the genealogical diagram (see preceding note) gives the date of August 10, as does Sepp in Vol. I, p. 11 (Christiaan Sepp, *Johannes Stinstra en zijn Tijd* (2 vols.; Amsterdam, 1865–66). Further, Stinstra ends Letter No. 9 with the statement: "My 46th birthday," while it was actually his forty-fifth birthday as birthdays are normally counted.

*5.* Sepp, I, 11.

*6.* Sepp, I, 20–36.

*7.* Sepp, I, 203–4.

*8.* Sepp, I, 204.

*9.* Sepp, II, 288.

*10.* Sepp, I, 204–7. See also Letter No. 3.

*11.* Such views included advocation of anti-Trinitarianism, rejection of both the deity of Christ and atonement by the blood of Christ, and strong emphasis on the free will of man. See *Mennonite Encyclopedia*, IV, 565. See also Letter No. 3.

*12. Request met bygevoegde Deductie voor het Regt van Vryheid van Geloove, Godsdienst en Conscientie op den naam van de Doops-gezinde Gemeenten in Friesland ingeleverd aan de E. M. Heeren Staaten der gemelde Provincie* (Leeuwarden, 1741).

*13.* Sepp, I, 218–25.

*14. De Natuure en Gesteldheid van Christus Koningrijk, onder-daanen, Kerke, en Godsdienst afgeschetst in vijf Predikatien* (Harlin-gen, 1741). Sepp summarized the sermons: (1) The true religion of Jesus is removed from all means of force and temporal gains or losses; (2) Shows the original simplicity and the true being of the Christian religion; (3) True sincerity is characteristic of a Christian; (4) There is no authority in the Christian church other than that of the Master, and no binding dogma may be recognized except that of the Scriptures; (5) The value of the personal conviction of each member of the Christian church must be recognized. Sepp felt that Stinstra was not successful in his general attack on dogma, because the Men-nonite Church itself was strongly attached to the dogma of baptism (I, 236–37). For mention of the *Five Sermons*, see Letters 2 and 3. See also *n.* 15, Introduction, and *nn.* 8 and 26, Letters.

*15.* Sepp, II, 1–73. One of Stinstra's views which disturbed the theological faculties was his bringing together as major figures of the Reformation the names of Luther, Calvin, Menno Simons (1496–1561), founder of the Mennonite sect, and Faustus Socinus (1539–1604). As Sepp points out, this was just too much, even though Stinstra defended his inclusion of Socinus with the others by arguing that Socinus, in breaking away from the papacy, had to be included as one who had worked seriously for and had stressed emphatically the principles of the Reformation. Stinstra granted that Socinus' name would frighten some of the readers of the *Five Sermons* and assumed that it would be clear proof to them of his holding Socinian beliefs (Sepp, I, 246–47). Unfortunately, he was right.

Stinstra was the last person in The Netherlands to be persecuted for Socinian beliefs, real or imagined. See Earl Morse Wilbur, *A History of Unitarianism: Socinianism and Its Antecedents* (Cam-bridge, Mass., 1947), p. 562. The Stinstra controversy produced more than forty published works; see S. Blaupot ten Cate, who listed the books in his *Geschiedenis der Doopsgezinden in Friesland* (Leeu-warden, 1839), pp. 351–53.

Stinstra stated to Richardson that he was not a Socinian; see Letter No. 3, and W. J. Kühler comes to the same conclusion after an examination of Stinstra's beliefs; see *Het Socinianisme in Nederland*

(Leiden, 1912), p. 267. But Stinstra was certainly interested in Socinianism as an expression of liberal belief; not only do we have his discussion of Socinus in his *Five Sermons*, but further possible evidence may be seen in a four-volume series of biographies "of the Most Prominent Dutch Men and Women," *Levensbeschryving van eenige meest voorname Nederlandsche Mannen en Vrouwen* (Amsterdam and Harlingen, 1774). It includes biographies of such diverse figures as Calvin, Jan Steen, Luther, Menno Simons, Jacob Arminius, Pope Adrian VI, Erasmus, Vondel, Rubens, and Rembrandt. A brief, sympathetic biography of Socinus (III, 18–27) was quite possibly written by Stinstra; although no authors' names appear on the title page or elsewhere, the work is attributed in part to Stinstra by The Royal Library, The Hague, and it was published in Harlingen by Stinstra's publisher. It would appear that Stinstra wrote at least some of the biographies of the religious leaders included.

Finally, the *Catalogue* of Stinstra's library lists a large number of theological works, some of which are Socinian; H. John McLachlan in his *Socinianism in Seventeenth-Century England* (Oxford, 1951), pp. 144–48, lists "Socinian Publications formerly in All Soul's Library Oxford." His list is limited to publications from Raków, Poland, the center for Socinian publications in the seventeenth century (Wilbur, p. 408). The *Catalogue* of Stinstra's library lists eighteen books published in Raków as well as other Socinian works, but it lists as well anti-Socinian books, and the inclusion of works on both sides of the Socinian controversy indicates Stinstra's interest in Theology without proving anything conclusively about his beliefs. See *n*. 14, Introduction, and *nn*. 8 and 26, Letters.

*16.* Sepp, II, 112–60.

*17.* Stinstra had read Fielding, however; see Letter No. 11; he also mentions *Tom Jones* briefly in his first Preface to *Clarissa* and his second Preface touches on Fielding's habit of digression in his novels.

*18.* I, sigs. *8–******2; III, sigs. *2–********3; V, sigs. *2–***ᵛ; VII, sigs. *2–**[7].

*19. Samuel Richardson: Printer and Novelist* (Chapel Hill, 1936), p. 265.

*20. Maendelyke Uittreksels, of de Boekzaal der geleerde Werrelt,* Pt. 75 (Dec., 1752), 734.

*21.* "Brief van Lugthart of 'er Zedenpreken uit Romans te haalen zyn," *De Nederlandsche Spectator,* V (1753), 139–40.

*22. Ibid.,* p. 141.

*23.* "Gedachten over 't Leezen van Vercierde Geschiedenissen en Romans," *De Nieuwe Vaderlandsche Letteroefeningen*, III (1788), 97–98.

*24.* Anna L. Barbauld (ed.), *The Correspondence of Samuel Richardson* (6 vols.; London), hereafter cited as *Correspondence*. The Dutch translation is entitled: *Briefwisseling van Samuel Richardson* (6 vols.; Amsterdam, 1805).

*25.* "Briefwisseling Tusschen den Eerw. Heer Joannes Stinstra, Leerar der Doopsgezinden te Harlingen, en den Heere Samuel Richardson, Schryver van de Pamela, Clarissa, en Grandison," *De Algemeene Vaderlandsche Letteroefeningen*, II (1804), 563. Three letters in translation follow: Stinstra's letters of Apr. 2, 1753, pp. 564–68; Dec. 24, 1753, pp. 603–6; and Richardson's letter of Mar. 20, 1754, pp. 606–9.

*26.* I, I–III.

*27.* Pt. 6 (Dec., 1796), 141–42.

*28.* I (1798), 143–44.

*29.* *Histoire de Sir Charles Grandison*, trans. J. G. Mounod (7 vols.; Göttingen and Leiden, 1755–56). See *n.* 38, Letters.

*30.* *Nouvelles lettres angloises, ou Histoire du Chevalier Grandisson* (4 vols.; Amsterdam, 1755–56). See *n.* 38, Letters.

*31.* *Clarisse Harlowe*, trans. Jules Janin (2 vols.; The Hague, 1846).

*32.* *De Geschiedenis van Sir Charles Grandison Verkort* (Leiden, 1793).

*33.* *De Algemeene Vaderlandsche Letteroefeningen*, I (1806), 48.

*34.* *Het Pad der Deugd* (Doordrecht, 1766).

*35.* McKillop, *Samuel Richardson*, p. 100.

*36.* I (1772), 270.

*37.* *De Nieuwe Vaderlandsche Oefeningen*, II (1769), 474–75.

*38.* *Ibid.*, III, 144.

*39.* *De Nieuwe Vaderlandsche Letteroefeningen*, V (1771), 439–40.

*40.* IV (1782), 557–58.

*41.* No. 9, Feb. 27, 1783, 71.

## PART ONE, The Correspondence

*1.* Printed in its entirety in Latin in Sepp, II, 248–49. Letters Nos. 3, 4, 7, and 9 are also translations from Latin.

*2.* See Letter No. 5 for nine excerpts of letters in praise of *Clarissa.* Professor McKillop conjectured that the bishop who had read *Clarissa* eleven times was Thomas Secker (1693–1768), Archbishop of Canterbury from 1758 to 1768; see *Samuel Richardson,* p. 266. See Letter No. 6 for Richardson's concern over Stinstra's revelation of this information in his second Preface and Letter No. 7 for Stinstra's reply.

*3. Answer to the Letter of a Very Reverend and Worthy Gentleman, Objecting to the Warmth of a Particular Scene in the History of Clarissa* [1749], Richardson's defense of the fire scene in Vol. IV. A copy of it is in the Forster Collection, Victoria and Albert Museum; it is described by Austin Dobson in *Samuel Richardson* (London, 1902), pp. 101–2, and more fully by T. C. Duncan Eaves and Ben D. Kimpel in "Richardsoniana," *Studies in Bibliography,* XIV (1961), 232–33. Eaves and Kimpel point out that Richardson based his defense on moral as well as on artistic grounds. Stinstra's translation of the *Answer,* appended to Vol. IV of his translation of *Clarissa,* is discussed by him in Letter No. 3; see also *n.* 16, Letters. There is no copy of the *Answer* listed in the *Catalogue* of Stinstra's library.

*4. Remarks on Clarissa* (London, 1749). Richardson referred to the work as a little piece by a lady, "published in Defence of the History of Clarissa." See William Merritt Sale, Jr., *Samuel Richardson A Bibliographical Record of His Literary Career with Historical Notes* (New Haven, 1936), p. 131. Professor McKillop attributed it to Sarah Fielding; see *Samuel Richardson,* p. 156.

*5. Meditations Collected from the Sacred Books,* printed 1750 but not published; described by Sale, *Samuel Richardson A Bibliographical Record,* p. 64.

*6.* Probably William Duncombe (1690–1769). See Letter No. 16 for excerpts from another letter from Duncombe to Richardson.

*7. Waarschuwinge tegen de Geestdrijverij, vervat in een Brief aan de Doopsgezinden in Friesland* (Harlingen, 1750). In this 81-page pamphlet, which is in the form of a letter to the Mennonites of Friesland, Stinstra sets forth his belief that Reason is an absolute necessity in religion—that it "is the noblest and loftiest gift which the merciful Creator has granted us . . ." (pp. 6–7) and that "an unreasonable religion is really no religion" (p. 28). Like Dr. Johnson, he believed that free play of the Imagination and the Passions could lead to madness (p. 40), and as an example of what can happen when Imagination overcomes Reason, he cites the emotional outbursts of religious fanatics: "screaming, shrieking, convulsions, and such clamor" (p. 22). Stinstra holds that because of the fanatic's lively Imagination, urged by his Passions, and because he puts himself above other people, he thinks that "the words which spring to his mouth and the images which come to his mind are the direct workings of God" (pp. 14–15). In his conclusion, Stinstra says the "mad people now more deserve our pity, compassion, and sympathy than our hatred, bias, and persecution" (p. 80).

For a further development of Stinstra's ideas on Imagination and Reason, see his Preface to Vols. v and vi of *Clarissa*.

Stinstra's *Waarschuwinge* was translated by Henry Rimius as *A Pastoral Letter Against Fanaticism* (London, 1753). Although Stinstra had not mentioned Count Zinzendorf or the Moravians by name, Rimius included on his title page the suggestion that the work "May Serve as an Excellent Antidote Against the Principles of *Enthusiasts* and *Fanaticks* in General, and the *Herrnhuters* or *Moravians* in Particular." Rimius had opened his attack on Zinzendorf with *A Candid Narrative of the Rise and Progress of the Herrnhuters* . . . (London, 1753); in it he states that Stinstra's *Waarschuwinge*, "tho' wrote with great Judgment, was no more than a Treatise against *Fanaticism* in general, and that the Account of the *Herrnhuters* prefixed thereto [Boissy's "Preface of the French Translator"], was imperfect . . . I changed my Purpose of barely translating this Work . . . I thence composed this Narrative of the Rise and Progress of Herrnhutism and its Doctrines . . ." (p. 7). Imperfect or not, Rimius had no hesitation in using part of Boissy's "Preface of the French Translator" in his "Preface" as if it were his own. Rimius brought out a second edition of the *Candid Narrative* (1755), and *A Solemn Call on Count Zinzendorf* . . . *to Answer All and Every Charge Brought Against Them* [the Moravians] *in the Candid Narrative* (1754); finally, *A Second Solemn Call* was published (1757) after Rimius' death. Rimius based his various attacks on unorthodox Moravian doctrines on the content of some of the Moravian hymns, which he felt to be blasphemous; on Zinzendorf's sermons; on the strong eroticism connected with Christ's wounds; and on what Rimius claimed were dishonest financial dealings by the Moravians in England.

A later translation of Stinstra's *Waarschuwinge* appeared as *An Essay on Fanaticism* (Dublin, 1774), translated by the Rev. Isaac Subremont from Boissy's French translation of 1752. Along with it he printed Boissy's "Preface" and a brief preface of his own in which he acknowledges his debt to Boissy, since he did not read Dutch and therefore could not translate from Stinstra's original. The *Catalogue* of Stinstra's library lists Rimius' translation of the *Waarschuwinge* and his *Candid Narrative*. See *nn.* 9, 12, 21, 22, 31, 41, and 55, Letters.

8. *De Natuure en Gesteldheid van Christus Koningrijk* . . . See *nn.* 14 and 15, Introduction, *n.* 26, Letters.

9. Count Nikolaus Ludwig von Zinzendorf (1700–1760), founder of the Herrnhut (Moravian) sect, which grew out of the persecuted Unitas Fratrum, or Bohemian Brethren. George Whitefield encouraged him to go to America, and from 1741 to 1743 he established a number of Moravian congregations in Pennsylvania. He lived mostly in London from 1749 to 1755. See *Encyclopædia Britannica* and *Webster's Biographical Dictionary*. See *n.* 7, Letters.

10. Thomas Herring (1693–1757), Archbishop of Canterbury, 1747–57.

11. They were not; see Letter No. 3.

12. John James Majendie (1709–83), author of several religious works in French and English, was Queen Charlotte's instructor in English and tutor to her sons, the Prince of Wales and the Duke of York. In his *Supplement to the Candid Narrative of the Rise and Progress of the Herrnhuters*, Henry Rimius refers to Majendie as "chaplain to the late Earl of Grantham, and prebendary of Sarum," and thanks him for his "kind assistance throughout the whole controversy . . ." over Zinzendorf and the Moravians (Preface, p. xviii). See *n.* 7, Letters.

13. The Grange, North End, Fulham. See William M. Sale Jr.'s article, "Samuel Richardson's House at Fulham," *Notes and Queries,* CLXIX (1935), 133–34.

14. Translation of original printed in part in *Correspondence,* v, 241–53. Mrs. Barbauld omitted pars. 1, 2, 3, 4, 6, 7, most of 8, part of 13, and combined pars. 9 and 10.

15. See *n.* 3, Letters.

16. Richardson wrote: "the Passion I found strongest in me, whenever I supposed myself a Reader only, and the Story real, was *Anger*, or *Indignation*: I had too great an Aversion to the intended Violator of the Honour of a CLARISSA, to suffer any-thing but alternate Admiration and Pity of her, and Resentment against him, to take place in my Mind, on the Occasion"; printed in the article by

T. C. Duncan Eaves and Ben D. Kimpel, "Richardsoniana," *Studies in Bibliography*, XIV (1961), 233.

*17.* See *n.* 4, Letters.

*18.* See *n.* 5, Letters.

*19.* Folkert van der Plaats, Stinstra's publisher; he too was a Mennonite and a deacon in the Harlingen Congregation.

*20.* William Duncombe; see *n.* 6, Letters.

*21.* Jean François Boissy (? –1753), a tutor at Leiden. See Sepp, II, 217–18. The translation referred to here is the *Lettre pastorale contre le Fanatisme* (Leiden, 1752).

*22.* August Wilhelm Sack (1703–86). The translation is the *Warnung vor dem Fanaticismus* (Berlin, 1752). Sack wrote the preface, but the work was translated by a certain Nolten or Noltenius. See Sepp, II, 218.

*23. Request met bygevoegde Deductie voor het Regt van Vryheid van Geloove, Godsdienst en Conscientie op den Naam van de Doopsgezinde Gemeenten in Friesland ingeleverd aan de E. M. Heeren Staaten der gemelde Provincie* (Leeuwarden, 1741). The "Suppliant Booklet" is entitled: *Remonstrantie aan de Ed. Mog. Heeren Staaten van Friesland ingeleverd op d. 27 Febr. 1742* (Amsterdam, 1742).

*24.* Samuel Clarke (1675–1729). See *n.* 66, Letters. Benjamin Hoadley (1676–1761), Bishop in succession of Bangor, Hereford, Salisbury, and Winchester. Stinstra owned copies of a number of his sermons.

*25.* Willem IV (1711–51); Stadhouder, 1747–51.

*26.* (August, 1747), pp. 569–88. The background of Stinstra's case is presented in a sympathetic light. Reprinted is a letter from Stinstra to the provincial government of Friesland of April 25, 1747, in which Stinstra states that he is sorry the publication of his *Five Sermons* has brought him into disfavor with the government but points out that he has never made any attempt to teach Socinian doctrines or anything else contrary to the teachings of Christ or to the country and even less to suggest that people should be indifferent towards religion (p. 578).

Also reprinted is Stinstra's letter of May 8, 1747, also to the provincial government, in which he argues that the States General do not have the authority to act as judges over "the belief, the teaching, and the religion of Christians." Stinstra recognizes God as the only authority in such matters, and he asserts that making promises to temporal authorities lessens the traditional freedom of the individual (pp. 583 and 585). See *nn.* 14 and 15, Introduction, and *n.* 8, Letters.

*27. Onregtvaardigheid der Sluikerije, aangewezen in eene Leer-Reden over Matth. XXII: 21* (Harlingen, 1739), literally: *The Injustice of Smuggling.* In this work, originally preached as a sermon on December 7, 1738 (Sepp, I, 216), Stinstra argues against evasion of import duties by stressing the text from Matthew: "Render therefore unto Caesar the things which are Caesar's; and unto God the things that are God's." He argues that while other thieves harm people, the smuggler is worse, because he harms the State (p. 19). He points out that smuggling is a common and frequent occurrence in the land (p. 3). Perhaps the significance of the subject lies in the fact that many of Stinstra's congregation in Harlingen were connected directly or indirectly with shipping, so that the sermon would have applied directly to them.

The other work mentioned is the *Gedagten over den Brief van den Heere Joan van den Honert* (Harlingen, 1742). Van den Honert (1693–1758) was instrumental in having Stinstra suspended and in having his *Five Sermons* suppressed.

*28. Vier en twintig Leerredenen* (Harlingen, 1746).

*29.* Stinstra's translation is entitled: *XVIII Predicatien en Nagelatene Predicatien* (Harlingen, 1749). For his translation of Clarke's work on natural and revealed religion, see *n.* 66, Letters.

*30.* Anna of Hanover (1709–59).

*31.* Isaac Tirion, who earlier had had business relationships with Stinstra's publisher, Folkert van der Plaats (both had published Stinstra's *Waarschuwinge tegen de Geestdrijverij* in 1750), later had a falling out with him. See Letters Nos. 9 and 10.

*32.* The translation appeared as: *Clarissa, oder die Geschichte eines vornehmen Frauenzimmers* (8 vols.; Göttingen, 1748–52). Johann David Michaelis (1717–91), Protestant theologian and Orientalist, was a professor at Göttingen from 1746–91.

*33.* See Letter No. 5, fifth par. from end, for Richardson's explanation.

*34.* The copy of this letter made by Martha Richardson has been printed in part several times: *Correspondence,* I, xxix–xliii *passim;* Iolo A. Williams, "Two Kinds of Richardsons," *London Mercury,* VII (1923), 382–88; McKillop, *Samuel Richardson,* pp. 4–7 and 16; it has been published in full twice: McKillop, *The Early Masters of*

*English Fiction* (Lawrence, Kan., 1956), pp. 47–51; John Carroll, *Selected Letters of Samuel Richardson* (Oxford, 1964), pp. 228–35. The copy lacks the first fourteen paragraphs of the original; the paragraph beginning, "But now, Sir, to your last Question . . ."; the two paragraphs preceding the excerpts; all of the excerpts from the letters in praise of *Clarissa*; and the last ten paragraphs.

*35.* See *n.* 3, Letters.

*36.* Albrecht von Haller (1708–77), anatomist, physiologist, botanist, physician, author. His criticism of *Clarissa* appeared in the *Bibliothèque raisonée*, XLII (1749), 325 ff., and was reprinted in the *Gentleman's Magazine*, XIX (1749), 245–46, 345–49. See McKillop, *Samuel Richardson*, p. 232.

*37.* *Lettres angloises; ou, Histoire de Miss Clarisse Harlove* (12 parts in 6 vols.; London [Paris], 1751). Richardson stated similar objections to Prévost's translation in a letter to Lady Braidshaigh of Feb. 24, 1753; see *Correspondence,* VI, 244–45. See *nn.* 63 and 104, Letters.

*38.* Two French translations of *Grandison* appeared at the same time: *Histoire de Sir Charles Grandison*, trans. J. G. Mounod (7 vols.; Göttingen and Leiden, 1755–56) and *Nouvelles lettres angloises, ou Histoire du Chevalier Grandisson*, trans. Prévost (8 parts in 4 vols.; Amsterdam, 1755–56). Gellert supervised the German translation by a group of Leipzig professors (see McKillop, *Samuel Richardson,* pp. 255–56). The completed work was entitled *Geschichte Herrn Carl Grandison. In Briefen entworfen von dem Verfasser der Pamela und der Clarissa* (7 vols.; Leipzig, 1754–55). See Letter No. 20 for a discussion of these translations.

*39.* Noordwijk (see Letter No. 9).

*40.* Folkert van der Plaats; see *n.* 19, Letters.

*41.* See *nn.* 7 and 55, Letters.

*42.* For the most recent investigation of Richardson's immediate family, see article by T. C. Duncan Eaves and Ben D. Kimpel, "Samuel Richardson and His Family Circle," *Notes and Queries,* XI (1964), 362–71.

*43.* Eaves and Kimpel present evidence that Richardson was born in Mackworth and baptized in October, 1689. *Ibid.*, pp. 364–66.

*44.* See McKillop, *The Early Masters of English Fiction*, pp. 51 and 222*n.*

*45.* The headings to the excerpts are in Richardson's handwriting; the excerpts are in the hand of William Richardson (1733–88), the nephew who succeeded to the business; see McKillop, *Samuel Richardson,* p. 284 and Eaves and Kimpel, "Samuel Richardson and His Family Circle," *Notes and Queries,* XI (1964), 403. See Letters Nos. 12 and 17.

*46.* Forster MS. xv, 2, fol. 7. I am indebted to Professor T. C. Duncan Eaves for this reference and for the further Forster Collection references in *nn.* 47, 48, 50, 51, 53, Letters. Patrick Delany (1685–1768) was Dean of Down from 1744 to 1767. Richardson published several of his works, including *The Life of David;* see William M. Sale, Jr., *Samuel Richardson: Master Printer* (Ithaca, 1950), pp. 164–166. Mary Granville (1700–1788) became his second wife. She was a friend of the Duchess of Portland and of Fanny Burney. To my knowledge this letter is unpublished, although in writing her sister, Anne, Mrs. Dewes, she twice praised *Clarissa.* See *Autobiography and Correspondence,* ed. Lady Llanover (1st ser.; 1861), II, 598: Letter of October 6, 1750, and II, 603: Letter of October 13, 1750.

*47.* For the original letter in its entirety see E. L. McAdam, Jr., "A New Letter from Fielding," *The Yale Review,* XXXVIII (1948), 300–310. For Fielding's published comments on *Clarissa* and the concept of the happy ending urged by others, see McKillop, *Samuel Richardson,* pp. 160–70.

*48.* Forster MS. xv, 2, fol. 24. Mrs. Barbauld conjectured that Channing was probably the friend who assisted Richardson with the letters of the pedant Brand in *Clarissa.* See *Correspondence,* II, 327–33.

*49.* Forster MS. xv, 2, fol. 24a.

*50.* For part of the original, with some variations from this copy, see *Correspondence,* II, 333–36.

*51.* Forster MS. xv, 2, foll. 25–26.

*52.* Forster MS. xv, 2, fol. 13.

*53.* See *n.* 64, Letters.

*54.* Forster MS. xv, 2, foll. 47–48. Philip Skelton (1707–87), Irish divine and author of *Ophiomaches, or Deism Revealed* (London, 1748). He was on friendly terms with Swift and Dr. Johnson. See *Correspondence,* v, 193–240 for letters between Richardson and him.

*55.* The advertisement is as follows: "A pastoral letter against fanaticism. By Mr. *Stinstra;* translated by *H. Rimius. Is. 6d. Robinson.* ------ This letter was occaiioned [sic] by the appearance of a new sect in the *Dutch* provinces, which greatly resembled the

*French* prophets. Persons who attended the preachers of this sect, suddenly cried out, sigh'd [,] groaned, fell into convulsions and cold sweats, complained of intolerable thirst, yet could not drink when water was offered them, and continued to call upon *Jesus* in broken and scarce articulate expressions, till on a sudden they recovered; declared that *Jesus* was come, and then fell into transports of joy, and strange extacies, by which the powers of nature were at length exhausted, and they became calm and silent. The work is a regular treatise of fanaticism, shewing its cause and effects, and prescribing rules to prevent and remove it." *Gentleman's Magazine*, XXIII (1753), 250. The information for the above advertisement was taken from Rimius' "Preface of the Translator," pp. iv–v, which Rimius took from Boissy's "Preface of the French Translator." See *nn.* 7 and 21, Letters.

56. Vols. I–IV of the octavo and duodecimo were published on November 13, 1753; Vols. V–VI of the duodecimo and Vol. V of the octavo on December 11, 1753; and Vol. VII of the duodecimo and Vol. VI of the octavo on March 14, 1754. See Sale, *Samuel Richardson A Bibliographical Record*, pp. 76, 81.

57. French hack writer who wrote a prefatory letter to *Pamela* (see McKillop, *Samuel Richardson*, p. 28). Also see *Correspondence*, V, 271–72 and 278, for de Freval's function as intermediary between Richardson and the proprietors of the French *Clarissa* and his efforts to obtain the French rights to *Sir Charles Grandison*.

58. Folkert van der Plaats.

59. See *n.* 31, Letters.

60. Isaac Tirion.

61. This announcement appeared in the *Amsterdamse Courant* for August 14, 1753: "FOLKERT VAN DER PLAATS, Boekverkoper te Harlingen, maekt bekent dat hy van voornemens is te drukken, als in het Engelsch uit is in 't Nederduits THE GOOD MAN, dat is de DEUGDZAME MAN; in 't Engelsch beschreven door S. Richarson [sic], Schryver van de Pamela en de HISTORIE VAN CLARISSE [sic], 't word in 't Engels gedrukt in 6 Delen, in 8 en 7 Delen in 12." The announcement was repeated on August 23 and August 30. The translation appeared as: *Historie van den Ridderbaronet Karel Grandison* (7 vols.; Harlingen, 1756–57). The brief praise of the novel in the Foreword to the translation was very probably written by Stinstra.

62. William Richardson.

*63.* Alexis Claude Clairaut (1713–65). See Alan D. McKillop's note, "A Letter from Samuel Richardson to Alexis Claude Clairaut," *MLN*, LXIII (1948), 109–13, for a discussion of Prévost's relationships with Richardson. John Carroll printed the letter again in *Selected Letters of Samuel Richardson*, pp. 236–38. See *n.* 97.

*64.* George Faulkner, Richardson's authorized publisher of *Grandison* in Ireland, joined with a group of Irish booksellers to bribe Richardson's workmen to steal advance sheets of the novel. Faulkner had earlier pirated *Pamela* and the *Familiar Letters*. See McKillop, *Samuel Richardson*, pp. 214–15 and William Merritt Sale, Jr., "*Sir Charles Grandison* and the Dublin Pirates," *Yale University Library Gazette*, VII (1933), 80–86.

*65.* For the original, with some deletions and differences, see *Correspondence*, V, 254–61.

*66.* Stinstra's friend was Jan Boelaard; the translation is entitled: *Eene Verhandeling over Gods Bestaen en Eigenschappen*; *als ook over de Verpligtingen van den natuurlijken Godsdienst, en de Waarheid en Zekerheid der Christelijke Openbaaringe* (Harlingen, 1753).

*67.* The Dutch translation to which Stinstra refers is *Over de Verzoeninge* (Harlingen, 1754).

*68.* Gooitjen Stinstra (1703–64), physician at Harlingen.

*69.* Evert Heeres Oosterbaan, who married Stinstra's sister, Grietje.

*70.* See *n.* 22, Letters.

*71.* Elizabeth Singer Rowe (1674–1737), writer of various types of religious verse. Catherine Cockburn (1679–1749), dramatist and moral essayist, author of *Remarks Upon the Principles and Reasonings of Dr. Rutherford's "Essay on the Nature and Obligations of Virtue."* Stinstra owned a copy of her *Works* (1751).

*72.* See *n.* 8, Letters. I have been unable to find evidence that Stinstra completed either this work or the two moral essays which he mentions a few lines further on.

*73.* William Wollaston (1660–1724), moral philosopher, author of *Religion of Nature Delineated* (1724). This work is a version of the "intellectual theory" of morality of which Samuel Clarke was the chief contemporary representative. Wollaston's rationalism led to suspicions of his orthodoxy. "Rauhson": Perhaps a misspelling of "Rawson"; John Taylor published *A Narrative of Joseph Rawson's Case . . . with a Prefatory Discourse in Defence of the Common Rights of Christians* (1737). It was published anonymously but was written by Rawson. A second edition appeared in 1742 with Rawson's name as author.

74. Pieter Adriaan Verwer, translator of *Amelia*; see McKillop, *Samuel Richardson*, p. 266.

75. See *n.* 64, Letters.

76. *The Case of Samuel Richardson, of London, Printer; with Regard to the Invasion of His Property in The History of Sir Charles Grandison, before Publication, by Certain Booksellers in Dublin* (London, 1753), described by Sale, *Samuel Richardson A Bibliographical Record*, p. 93.

77. Anna Williams (1706–83), whom Dr. Johnson befriended for many years. *Verses Addressed to Mr. Richardson, on His History of Sir Charles Grandison* (London, 1753).

78. See *nn.* 64 and 76, Letters.

79. Printed in *Correspondence*, v, 261–70. The postscript in Barbauld's edition is actually from Richardson's autobiographical letter (No. 5) and the following paragraphs are omitted: 2, 5, 12–14, 17–19.

80. See Letter No. 2.

81. See Letter No. 11 for Stinstra's earlier conjecture that Richardson was a reformed rake; see Letter No. 14 for his reply to Richardson's statement.

82. See Letter No. 11 for Stinstra's comments.

83. Stinstra felt that Harriet Byron's "generous Love" might, for female readers, "lay open more than is convenient for the less prudent of that Sex, to the allurements of specious Lovers." See Letter No. 11.

84. John Balguy (1686–1748), author of *The Foundation of Moral Goodness* and *Essay on Redemption*. An admirer of Samuel Clarke, he was vicar of Northallerton, York. Stinstra owned copies of several of his works.

85. See *n.* 76, Letters. Stinstra had not yet received William Richardson's letter of March 12, 1754.

86. See *n.* 76, Letters.

87. See *n.* 84, Letters.

88. His publications consisted of a few single sermons, which were collected and published in 1763 by William Duncombe. His letters to Duncombe were edited by the Rev. John Duncombe, William's son, in 1777.

89. (1754), by Isaac Hawkins Browne, the elder (1705–60); it

was well received by scholars of his time. The best known English translation is by Soame Jenyns. Browne was a friend of Dr. Johnson, who praised him highly as a conversationalist.

*90.* See *n.* 73. Stinstra owned a copy.

*91.* James Foster (1697–1753), dissenting divine. The work referred to here is *Discourses on All the Principal Branches of Natural Religion and Social Virtue* (2 vols.; London, 1749 and 1752). Stinstra owned a copy. Sepp conjectured that Stinstra was the translator of 16 of Foster's sermons as: *Zestien Predikaetsien over zeer gewichtige Stoffen* (Harlingen, 1737), although Stinstra was not in complete agreement with Foster's views. See Sepp, II, 166–67. Several of Foster's works were in Stinstra's library.

*92.* (London, 1731), an answer to the named work, by Matthew Tindal (1657–1733), who called himself a "Christian Deist."

*93.* This work was originally published as an article, "Moral Philosophy," for the *Modern Preceptor*; it was published separately in 1754 under the title given here. David Fordyce (1711–51) was Professor of Moral Philosophy in Marischal College.

*94.* *A System of Moral Philosophy* (2 vols.; London, 1749) by Henry Grove (1684–1738); Thomas Amory (1701–74) wrote the last eight chapters. The system is mild Christian Stoicism. The function of morality is to meet the universal demand for happiness.

*95.* *De Legibus Naturae Disquisitio Philosophica . . .* (London, 1672) by Richard Cumberland (1631–1718). The work holds that "universal benevolence" is the source of all virtues. It was one of the treatises called out by opposition to Hobbes. English translations appeared in 1692, 1727, and 1750.

*96.* See McKillop, *Samuel Richardson*, p. 215*n.*

*97.* See *n.* 64, Letters.

*98.* *Copy of a Letter to a Lady* and *Answer to a Letter from a Friend . . .* , described by Sale, *Samuel Richardson A Bibliographical Record*, p. 94.

*99.* See *n.* 110, Letters.

*100.* *A Collection of the Moral and Instructive Sentiments, Maxims, Cautions, and Reflexions, Contained in the Histories of Pamela, Clarissa, and Sir Charles Grandison* (London, 1755), described by Sale, *Samuel Richardson A Bibliographical Record*, pp. 95–97.

*101.* See *n.* 100, Letters, and beginning of Letter No. 18.

*102.* See *n.* 100, Letters.

*103.* Isaac Tirion.

*104.* Elie Luzac (1723–96), who founded several journals and reviews which gave accounts of important works which appeared in The Netherlands and abroad. "Weidmann's": the Leipzig publishing house of Weidmann. See *n.* 38, Letters, for the French and German translations of *Grandison.* See also *n.* 63, Letters.

*105.* Richardson's portrait does not appear in the only copy of the translated *Grandison* which I have seen.

*106.* See *nn.* 99 and 110, Letters; see also Letters Nos. 5 and 15.

*107.* Hans Buma (1716–72). He had had some difficulties with his congregation. It is probable that one of the arguments was about his opposition to combining the administration of pastoral and church property in 1755. A development of this disagreement was his action in 1757 to appoint the elders and deacons of his pastorate on a yearly rotating basis rather than for life. He remained pastor at IJsbrechtum until his death. See Sepp, II, 250–51.

*108.* At the time that Stinstra mentions him he was pastor of the Remonstrant Congregation at Haarlem. Nozeman published numerous controversial religious works, and two of them were owned by Stinstra. See Sepp, II, 251.

*109.* See *n.* 100, Letters.

*110.* For a full discussion of Richardson's changes, see article by T. C. Duncan Eaves and Ben D. Kimpel, "Richardson's Revisions of *Pamela,*" *Studies in Bibliography,* xx (1967), 61–88.

*111.* See article by Eaves and Kimpel, "Samuel Richardson's London Houses," *Studies in Bibliography,* xv (1962), 145–46.

*112.* William Caslon (1692–1766), typefounder. His type was used extensively until the end of the century and was brought back into use about 1845 by the Chiswick Press.

*113.* Claude Garamond (1480–1561). His typefaces appeared in books printed in Paris around 1532. See W. Turner Berry *et al., The Encyclopaedia of Type Faces* (3d ed.; London, 1962), p. 85.

*114.* Matthieu Maty (1718–76), son of a refugee minister. He received his degree at the University of Leiden, went to England in 1740, where he became acquainted with Lord Chesterfield. He was appointed assistant librarian at the British Museum in 1753, was made a member of the Royal Society in 1758 and permanent secretary in 1765. He edited the *Journal brittanique* (21 vols.; The Hague, 1750–55); the success of this journal was so great that a continuation of it appeared under the name of the *Nouvelle bibliothèque anglaise* under the editorship of de Joncourt.

*115.* Cornelis Nozeman. See *n.* 108, Letters.

*116.* See *n.* 112, Letters.

*117.* (1694–1761), dissenting divine and Hebraist who published numerous religious works. See *nn.* 67, 73, Letters.

## PART TWO, *Johannes Stinstra's Prefaces*

*1.* Stinstra's footnotes are indicated parenthetically in the text. See A Note on the Text for my method of translation.

*2.* See Introduction and Stinstra's letter of April 2, 1753 (Letter No. 3).

*3.* Pierre-Daniel Huet (1630–1721), Bishop of Avranches. In 1670 Louis XIV appointed him tutor to the Dauphin, for whom he published an edition of the classics. Other works include: *Traité de la traduction* (1661) and *Essai sur l'origine des romans,* which was prefixed to Mme de La Fayette's *Zaïde* (1670).

*4.* See McKillop, *Samuel Richardson,* pp. 126–27.

*5.* See *nn.* 29 and 66, Letters.

*6.* Formal Dutch forms of address, comparable to "Your Reverence," "Your Most Noble," etc.

*7.* Stinstra's lack of knowledge of English epistolary fiction before Richardson is apparent here.

*8.* I, facing sig. *2. They appear as follows:
"The Work is *Nature's,* every title in 't.
She wrote, and gave it *Richardson* to print.
But he (so loose to trust Mankind are grown)
The Goddess braved, and claims it as his own."
Journ. Britann. Decemb. 1750. p. 438.
Dus overgebragt. [Translated thus:]
"Dit's de arbeid van Natuur, elk blad vertoont haar merk.
Zij schreef, en gaf het boek aan *Richardson* te drukken.
Maar hij (zo kan belang het menschelijk hart verrukken)
Braveert Natuur, en zegt; het is mijn eigen werk."
The original differs slightly from that quoted by McKillop; see *Samuel Richardson,* p. 158.

*9.* See McKillop, *Samuel Richardson,* pp. 154–55, for a brief discussion of changes in the various editions of *Clarissa.*

*10.* This is Lovelace's letter to Belford in which he outlines his fantastic plan of raping Mrs. Howe, Anna, and their maidservant at sea. (IV, 61–69, 4th ed., 1751)

The reference to medical doctors: Lovelace has deliberately made himself ill, in order to gain Clarissa's sympathy, by taking ipecacuanha, an emetic. He makes the "cutting remark" against doctors in reply to Clarissa's statement: "God made physicians," when he thinks to himself that if she means "physic" instead of "physicians," the phrase would then mean what the vulgar phrase means: "God sends meat, the Devil cooks." (IV, 84, 4th ed., 1751)

Clarissa's remark which clears up Richardson's meaning of the above is made in a letter to Anna Howe in which she relates that she has suggested a physician for Lovelace but he has declined; she adds: "I have great honour for the faculty; and the greater, as I have always observed, that those who treat the professors of the Art of Healing contemptuously, too generally treat higher institutions in the same manner." (IV, 86, 4th ed., 1751)

The reference to IV, 307 has to do with Clarissa's berating herself for her vanity and her hoping that she has suffered enough for it. She adds: "Since now, I verily think, I more despise myself for my presumptuous self-security, as well as vanity, than ever I secretly vaunted myself on my good inclinations: *Secretly,* I say, however; for indeed I had not given myself leisure to reflect, till I was thus mortified, how very imperfect I was; nor how much truth there is in what Divines tell us, That we sin in our best performances." (IV, 9, 4th ed., 1751)

*11.* See *n.* 2, Letters, and Letters Nos. 6 and 7.

*12.* The pedant Brand.

*13.* See *n.* 3, Letters.

*14.* Stinstra is referring here specifically to his *Waarschuwinge tegen de Geestdrijverij*; see *n.* 7, Letters.

*15.* Francis Hutcheson (1694–1746), follower of Shaftesbury, was elected to the Chair of Moral Philosophy at Glasgow in 1729. Stinstra here refers to Hutcheson's *An Inquiry into the Original of our Ideas of Beauty and Virtue . . .* (1725), published anonymously. Stinstra owned a copy of Hutcheson's later work, *System of Moral Philosophy* (London, 1755). For Fordyce, see *n.* 93, Letters.

*16.* The Dutch translation, however, does not contain a dedication.

*17.* Lovelace, in relating a conversation between Clarissa and him to Belford, states his "aversion to tragedies": "I had too much *feeling,* I said. There was enough in the world to make our hearts sad, without carrying grief into our diversions, and making the distresses of others our own." (III, 358, 4th ed., 1751)

# Index

# Index

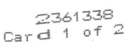